PARISH HYMNS.

A

COLLECTION OF HYMNS

FOR

PUBLIC, SOCIAL, AND PRIVATE

WORSHIP.

SELECTED AND ORIGINAL.

PHILADELPHIA:
PUBLISHED BY HENRY PERKINS.
1850.

Entered according to Act of Congress, in the year 1843, by PERKINS & PURVES, in the Clerk's Office of the District Court of the Eastern District of Pennsylvania.

Stereotyped by
S. DOUGLAS WYETH.

I. ASHMEAD, Printer

PREFACE.

The following collection of hymns has been prepared with reference to that standard which is found in *the general judgment of the Christian public.* Of the many speculations concerning devotional lyric poetry, which have been at different times proposed, it has not seemed proper to allow to any one an influence in advance of the settled decisions of public opinion; but much care has been exercised in seeking to ascertain those decisions, and to conform the character of the book to them. In pursuance of this plan, favorite standard hymns have been retained, as the basis of the collection; while a laborious examination has been made of a large number of Hymn Books and other volumes of religious poetry, British and American, for the purpose of giving it variety and freshness. Every stanza inserted has been carefully considered; and while it has not been thought proper to exclude every one which does not possess high poetic merit, or to torture every one which is not perfectly accommodated to musical accent, it is hoped that the attention which has been paid, in the preparation of the book, to the claims of literary and musical taste, will be found to have effected as much as was advisable. Above all, it is hoped that nothing has been admitted which is at variance with the word of God.

Alterations in language have been made only where, with a full knowledge of the reasonable jealousy of the public on that point, they were judged to be indispensable. A Hymn Book fitted to meet the demands of worshiping assemblies, cannot be produced without the labor of abridgment and alteration; but that wantonness of change and mutilation, which has proved so offensive to the community, is most justly condemned. In the following collection are a few hymns, (not hitherto familiar to the public,) in which considerable alterations have been made. They are such as were seen to admit of changes which would render them highly valuable, while, in their original form, they could not have been inserted. Most of these are designated in the Index. In many hymns, what will appear to some to be alterations, are but restorations of the original language, with which unnecessary liberties had been taken.

Among the leading objects kept in view, has been that of gratifying the wish, so generally entertained by those whose feelings are chiefly to be regarded in the preparation of such a book, for that class of hymns which is felt to be peculiarly suited to evening meetings and other occasions of social worship—a class characterized by somewhat more of free expression and enlivening fervor, than belongs to the stately compositions which better accord with the dignity of the sanctuary. It is believed that the book will be found unusually rich in this department.

The original hymns are designated as such in the Index.

Much labor has been employed upon the classification of the hymns; but any one who has attempted such a task will be convinced that no two persons could be found who would perform it in precisely the same manner. The schedule which exhibits this classification may often be found more convenient than the alphabetical Index of Subjects.

The collection is submitted to the public, under a sense of the responsibility of attempting to furnish, for those who worship God, the language of devotional song; and with pleasure in the reflection that many a soul may find here the expression of its faith, adoration, and hope, and the means of advancing preparation for the songs of heaven.

HYMNS.

WORSHIP.

---

1 *Assembling for Worship.* L. M.

1 ASSEMBLED in thy name, O Lord,
We plead the promise of thy word;
We gather now to seek thy face—
Oh may thy presence fill the place.

2 When 'mid the sad forsaken band
Of thy disciples thou didst stand,
Thy voice, divinely speaking "Peace,"
Bade doubt and fear and sorrow cease.

3 Now may we hear the voice of love
Speak peace and pardon from above;
Sweet intercourse with Jesus find,
And prove him powerful, faithful, kind.

4 Oh send us not away unbless'd,
For on thy gracious word we rest;
We, sinners, to our Saviour flee,
Helpless and hopeless but in thee.

2

The Blessing of God implored. C. M

1 IN thy great name, O Lord, we come
To worship at thy feet;
Oh pour thy Holy Spirit down
On all that now shall meet.

2 We come to hear Jehovah speak,
To hear the Saviour's voice;
Thy face and favor, Lord, we seek;
Now make our hearts rejoice.

3 Teach us to pray and praise—to hear
And understand thy word;
To feel thy blissful presence near,
And trust our living Lord.

4 Let sinners now thy goodness prove,
And saints rejoice in thee;
Let rebels be subdued by love,
And to the Saviour flee.

3

Divine Aid sought. 7s

1 LORD, we come before thee now,
At thy feet we humbly bow;
Oh do not our suit disdain;
Shall we seek thee, Lord, in vain?

2 Lord, on thee our souls depend;
In compassion now descend;
Fill our hearts with thy rich grace,
Tune our lips to sing thy praise.

3 In thine own appointed way,
Now we seek thee, here we stay;

Lord, we know not how to go,
Till a blessing thou bestow.

4 Send some message from thy word,
That may peace and joy afford;
Let thy Spirit now impart
Full salvation to each heart.

4

Social Worship. C. M.

1 O LORD, our languid souls inspire,
For here we trust thou art;
Send down a coal of heavenly fire,
To warm each waiting heart.

2 Show us some token of thy love,
Our fainting hope to raise;
And pour thy blessing from above,
That we may render praise.

3 The feeling heart, the melting eye,
The humble mind bestow;
And shine upon us from on high,
To make our graces grow.

4 May we in faith receive thy word,
In faith present our prayers;
And, in the presence of our Lord,
Unbosom all our cares.

5 And may the gospel's joyful sound,
Enforced by mighty grace,
Awaken many sinners round
To come and fill the place.

5

Social Worship. C. M.

1 O THOU in whom thy saints are one,
Permit us now to see,
In this short hour of prayer and praise,
A glimpse of heaven and thee.

2 While, with one heart and one desire,
Low at thy feet we kneel,
Oh warm our hearts with heavenly love,
And all thy grace reveal.

3 Thy gracious presence, Lord, alone
Can make our worship bless'd,
Drive from our thoughts a vexing world,
And lay our griefs to rest.

4 Descend, and bless our waiting souls,
And meet us as thine own;
And fit us to ascend and praise
Before th' eternal throne.

6

The Praises of Heaven. C. M.

1 COME, Lord, and warm each languid
Inspire each lifeless tongue; [heart,
And let the joys of heaven impart
Their influence to our song.

2 The saints, from sin for ever free,
There mourn its power no more;
But, clothed in spotless purity,
Redeeming love adore.

3 There the bless'd followers of the Lamb
Join in immortal songs;

And endless honors to his name
Employ their tuneful tongues.

4 Lord, tune our hearts to praise and love;
Our feeble notes inspire;
Till in thy blissful courts above
We join th' angelic choir.

7 *Invocation of the Saviour.* C. M.

1 COME, thou desire of all thy saints,
Our humble strains attend;
While, with our praises and complaints,
Low at thy feet we bend.

2 When we thy wondrous glories hear,
And all thy sufferings trace,
What sweetly awful scenes appear!
What rich, unbounded grace!

3 How should our songs, like those above,
With warm devotion rise!
How should our souls, on wings of love,
Mount upward to the skies!

4 Come, Lord, thy love alone can raise
In us the heavenly flame;
Then shall our lips resound thy praise,
Our hearts adore thy name.

5 Dear Saviour, let thy glory shine,
And fill thy dwellings here,
Till life and love and joy divine
A heaven on earth appear.

8

Praise to the Saviour. 5. 6.

1 ALL praise to his name
  Who gives us to meet,
His love to proclaim,
  His mercies repeat:
Who offers his blessing,
  And bids us draw near;
Whose favor possessing,
  We nothing should fear.

2 In him we have peace,
  In him we have power;
His smiles never cease
  To cheer the dark hour:
In every temptation,
  He sends from above
His wondrous salvation,
  His rescuing love.

3 Bless'd Jesus, thy word
  Can bid us be free;
Our Saviour and Lord,
  We hasten to thee:
Oh give us some token
  That thou art still nigh;
Our faith is unbroken,
  Our help is on high.

9

Presence of the Saviour. L. M.

1 JESUS, where'er thy people meet,
  There they behold thy mercy-seat;
Where'er they seek thee, thou art found;
And every place is hallowed ground.

2 Dear Shepherd of thy chosen few,
Thy former mercies here renew;
Here to our waiting hearts proclaim
The sweetness of thy saving name.

3 Here may we prove the power of prayer
To strengthen faith and banish care;
To teach our faint desires to rise
To things unseen beyond the skies.

4 Lord, we are few, but thou art near,
Nor short thine arm, nor deaf thine ear;
Oh rend the heavens this favored hour—
Let thousands feel thy saving power.

10

Sincerity. C. M

1 LORD, when we bend before thy throne
And our confessions pour,
Teach us to feel the sins we own,
And hate what we deplore.

2 Our burdened spirits pitying see;
True penitence impart;
And let a healing ray from thee
Beam hope on every heart.

3 When our responsive tongues essay
Their grateful songs to raise,
Grant that our souls may join the lay,
And rise to thee in praise.

4 When we disclose our wants in prayer,
May we our wills resign;
And not a thought our bosom share,
Which is not wholly thine.

5 Let faith each meek petition fill,
And waft it to the skies;
And teach our hearts 'tis goodness still
That grants it, or denies.

11 *The Sanctuary.* 7s

1 SAFELY through another week
God has brought us on our way;
Let us now a blessing seek,
Waiting in his courts to-day;
Day of all the week the best,
Emblem of eternal rest.

2 While we seek supplies of grace,
Through the dear Redeemer's name,
Show thy reconciling face,
Take away our sin and shame;
From our worldly cares set free,
May we rest this day in thee.

3 Here we come thy name to praise;
Let us feel thy presence near:
May thy glory meet our eyes,
While we in thy house appear:
Here afford us, Lord, a taste
Of our everlasting feast.

4 May the gospel's joyful sound
Conquer sinners, comfort saints,
Make the fruits of grace abound,
Bring relief from all complaints:
Thus let all our Sabbaths prove,
Till we join the church above.

12 *Praise for Restoration.* C. M.

1 WHAT shall I render to my God,
For all his kindness shown?
My feet shall visit thine abode,
My songs address thy throne.

2 Among the saints who fill thy house,
My offering shall be paid;
There shall my zeal perform the vows
My soul in anguish made.

3 How happy all thy servants are!
How great thy grace to me!
My life, which thou hast made thy care,
Lord, I devote to thee.

4 Now I am thine—for ever thine—
Nor shall my purpose move;
Thy hand hath loosed my bonds of pain,
And bound me with thy love.

5 Here, in thy courts, I leave my vow,
And thy rich grace record;
Witness, ye saints, who hear me now,
If I forsake the Lord.

13 *Welcome to Christian Friends.* L. M.

1 KINDRED in Christ, for his dear sake
A hearty welcome here receive;
May we together now partake
The joys which only he can give.

2 May he by whose kind care we meet,
Send his good Spirit from above,

Make our communications sweet,
  And cause our hearts to burn with love.

3 Forgotten be each worldly theme,
  When Christians see each other thus;
We only wish to speak of him
  Who lived, and died, and reigns for us.

4 We'll talk of all he did and said
  And suffered for us here below;
The path he marked for us to tread,
  And what he's doing for us now.

5 Thus, as the moments pass away,
  We'll love and wonder and adore,
And hasten on the glorious day
  When we shall meet to part no more.

14 *Heavenly Joy on Earth.* S. M

1 COME, we who love the Lord,
  And let our joys be known;
Join in a song, with sweet accord,
  And thus surround the throne.

2 Let those refuse to sing,
  Who never knew our God;
But children of the heavenly King
  Should speak their joys abroad.

3 The men of grace have found
  Glory begun below;
Celestial fruits on earthly ground
  From faith and hope may grow.

4 The hill of Zion yields
  A thousand sacred sweets,

Before we reach the heavenly fields,
Or walk the golden streets.

5 Then let our songs abound,
And every tear be dry; [ground,
We're marching through Immanuel's
To fairer worlds on high.

15 *Worthy the Lamb.* 6. 4.

1 GLORY to God on high!
Let heaven and earth reply—
"Praise ye his name;"
His love and grace adore,
Who all our sorrows bore:
Sing loud for evermore—
"Worthy the Lamb."

2 They who surround the throne
Join cheerfully in one,
Praising his name;
We who have felt his blood
Sealing our peace with God,
Sound through the earth abroad—
"Worthy the Lamb."

3 Join, all ye ransomed race,
Jesus our Lord to bless;
Praise ye his name;
In him we will rejoice,
Making a joyful noise,
Shouting with heart and voice—
"Worthy the Lamb."

4 Soon must we change our place,
Yet will we never cease

Praising his name:
Still will we tribute bring,
Hail him our gracious King,
And through all ages sing—
"Worthy the Lamb."

16 *The Song of the Redeemed.* S. M

1 AWAKE, and sing the song
Of Moses and the Lamb;
Wake, every heart and every tongue
To praise the Saviour's name.

2 Sing of his dying love;
Sing of his rising power:
Sing how he intercedes above,
For those whose sins he bore.

3 Sing till we feel the heart
Ascending with the tongue;
Sing till the love of sin depart,
And grace inspire the song.

4 Sing on your heavenly way,
Ye ransomed sinners, sing;
Sing on, rejoicing every day
In Christ, th' eternal King.

5 Soon shall we hear him say—
"Ye blessed children, come;"
Soon will he call us hence away,
And take his wanderers home.

6 Soon shall our raptured tongue
His endless praise proclaim;
And sweeter voices tune the song
Of Moses and the Lamb.

17

Exhortation to Praise. S. M.

1 STAND up and bless the Lord,
Ye people of his choice;
Stand up and bless the Lord your God,
With heart and soul and voice.

2 Oh for the living flame
From his own altar brought,
To touch our lips, our souls inspire,
And wing to heaven our thought.

3 God is our strength and song,
And his salvation ours;
Then be his love in Christ proclaimed
With all our ransomed powers.

4 Stand up and bless the Lord,
The Lord your God adore;
Stand up and bless his glorious name,
Henceforth, for evermore.

18

Praise to the Saviour. 5. 6.

1 YE servants of God,
Your Master proclaim,
And publish abroad
His wonderful name;
The name all victorious
Of Jesus extol;
His kingdom is glorious,
And rules over all.

2 God ruleth on high,
Almighty to save;

And still he is nigh,
His presence we have;
The great congregation
His triumph shall sing,
Ascribing salvation
To Jesus our king.

3 Salvation to God
Who sits on the throne;
Let all cry aloud
And honor the Son;
Immanuel's praises
The angels proclaim,
Fall down on their faces,
And worship the Lamb.

4 Then let us adore,
And give him his right—
All glory and power,
And wisdom and might;
All honor and blessing,
With angels above,
And thanks never ceasing,
And infinite love.

19 *Thanksgiving.* 7s.

1 SWELL the anthem, raise the song,
Praises to our God belong;
Saints and angels join to sing
Praises to the heavenly King.

2 Blessings from his liberal hand
Flow around this happy land;

Guarded by his watchful eye,
Peace and freedom we enjoy.

3 Here, beneath a virtuous sway,
May we cheerfully obey;
Never feel oppression's rod,
Ever own and worship God.

4 Hark! the voice of nature sings
Praises to the King of kings;
Let us join the choral song,
And the grateful notes prolong.

20 *Retirement.* C. M.

1 FAR from the world, O Lord, I flee,
From strife and tumult far;
From scenes where Satan wages still
His most successful war.

2 The calm retreat, the silent shade,
With prayer and praise agree;
And seem by thy sweet bounty made
For those who follow thee.

3 Then, if thy Spirit touch the soul,
And grace her mean abode,
Oh, with what peace and joy and love
She there communes with God!

4 There, like the nightingale, she pours
Her solitary lays;
Nor asks a witness of her song,
Nor thirsts for human praise.

5 Author and guardian of my life,
Sweet source of light divine,

And—all harmonious names in one—
My Saviour, thou art mine.

6 What thanks I owe thee, and what love!
A boundless, endless store
Shall echo through the realms above,
When time shall be no more.

21 *Closet Hymn.* L. M.

1 RETIRE—all meaner things retire,
And leave me to my soul's desire—
To meet her God, where, all subdued,
The cares of earth no more intrude.

2 I'm now alone, O Lord, with thee,
But thou art more than worlds to me;
And were surrounding worlds my own,
Without thee I were poor and lone.

3 Do troubles from the world increase?
In thee I find the promised peace;
Nor could my soul sustain the wo
Of earth my friend, and God my foe.

4 With thee my shield, my portion here,
What can I lack—what need I fear?
And if thou call me hence, I know
'Tis to my Rock of trust I go.

5 Oh hold me, Father, Friend, and Guide,
Nor let my feet be drawn aside,
In bright or shadowy wilds to roam,
From keeping life's straight pathway home.

22 *Retirement and Meditation.* L. M.

1 RETURN, my roving heart, return,
And chase these shadowy forms no
Seek out some solitude to mourn, [more:
And thy forsaken God implore.

2 O thou great God, whose piercing eye
Distinctly marks each deep recess,
In these sequestered hours draw nigh,
And with thy presence fill the place.

3 Through all the windings of my heart,
My search let heavenly wisdom guide;
And still its radiant beams impart,
Till all be cleansed and purified.

4 Then, with the visits of thy love,
Vouchsafe my inmost soul to cheer;
Till every grace shall join to prove
That God has fixed his dwelling there.

23 *Prayer for the Divine Presence.* L. M.

1 FAR from my thoughts, vain world, be-
Let my religious hours alone; [gone;
Fain would my eyes my Saviour see;
I wait a visit, Lord, from thee.

2 Oh warm my heart with holy fire,
And kindle there a pure desire:
Come, blessed Jesus, from above,
And fill my soul with heavenly love.

3 Hail, great Immanuel, all divine!
In thee the Father's glories shine;

Thy grace the rebel heart can move—
Redeeming grace and dying love.

24 *Delight in God.* C. M.

1 WHILE thee I seek, protecting Power,
Be my vain wishes stilled;
And may this consecrated hour
With better hopes be filled.

2 Thy love the power of thought bestowed;
To thee my thoughts would soar;
Thy mercy o'er my life has flowed;
That mercy I adore.

3 In each event of life, how clear
Thy ruling hand I see!
Each blessing to my soul most dear,
Because conferred by thee.

4 In every joy that crowns my days,
In every pain I bear,
My heart shall find delight in praise,
Or seek relief in prayer.

5 When gladness wings my favored hour.
Thy love my thoughts shall fill;
Resigned, when storms of sorrow lowei
My soul shall meet thy will.

6 My lifted eye, without a tear,
The gathering storm shall see;
My steadfast heart shall know no fear;
That heart will rest on thee.

25

The Throne of Grace. H. M.

1 O THOU that hearest prayer,
And teachest how to pray,
My groveling heart prepare
To wing its heavenward way;
High as thy mercy-seat to rise,
And there pour out its earnest cries.

2 Too oft, when faith is weak,
I fear my prayers are vain;
The blessings which I seek
I scarcely hope to gain;
My wants appear to mount too high;
My hopes, o'erborne with sorrow, die.

3 Lord, give me faith and light,
Humility and love;
And from my feeble sight
The darkening film remove;
Kindle devotion's languid flame,
And bid me come in Jesus' name.

26

Morning and Evening. L. M. 6 lines.

1 WHEN, streaming from the eastern skies,
The morning light salutes my eyes,
O Sun of Righteousness divine,
On me with beams of mercy shine;
Chase the dark clouds of guilt away,
And turn my darkness into day.

2 When each day's scenes and labors close,
And wearied nature seeks repose,

With pardoning mercy richly bless'd,
Guard me, my Saviour, while I rest;
And, as each morning sun shall rise,
Oh lead me onward to the skies.

3 And at my life's last setting sun,
My conflicts o'er, my labors done,
Jesus, thy heavenly radiance shed,
To cheer and bless my dying bed;
And from death's gloom my spirit raise,
To see thy face, and sing thy praise.

27 *Morning Thanksgiving.* C. P. M.

1 ONCE more my eyes behold the day,
And to my God my soul would pay
Its tributary lays;
Oh may the life preserved by thee,
With all its powers and blessings, be
Devoted to thy praise.

2 How many, since I laid me down,
Have launched into a world unknown,
To meet a dreadful doom!
But I am spared to seek thy face,
To hear the message of thy grace,
And to my Saviour come.

3 Still be thou near, my gracious Lord,
To guide my footsteps by thy word,
And lead me in thy way;
And when my days on earth are past,
Oh let me wake with thee at last,
In an eternal day.

28 *A Hymn for Morning or Evening.* C. M.

1 ON thee, each morning, O my God,
My waking thoughts attend;
In thee are founded all my hopes,
In thee my wishes end.

2 My soul, in pleasing wonder lost,
Thy boundless love surveys;
And, fired with grateful zeal, prepares
The sacrifice of praise.

3 When evening slumbers press my eyes,
With thy protection blessed,
In peace and safety I commit
My weary limbs to rest.

4 My spirit, in thy hands secure,
Fears no approaching ill;
For whether waking or asleep,
Thou, Lord, art with me still.

29 *Morning Praise.* C. M.

1 LORD of my life, oh may thy praise
Employ my noblest powers,
Whose goodness lengthens out my days,
And fills the circling hours.

2 Preserved by thine almighty arm,
I passed the shades of night,
Secure and safe from every harm,
And see returning light.

3 While many spent the night in sighs,
And restless pains and woes,

In gentle sleep I closed my eyes,
And undisturbed repose.

4 When sleep death's image o'er me spread,
And I unconscious lay,
Thy watchful care was round my bed,
To guard my feeble clay.

5 Oh let the same almighty care
My waking hours attend;
From every danger, every snare,
My heedless steps defend.

6 Smile on my minutes as they roll,
And guide my future days;
And let thy goodness fill my soul
With gratitude and praise.

30 *Morning Praise.* C. M.

1 ONCE more, my soul, the rising day
Salutes thy waking eyes;
Once more, my voice, thy tribute pay
To him that rules the skies.

2 'Tis he supports my mortal frame;
My tongue shall speak his praise;
My sins would rouse his wrath to flame,
And yet his wrath delays.

3 On a poor worm thy power might tread,
And I could ne'er withstand;
Thy justice might have crushed me dead,
But mercy held thy hand.

4 How many wretched souls are fled
Since the last setting sun!

And yet thou lengthenest out my thread,
And yet my moments run.

5 Great God, let all my hours be thine,
While I enjoy the light;
Then shall my sun in smiles decline,
And bring a pleasant night.

31 *An Evening Song.* C. M.

1 DREAD Sovereign, let my evening song
Like holy incense rise:
Assist the offerings of my tongue
To reach the lofty skies.

2 Perpetual blessings from above
Encompass me around;
But oh, how few returns of love
Hath my Creator found!

3 What have I done for him who died
To save my wretched soul?
How are my follies multiplied,
Fast as the minutes roll!

4 Lord, with this guilty heart of mine,
To thy dear cross I flee;
And to thy grace my soul resign,
To be renewed by thee.

5 Sprinkled afresh with pardoning blood,
I lay me down to rest,
As in the embraces of my God,
Or on my Saviour's breast.

32 *Divine Protection.* 8s.

1 INSPIRER and hearer of prayer,
 Protector and Saviour divine—
My all to thy covenant care
 I sleeping or waking resign.

2 If thou art my shield and my sun,
 The night is no darkness to me;
And fast as my moments roll on,
 They bring me but nearer to thee.

3 Thy minist'ring spirits descend,
 To watch while thy saints are asleep;
By day and by night they attend,
 The heirs of salvation to keep.

4 Their worship no interval knows;
 Their fervor is still on the wing;
And while they protect my repose,
 They chant to the praise of my King.

5 I too, at the season ordained,
 Their chorus for ever shall join;
And love and adore, without end,
 Their faithful Creator and mine.

33 *Evening Thanksgiving.* L. M.

1 GREAT God, to thee my evening song
 With humble gratitude I raise;
Oh let thy mercy tune my tongue,
 And fill my heart with lively praise.

2 My days, unclouded, as they pass,
 And every gently rolling hour,

Are monuments of wondrous grace,
  And witness to thy love and power.

3 Seal my forgiveness in the blood
  Of Jesus; his dear name alone
I plead for pardon, gracious God,
  And kind acceptance at thy throne.

4 Let this bless'd hope my eyelids close;
  With sleep refresh my feeble frame;
Safe in thy care may I repose,
  And wake with praises to thy name.

34 "*The Night cometh.*"—John ix. 4. 7s.

1 AS the twilight shadows fall,
  Let us, in the closing day,
Mark the solemn hour when all
  Earthly things shall fade away.

2 In the grave to which we haste,
  No repentance can be found;
Shall we then our moments waste,
  While we stand on trial-ground?

3 Ere the coming of that night,
  (When its coming who shall say?)
Let us do with all our might,
  Strive and labor, watch and pray.

4 Lord, do thou thy grace impart;
  Penitence and faith bestow;
Come and sanctify each heart,
  Let us thy salvation know.

5 That when waning years have fled,
  And these scenes have passed away,

Rising with the summoned dead,
We may wake to endless day.

35

Close of the Day. 7s.

1 SOFTLY now the light of day
Fades upon my sight away;
Free from care, from labor free,
Lord, I would commune with thee.

2 Soon for me the light of day
Shall for ever pass away;
Then, from sin and sorrow free,
Take me, Lord, to dwell with thee.

36

Retiring to Rest. S. M.

1 THE day is past and gone,
The evening shades appear;
Oh may I ever keep in mind,
The night of death draws near.

2 I lay my garments by,
Upon my bed to rest;
So death will soon remove me hence,
And leave my soul undressed.

3 Lord, keep me safe this night,
Secure from all my fears;
May angels guard me while I sleep,
Till morning light appears.

4 And when I early rise,
To view th' unwearied sun,
May I set out to win the prize,
And after glory run.

5 That when my days are past
  And I from time remove,
Lord, I may in thy bosom rest,
  The bosom of thy love.

37 *Retiring to Rest.* 7s.

1 INTERVAL of grateful shade,
  Welcome to my wearied head:
Welcome slumber to my eyes,
Tired with glaring vanities.

2 Lord, thine eye, which cannot sleep,
These defenceless hours shall keep;
Bless'd vicissitude to me—
Day and night I'm still with thee.

3 What though downy slumbers flee,
Strangers to my couch and me?
My Redeemer will impart
Secret comfort to my heart.

4 What if death my sleep invade,
Should I be of death afraid?
While encircled by thine arm,
Death may strike, but cannot harm.

5 With thy heavenly presence bless'd,
Death is life, and labor rest:
Welcome sleep or death to me,
Still secure, if still with thee.

38 *Evening Worship.* C. M.

1 O LORD, another day is flown;
  And we, a little band,

Are met once more before thy throne,
To bless thy fostering hand.

2 And, Jesus, thou thy smiles wilt deign,
As we before thee pray;
For thou didst bless the infant train,
And we are less than they.

3 Thy heavenly grace to each impart;
All evil far remove;
And shed abroad in every heart
Thine everlasting love.

4 Oh still restore our wandering feet,
And still direct our way;
Till worlds shall fail, and faith shall greet
The dawn of endless day.

39 *Family Worship.* L. M.

1 FATHER of all, thy care we bless,
Which crowns our families with peace;
From thee they spring, and by thy hand
They have been, and are still sustained.

2 To God, most worthy to be praised,
Be our domestic altars raised;
Who, Lord of heaven, scorns not to dwell
With saints, in their obscurest cell.

3 To thee may each united house,
Morning and night, present its vows;
Our servants there, and rising race,
Be taught thy precepts and thy grace.

4 Oh may each future age proclaim
The honors of thy glorious name;

While, pleased and thankful, we remove
To join the family above.

40 *Delight in God.* C. M.

1 LORD, with our household deign to stay,
And bid our hearts rejoice;
Our willing hearts shall own thy sway,
And echo to thy voice.

2 With thee conversing, we forget
All time and toil and fear;
Labor is rest, and pain is sweet,
If thou, our God, art here.

3 Thou callest us to seek thy face—
Thy face with joy we seek;
Wait for the whispers of thy grace,
And hear what thou dost speak.

4 Thus would we every hour employ,
Till we thy glory see;
Till we partake our Master's joy,
And find our heaven in thee.

41 *Dismission.* 8. 7. 4.

1 LORD, dismiss us with thy blessing,
Fill our hearts with joy and peace;
Let us, each thy love possessing,
Triumph in redeeming grace:
Oh refresh us,
Travelling through this wilderness.

2 Thanks we give, and adoration,
For thy gospel's joyful sound;

May the fruits of thy salvation
In our hearts and lives abound;
May thy presence
With us evermore be found.

3 So, whene'er the signal's given,
Us from earth to call away,
Borne on angels' wings to heaven,
Glad the summons to obey—
May we, ready,
Rise and reign in endless day.

42 *Dismission.* L. M.

1 DISMISS us with thy blessing, Lord;
Help us to feed upon thy word;
All that has been amiss forgive,
And let thy truth within us live.

2 Though we are guilty, thou art good;
Wash all our works in Jesus' blood;
Give every burdened soul release,
And bid us all depart in peace.

43 *Parting Hymn.* L. M.

1 NOW, Christian brethren, ere we part,
Join every voice and every heart;
One solemn hymn to God we raise,
One closing song of grateful praise.

2 Christians, we here may meet no more,
But there is yet a happier shore;
And there, released from toil and pain,
Dear brethren, we shall meet again.

44 *Prayer at Parting.* 7s.

1 FOR a season called to part,
Let us now ourselves commend
To the gracious eye and heart
Of our ever-present Friend.

2 Jesus, hear our humble prayer:
Tender Shepherd of thy sheep,
Let thy mercy and thy care
All our souls in safety keep.

3 In thy strength may we be strong;
Sweeten every cross and pain;
Spare us, that we may, ere long,
Meet and worship thee again.

4 Then, if thou thy help afford,
Songs of gladness will we raise;
And our souls shall bless the Lord,
And speak forth his glorious praise.

45 *The Saints one in Christ.* C. M.

1 BLESS'D be the dear, uniting love,
That will not let us part;
Our bodies may far off remove—
We still are one in heart.

2 Joined in one Spirit to our Head,
Where he appoints, we go;
And still in Jesus' footsteps tread,
And show his praise below.

3 Partakers of the Saviour's grace,
The same in mind and heart—

Nor joy, nor grief, nor time, nor place,
  Nor life, nor death can part.

4 But let us hasten to the day
  Which shall our flesh restore,
When death shall all be done away;
  And we shall part no more.

46 *The meeting of Friends in Heaven.* 6. 5

1 WHEN shall we meet again—
    Meet ne'er to sever?
  When will peace wreathe her chain
    Round us for ever?
  Our hearts will ne'er repose,
  Safe from each blast that blows,
  In this dark vale of woes—
    Never—no, never.

2 When will love freely flow,
    Pure as life's river?
  When will sweet friendship glow,
    Changeless for ever?
  Where joys celestial thrill,
  Where bliss each heart shall fill,
  And fears of parting chill
    Never—no, never.

3 Up to that world of light
    Take us, dear Saviour;
  May we all there unite,
    Happy for ever:
  Where kindred spirits dwel
  There may our music swell
  And time our joys dispel
    Never—no, never.

4 Soon shall we meet again—
  Meet ne'er to sever;
Soon will peace wreathe her chain
  Round us for ever:
Our hearts will then repose
Secure from worldly woes;
Our songs of praise shall close
  Never—no, never.

47 *Christian Love and Fellowship.* S. M.

1 BLESS'D be the tie that binds
  Our hearts in Christian love;
The fellowship of kindred minds
  Is like to that above.

2 Before our Father's throne
  We pour our ardent prayers;
Our fears, our hopes, our aims are one—
  Our comforts and our cares.

3 We share our mutual woes,
  Our mutual burdens bear;
And often for each other flows
  The sympathizing tear.

4 When we asunder part,
  It gives us inward pain;
But we shall still be joined in heart,
  And hope to meet again.

5 This glorious hope revives
  Our courage by the way;
While each in expectation lives,
  And longs to see the day.

6 From sorrow, toil, and pain,
  And sin we shall be free;
And perfect love and friendship reign
  Through all eternity.

THE SCRIPTURES.

48 *Consolations of the Bible.* 7. 6. Iambic.

1 SEE sacred waters springing;
  From Zion's fount they flow:
Come, then, your sorrows bringing,
  And lose your every wo.

2 Drink for the soul that's thirsting,
  Comfort for those who fear,
Balm for the heart when bursting,
  May all be gathered here.

3 What added boon is wanting?
  Thy blessing, Lord, must give
The gift of faith, by granting
  To read, believe, and live.

49 *The Bible Precious.*—Ps. cxix. 105. C. M.

1 HOW precious is the book divine,
  By inspiration given!
Bright as a lamp its doctrines shine,
  To guide our souls to heaven.

2 It sweetly cheers our drooping hearts,
  In this dark vale of tears;

Life, light, and heavenly joy imparts,
  And quells our rising fears.

3 This lamp, through all the tedious night
  Of life, shall guide our way,
Till we behold the clearer light
  Of an eternal day.

50 *Excellence of the Scriptures.* C. M.

1 FATHER of mercies, in thy word
  What endless glory shines!
For ever be thy name adored
  For these celestial lines.

2 Here the Redeemer's welcome voice
  Spreads heavenly peace around;
And life and everlasting joys
  Attend the blissful sound.

3 Oh may these heavenly pages be
  My ever dear delight;
And still new beauties may I see,
  And still increasing light.

4 Divine Instructor, gracious Lord,
  Be thou for ever near;
Teach me to love thy sacred word,
  And view my Saviour there.

51 *Joy in the Gospel.* C. M.

1 LADEN with guilt, and full of fears,
  I fly to thee, my Lord;
And not a glimpse of hope appears,
  But in thy written word.

2 The volume of my Father's grace
Does all my grief assuage;
Here I behold my Saviour's face,
Almost in every page.

3 This is the field where hidden lies
The pearl of price unknown;
That merchant is divinely wise,
Who makes the pearl his own.

4 Here consecrated water flows
To quench my thirst of sin;
Here the fair tree of knowledge grows,
Nor danger dwells therein.

5 Oh may thy counsels, mighty God,
My roving feet command;
Nor I forsake the happy road
That leads to thy right hand.

52 *The Glory of the Word.* C. M.

1 THE Spirit breathes upon the word,
And brings the truth to sight;
Precepts and promises afford
A sanctifying light.

2 A glory gilds the sacred page,
Majestic like the sun;
It gives a light to every age,
It gives—but borrows none.

3 The hand that gave it still supplies
The gracious light and heat;
His truths upon the nations rise,
They rise, but never set.

4 Let everlasting thanks be thine,
For such a bright display,
As makes a world of darkness shine
With beams of heavenly day.

GOD.

53 *Divine Sovereignty.* C. M.

1 KEEP silence, all created things,
And wait your Maker's nod;
My soul stands trembling, while she sings
The honors of her God.

2 Life, death, and hell, and worlds unknown,
Hang on his firm decree;
He sits on no precarious throne,
Nor borrows leave to be.

3 Chained to his throne, a volume lies,
With all the fates of men,
With every angel's form and size,
Drawn by th' eternal pen.

4 His providence unfolds the book,
And makes his counsels shine;
Each opening leaf, and every stroke,
Fulfills some deep design.

5 Not Gabriel asks the reason why,
Nor God the reason gives;
Nor dares the favorite angel pry
Between the folded leaves.

6 My God, I would not long to see
  My fate, with curious eyes,
What gloomy lines are writ for me,
  Or what bright scenes may rise.

7 In thy fair book of life and grace,
  Oh may I find my name
Recorded in some humble place,
  Beneath my Lord, the Lamb.

54 *The Designs of God hidden* C. M.

1 THY way, O God, is in the sea,
  Thy paths I cannot trace;
Nor comprehend the mystery
  Of thy unbounded grace.

2 Here the dark vails of flesh and sense
  My captive soul surround;
Mysterious deeps of Providence
  My wondering thoughts confound.

3 As through a glass, I dimly see
  The wonders of thy love:
How little do I know of thee,
  Or of the joys above!

4 Though but in part I know thy will,
  I bless thee for the sight;
When will thy love the rest reveal,
  In glory's clearer light?

5 With rapture shall I then survey
  Thy providence and grace;
And spend an everlasting day
  In wonder, love, and praise.

55 *The Divine Purposes.* C. M.

1 GOD moves in a mysterious way,
His wonders to perform;
He plants his footsteps in the sea,
And rides upon the storm.

2 Deep in unfathomable mines
Of never-failing skill,
He treasures up his bright designs,
And works his sovereign will.

3 Ye fearful saints, fresh courage take;
The clouds ye so much dread
Are big with mercy, and shall break
In blessings on your head.

4 Judge not the Lord by feeble sense,
But trust him for his grace;
Behind a frowning providence
He hides a smiling face.

5 His purposes will ripen fast,
Unfolding every hour;
The bud may have a bitter taste,
But sweet will be the flower.

6 Blind unbelief is sure to err,
And scan his work in vain;
God is his own interpreter,
And he will make it plain.

56 *Thanks for Preserving Goodness.* C. M.

1 WHEN all thy mercies, O my God,
My rising soul surveys,

Transported with the view, I'm lost
In wonder, love, and praise.

2 Unnumbered comforts on my soul
Thy tender care bestowed,
Before my infant heart conceived
From whom those comforts flowed.

3 When in the slippery paths of youth
With heedless steps I ran,
Thine arm, unseen, conveyed me safe,
And led me up to man.

4 Ten thousand thousand precious gifts
My daily thanks employ;
Nor is the least a cheerful heart,
That tastes those gifts with joy.

5 Through every period of my life,
Thy goodness I'll pursue;
And after death, in distant worlds,
The glorious theme renew.

6 Through all eternity, to thee
A joyful song I'll raise:
But oh, eternity's too short
To utter all thy praise.

57 *The Servants of God safe.* C. M.

1 HOW are thy servants blessed, O Lord,
How sure is their defence!
Eternal wisdom is their guide,
Their help Omnipotence.

2 In foreign realms, and lands remote,
Supported by thy care,

Through burning climes they pass unhurt,
And breathe in tainted air.

3 When by the dreadful tempest borne,
High on the broken wave,
They know thou art not slow to hear,
Nor impotent to save.

4 The storm is laid—the winds retire,
Obedient to thy will:
The sea, that roars at thy command,
At thy command is still.

5 In midst of dangers, fears, and deaths,
Thy goodness we'll adore;
We'll praise thee for thy mercies past,
And humbly hope for more.

6 Our life, while thou preserv'st that life,
Thy sacrifice shall be;
And death, when death shall be our lot,
Shall join our souls to thee.

58 *Providence and Grace.* C M.

1 ALMIGHTY Father, gracious Lord,
Kind Guardian of my days,
Thy mercies let my heart record,
In songs of grateful praise.

2 In life's first dawn, my tender frame
Was thy indulgent care,
Long ere I could pronounce thy name,
Or breathe the infant prayer.

3 Each rolling year new favors brought
From thine exhaustless store;

But ah, in vain my laboring thought
  Would count thy mercies o'er.

4 While sweet reflection through my days
  Thy bounteous hand would trace,
Still dearer blessings claim my praise,
  The blessings of thy grace.

5 Yes, I adore thee, gracious Lord,
  For favors more divine;
That I have known thy sacred word,
  Where all thy glories shine.

6 Lord, when this mortal frame decays,
  And every weakness dies,
Complete the wonders of thy grace,
  And raise me to the skies.

7 Then shall my joyful powers unite
  In more exalted lays;
And join the happy sons of light,
  In everlasting praise.

59 *Trust in God.* S. M.

1 O THOU, my life, my joy,
  My glory and my all—
Unsent by thee, no good can come,
  No evil can befall.

2 Such are thy wondrous works,
  And methods of thy grace,
That I may safely trust in thee,
  Through all this wilderness.

3 'Tis thine all-powerful arm
  Upholds me in the way;

And thy rich bounty well supplies
 The wants of every day.

4 For such compassions, Lord,
 Ten thousand thanks are due;
For such compassions, I esteem
 Ten thousand thanks too few.

60 *The Divine Protection.*—Ps. xci. 8. 7.

1 CALL Jehovah thy salvation,
 Rest beneath th' Almighty's shade;
In his secret habitation
 Dwell, and never be dismayed:
There no tumult can alarm thee,
 Thou shalt dread no hidden snare;
Guile nor violence can harm thee,
 In eternal safeguard there.

2 From the sword at noonday wasting,
 From the noisome pestilence,
In the depth of midnight blasting,
 God shall be thy sure defence:
Fear not thou the deadly quiver,
 When a thousand feel the blow;
Mercy shall thy soul deliver,
 Though ten thousand be laid low.

3 Since, with pure and firm affection,
 Thou on God hast set thy love,
With the wings of his protection
 He will shield thee from above;
Thou shalt call on him in trouble,
 He will hearken, he will save;
Here for grief reward thee double,
 Crown with life beyond the grave.

61

"Casting all your care upon Him." S. M.

1 WHY wilt thou cast thy care
Upon a feeble arm,
Which, like thy own, doth shrink to bear
Adversity or harm?

2 Why wilt thou cast thy care
Upon an erring heart,
Which hath of secret ills a share,
And dreads affliction's dart?

3 Why wilt thou cast thy care
On any born of clay?
Like flowers beneath the frosty air,
They fade and pass away.

4 But cast thy care on him
Who hath eternal might,
And will not scorn the contrite soul
That trembleth in his sight.

5 Whose glorious throne shall stand
When every star is dim;
Whose tender mercies have no bound—
Yea, cast thy care on him.

62

Divine Aid withdrawn. C. M

1 A PRESENT God is all our strength,
And all our joy and hope;
When he withdraws, our comforts die,
And every grace must droop.

2 But flattering trifles charm our hearts
To court their false embrace,

Till justly this neglected friend
Averts his angry face.

3 He leaves us, and we miss him not,
But go presumptuous on,
Till, baffled, wounded, and enslaved,
We learn that God is gone.

4 And what, my soul, can then remain,
One ray of light to give?
Severed from him, their better life,
How can his children live?

5 Hence, all ye painted forms of joy,
And leave my heart to mourn:
I would devote these eyes to tears,
Till cheered by his return.

63 *Trust in God.* C. M.

1 WHO knoweth of his safety, Lord—
Who here in tents of clay
Doth 'bide the buffet of the storm,
The footsteps of decay;
Whose life by fleeting air is fed,
Whose thread-like nerves do thrill
At every sympathy with pain,
At every thought of ill?

2 Who knoweth of his safety, Lord—
Who o'er the crumbling verge
Of fearful floods, with blinded eyes,
His slippery course doth urge;
Who, dreaming but to pluck the flowers,
May on a serpent tread,

And, in the glory of his hours,
Be numbered with the dead?

3 He knoweth, Lord, whose soul doth rest
On thy eternal might;
The anchor of whose hope is sure,
Though earth eludes his sight:
Who, when the hoarded joys of time
All like a vision fly,
Can, from this falling tent of clay,
Rise to a home on high.

64 *The Works of God.* C. M.

1 LORD, when our raptured thought surveys
Creation's beauties o'er,
All nature joins to teach thy praise,
And bid our souls adore.

2 Where'er we turn our gazing eyes,
Thy radiant footsteps shine;
Ten thousand pleasing wonders rise,
And speak their source divine.

3 On us thy providence has shone
With gentle, smiling rays;
Oh may our lips and lives make known
Thy goodness and thy praise.

65 *"Whom have I,"* &c.—Ps. lxxiii. 25. 7s.

1 LORD of earth, thy forming hand
Well this beauteous frame hath planned;
Yet, amidst this scene so fair,
Should I cease thy smile to share,

What were all its joys to me?
Whom have I on earth but thee?

2 Lord of heaven, beyond our sight
Lies a world of purer light;
There, in love's unclouded reign,
Parted hands shall clasp again;
While immortal music rings
From unnumbered seraph strings.

3 There, in bliss and praises high,
Dwells a glorious company;
Oh, that world is passing fair,
Yet, if thou wert absent there,
What were all its joys to me?
Whom have I in heaven but thee?

4 Lord of earth and heaven, my breast
Seeks in thee its only rest;
I was lost—thy accents mild
Homeward lured thy wandering child;
I was blind—thy healing ray
Charmed the long eclipse away.

5 Source of every joy I know,
Solace of my every wo—
Oh, if once thy smile divine
Ceased upon my soul to shine,
What were earth or heaven to me?
Whom have I in each but thee?

66 *Preserving Grace.*—Jude 24, 25. S. M

1 TO GOD, the only wise,
Our Saviour and our King,

Let all the saints below the skies
Their humble praises bring.

2 'Tis his almighty love,
His counsel and his care,
Preserves us safe from sin and death,
And every hurtful snare.

3 He will present our souls
Unblemished and complete,
Before the glory of his face,
With joys divinely great.

4 Then all the chosen seed
Shall meet around the throne;
Shall bless the conduct of his grace,
And make his wonders known.

5 To our Redeemer God
Wisdom and power belongs;
Immortal crowns of majesty,
And everlasting songs.

67 *The Love of God.* C. P. M.

1 MY God, thy boundless love I praise;
How bright on high its glories blaze!
How sweetly bloom below!
It streams from thy eternal throne;
Through heaven its joys for ever run,
And o'er the earth they flow.

2 'Tis love that paints the purple morn,
And bids the clouds, in air upborne,
Their genial drops distill;
In every vernal beam it glows,

And breathes in every gale that blows,
And glides in every rill,
But in the gospel it appears
In sweeter, fairer characters,
And charms the ravished breast:
There love immortal leaves the sky,
To wipe the drooping mourner's eye,
And give the weary rest.

4 Then let the love that makes me bless'd,
With cheerful praise inspire my breast,
And ardent gratitude;
And all my thoughts and passions tend
To thee, my Father and my Friend,
My soul's eternal good.

68 *Disobedience and Ingratitude.* C. M.

1 INFINITE power, eternal Lord,
How mighty is thy hand!
All nature rose t' obey thy word,
And moves at thy command.

2 Fire, air, and earth, and stormy sea,
Perform thy sovereign will;
And every beast and every tree
Thy great designs fulfill.

3 But ah, how wide my spirit flies,
And wanders from her God;
My soul forgets the heavenly prize,
And treads the downward road.

4 The creatures of a meaner frame
Pay all their dues to thee;

But they have never known thy name,
  Nor e'er been loved like me.

5 Great God, create my soul anew;
  To thee my powers I bring;
Make all the wheels of nature true,
  And govern every spring.

6 Then shall my feet no more depart,
  Nor my affections rove;
Devotion shall be all my heart,
  And all my passions—love.

69 *God our Father.* C. M.

1 COME, shout aloud the Father's grace,
  And sing the Saviour's love;
Soon shall you join the glorious theme,
  In loftier strains, above.

2 God, the eternal, mighty God,
  To dearer names descends;
Calls you his treasure and his joy,
  His children and his friends.

3 My Father—God! and may these lips
  Pronounce a name so dear?
Not thus could heaven's sweet harmony
  Delight my list'ning ear.

4 Thanks to my God for every gift
  His bounteous hands bestow;
And thanks eternal for that love
  Whence all those comforts flow.

5 For ever let my grateful heart
  His boundless grace adore,

Which gives ten thousand blessings now,
  And bids me hope for more.

70 "*The Spirit of Adoption.*"—Rom. viii. 15. C. M.

1 SOVEREIGN of all the worlds on high,
  Allow my humble claim;
Nor, when I raise my guilty head,
  Disdain a father's name.

2 My Father—God! how sweet the sound!
  How tender, and how dear!
Not all the harmony of heaven
  Could so delight the ear.

3 Come, sacred Spirit, seal the name
  On my expanding heart;
And show that in Jehovah's grace
  I share a filial part.

4 Cheered by a signal so divine,
  Unwavering I believe;
And Abba, Father, humbly cry;
  Nor can the sign deceive.

71 *Support from God.*—Ps. xvi. C. M.

LET heathens to their idols haste,
  And worship wood or stone;
But my delightful lot is cast
  Where the true God is known.

2 His hand provides my constant food,
  He fills my daily cup;
Much am I pleased with present good,
  But more rejoice in hope.

3 God is my portion and my joy;
His counsels are my light;
He gives me sweet advice by day,
And gentle hints by night.

4 My soul would all her thoughts approve
To his all-seeing eye;
Nor death nor hell my hope shall move,
While such a friend is nigh.

72 *God the Portion of the Soul.* C. M

1 MY God, the spring of all my joys,
The life of my delights,
The glory of my brightest days,
And comfort of my nights,—

2 In darkest shades, if thou appear,
My dawning is begun;
Thou art my soul's bright morning star,
And thou my rising sun.

3 The opening heavens around me shine
With beams of sacred bliss,
While Jesus shows his love is mine,
And whispers I am his!

4 My soul would leave this heavy clay,
At that transporting word;
Run up with joy the shining way,
And haste to meet my Lord.

5 Fearless of hell and ghastly death,
I'd break through every foe;
The wings of love and arms of faith
Should bear me conqueror through.

CHRIST.

73

The Song of the Angels. 8. 7.

1 HARK! what mean those holy voices,
Sweetly sounding through the skies?
Lo, th' angelic host rejoices;
Heavenly hallelujahs rise!

2 Christ is born, the great Anointed;
Him, in bursts of praise, they sing;
He hath come, of God appointed
Saviour, Prophet, Priest, and King.

3 Sinners, learn that song of glory;
Hail the heavenly kingdom nigh;
Spread abroad the wondrous story;
Shout in praise to God most high.

74

The Incarnation. 7s

1 HARK! the herald angels sing
"Glory to the new-born King;
Peace on earth and mercy mild—
God and sinners reconciled."

2 Joyful, all ye nations, rise,
Join the triumph of the skies;
With th' angelic host proclaim,
"Christ is born in Bethlehem!"

3 Vailed in flesh, the Godhead see,
Hail th' incarnate Deity!
Pleased as man with men to dwell,
Jesus, our Immanuel.

4 Mild, he lays his glory by,
Born that man no more may die;
Born to raise the sons of earth,
Born to give them second birth.

5 Sing we then—with angels sing
Glory to the new-born King:
Glory in the highest heaven,
Peace on earth, and man forgiven.

75 *The Star of the East.*—Matt. ii. 2. 11. 10.

1 BRIGHTEST and best of the sons of the morning—
Dawn on our darkness, and lend us thine aid;
Star of the East, the horizon adorning—
Guide where the infant Redeemer is laid.

2 Cold on his cradle the dew-drops are shining;
Low lies his head, with the beasts of the stall;
Angels adore him, in slumbers reclining—
Maker and Monarch and Saviour of all.

3 Say, shall we yield him, in costly devotion,
Odors of Edom, and off'rings divine?
Gems of the mountain, and pearls of the ocean,
Myrrh from the forest, and gold from the mine?

4 Vainly we offer each ample oblation;
Vainly with gifts would his favor secure;

Richer, by far, is the heart's adoration;
Dearer to God are the prayers of the poor.

5 Brightest and best of the sons of the morning—
Dawn on our darkness, and lend us thine aid;
Star of the East, the horizon adorning—
Guide where our infant Redeemer is laid.

76 *Christ's Mission attested.* L. M.

1 BEHOLD, the blind their sight receive!
Behold, the dead awake and live!
The dumb speak wonders! and the lame
Leap like the hart, and bless his name!

2 Thus does th' eternal Spirit own
And seal the mission of the Son;
The Father vindicates his cause,
While he hangs bleeding on the cross.

3 He dies!—the heavens in mourning stood!
He rises—and appears a God!
Behold the Lord ascending high,
No more to bleed, no more to die.

4 Hence and for ever from my heart
I bid my doubts and fears depart;
And to those hands my soul resign,
Which bear credentials so divine.

77 *Healing Mercy.* C. M.

1 JESUS, and didst thou condescend,
When vailed in human clay,

To heal the sick, the lame, the blind,
And drive disease away?

2 Didst thou regard the beggar's cry,
And give the blind to see?—
Jesus, thou Son of David, hear—
Have mercy, too, on me.

3 And didst thou pity mortal wo,
And sight and health restore?
Then pity, Lord, and save my soul,
Which needs thy mercy more.

4 Didst thou regard thy servant's cry,
When sinking in the wave?
I perish, Lord,—oh save my soul,
For thou alone canst save.

78 *Repentance at the Cross.* C. M.

1 ALAS, and did my Saviour bleed,
And did my Sovereign die?
Would he devote that sacred head,
For such a worm as I?

2 Was it for crimes that I had done
He groaned upon the tree?
Amazing pity! grace unknown!
And love beyond degree!

3 Well might the sun in darkness hide,
And shut his glories in,
When God, the mighty Maker, died
For man the creature's sin.

4 Thus might I hide my blushing face,
While his dear cross appears;

Dissolve my heart in thankfulness,
And melt my eyes to tears.

5 But floods of tears can ne'er repay
The debt of love I owe:
Here, Lord, I give myself away—
'Tis all that I can do.

79 *Redemption finished.* 8. 7. 4

1 HARK! the voice of love and mercy
Sounds aloud from Calvary!
See! it rends the rocks asunder—
Shakes the earth—and vails the sky!
"It is finished!"—
Hear the dying Saviour cry.

2 "It is finished!"—oh, what pleasure
Do these precious words afford!
Heavenly blessings, without measure,
Flow to us through Christ the Lord.
"It is finished!"
Saints, the dying words record.

3 Tune your harps anew, ye seraphs,
Join to sing the pleasing theme:
All in earth and all in heaven,
Join to praise Immanuel's name:
Hallelujah!
Glory to the bleeding Lamb.

80 *Christ our Sacrifice.*—Lam. i. 12. 5. 11.

1 ALL ye that pass by,
To Jesus draw nigh;
To you is it nothing that Jesus should die?

For sins not his own
He dies to atone;
Were sorrow and pity like his ever known?

2 The Lord, in the day
Of his anger, did lay
Our sins on the Lamb; and he bore them [away;
He answered for all;
Oh come at his call,
And low at his cross in astonishment fall.

3 Oh lift up your eyes;
"'Tis finished," he cries:
Almighty, he suffers; immortal, he dies:
For you and for me
He prayed on the tree;
The prayer is accepted—the sinner is free.

81

Christ our Example in Suffering. 7s. 6 lines.

1 GO to dark Gethsemane,
Ye who feel the tempter's power;
Your Redeemer's conflict see;
Watch with him one bitter hour:
Turn not from his griefs away;
Learn of Jesus Christ to pray.

2 Follow to the judgment-hall,
View the Lord of life arraigned:
Oh the wormwood and the gall!
Oh the pangs his soul sustained!
Shun not suffering, shame, or loss;
Learn of Christ to bear the cross.

3 Calvary's mournful mountain climb;
There, adoring at his feet,

Mark that miracle of time—
God's own sacrifice complete:
"It is finished," hear him cry;
Learn of Jesus Christ to die.

4 Early hasten to the tomb,
Where they laid his breathless clay;
All is solitude and gloom;
Who hath taken him away?
Christ is risen!—he seeks the skies;
Saviour, teach us so to rise.

82 *A Look from the Cross.* C. M.

1 I SAW One hanging on a tree,
In agony and blood,
Who fixed his languid eyes on me,
As near the cross I stood.

2 Sure never, till my latest breath,
Can I forget that look;
It seemed to charge me with his death,
Though not a word he spoke.

3 My conscience felt and owned the guilt,
And plunged me in despair;
I saw my sins his blood had spilt,
And helped to nail him there.

4 A second look he gave, which said—
"I freely all forgive;
This blood is for thy ransom paid,
I die that thou mayst live."

5 Thus, while his death my sin displays,
In all its blackest hue,
Such is the mystery of grace
It seals my pardon too.

83 *The Lamb of God.* 6.

1 GOD of my salvation, hear,
  And help me to believe;
Now to thee do I draw near,
  Thy blessing to receive:
Full of sin, alas, I am,
  But to thee for refuge flee;
Friend of sinners, spotless Lamb,
  Thy blood was shed for me.

2 No good word or work or thought
  I bring to buy thy grace;
Pardon I accept, unbought;
  Thy proffer I embrace.
Needy, guilty, vile I am,
  Yet I know thy love is free;
Friend of sinners, spotless Lamb,
  Thy blood was shed for me.

3 Saviour, from thy wounded side
  I never will depart;
At thy cross will I abide,
  And give thee there my heart;
When my place above I claim,
  I will make the cross my plea;
Friend of sinners, spotless Lamb,
  Thy blood was shed for me.

84 *Crucifixion to the World.*—Gal. vi. 14. L. M.

1 WHEN I survey the wondrous cross
  On which the Prince of glory died,
My richest gain I count but loss,
  And pour contempt on all my pride.

2 Forbid it, Lord, that I should boast,
Save in the death of Christ, my God;
All the vain things that charm me most,
I sacrifice them to his blood.

3 See, from his head, his hands, his feet,
Sorrow and love flow mingled down!
Did e'er such love and sorrow meet,
Or thorns compose so rich a crown?

4 Were the whole realm of nature mine,
That were a present far too small;
Love so amazing, so divine,
Demands my soul, my life, my all.

85 *Christ our Sacrifice.* S. M.

1 NOT all the blood of beasts
On Jewish altars slain,
Could give the guilty conscience peace,
Or wash away the stain.

2 But Christ, the heavenly Lamb,
Takes all our sins away;
A sacrifice of nobler name,
And richer blood than they.

3 My faith would lay her hand
On that dear head of thine,
While like a penitent I stand,
And there confess my sin.

4 My soul looks back to see
The burdens thou didst bear,
When hanging on the cursed tree,
And hopes her guilt was there.

5 Believing, we rejoice
To see the curse remove;
We bless the Lamb with cheerful voice,
And sing his bleeding love.

86

Remember Calvary. 7. 6.

1 LAMB of God, whose bleeding love
We now recall to mind,
Send the answer from above,
And let us mercy find:
Think on us who think on thee;
Every burdened soul release;
Oh remember Calvary,
And bid us go in peace.

2 Let thy blood, by faith applied,
The sinner's pardon seal;
Speak us freely justified,
And all our sickness heal:
By thy passion on the tree,
Let our griefs and troubles cease;
Oh remember Calvary,
And bid us go in peace.

3 Do not bid us hence depart,
Till thou our wants relieve;
Write forgiveness on our heart,
And all thine image give:
Still our souls shall cry to thee,
Cry for pardon and release;
Oh remember Calvary,
And bid us go in peace.

87 *The Robe of Righteousness.*—Isa. lxi. 10. C. M.

1. AWAKE, my heart, arise my tongue,
Prepare a tuneful voice;
In God the life of all my joys,
Aloud will I rejoice.

2 'Tis he adorned my naked soul,
And made salvation mine;
Upon a poor polluted worm
He makes his graces shine.

3 And lest the shadow of a spot
Should on my soul be found,
He took the robe the Saviour wrought,
And cast it all around.

4 How far the heavenly robe exceeds
What earthly princes wear!
These ornaments, how bright they shine!
How white the garments are!

5 Strangely, my soul, art thou arrayed
By the great sacred Three;
In sweetest harmony of praise
Let all thy powers agree.

88 *The Hiding-Place.*—Isa. xxxii. 2. L. M.

1 HAIL, sovereign love, that first began
The scheme to rescue fallen man!
Hail, matchless, free, eternal grace,
That gave my soul a hiding-place.

2 Against the God that rules the sky,
I fought with hands uplifted high;

Despised the offers of his grace,
Too proud to seek a hiding-place.

3 But thus th' eternal counsel ran—
"Almighty love—arrest the man;"
I felt the arrows of distress,
And found I had no hiding-place.

4 Vindictive Justice stood in view;
To Sinai's fiery mount I flew;
But Justice cried, with frowning face—
"This mountain is no hiding-place."

5 But lo, a heavenly voice I heard—
And mercy's angel soon appeared;
Who led me on, a pleasing pace,
To Jesus Christ, my hiding-place.

6 On him almighty vengeance fell,
Which must have sunk a world to hell;
He bore it for his chosen race,
And now he is my hiding-place.

89 *Glorying in the Cross.* C. M. Double.

1 THOU art my hiding-place, O Lord,
In thee I fix my trust,
Encouraged by thy holy word—
A feeble child of dust:
I have no argument beside,
I urge no other plea,
And 'tis enough—the Saviour died,
The Saviour died for me.

2 When storms of fierce temptation beat,
And furious foes assail,

My refuge is the mercy-seat,
  My hope within the vail;
From strife of tongues and bitter words,
  My spirit flies to thee:
Joy to my heart the thought affords—
  My Saviour died for me.

3 'Mid trials heavy to be borne,
  When mortal strength is vain,
A heart with grief and anguish torn,
  A body racked with pain—
Ah, what could give the sufferer rest,
  Bid every murmur flee—
But this—the witness in my breast
  That Jesus died for me?

4 And when thine awful voice commands
  This body to decay,
And life, in its last lingering sands,
  Is ebbing fast away—
Then, though it be in accents weak,
  My voice shall call on thee,
And ask for strength in death to speak—
  "My Saviour died for me."

90 *Christ's voluntary Sacrifice.* C. M

1 HOW condescending and how kind
  Was God's eternal Son!
Our misery reached his heavenly mind,
  And pity brought him down.

2 He sunk beneath our heavy woes,
  To raise us to his throne:

There's ne'er a gift his hand bestows
But cost his heart a groan.

3 This was compassion like a God—
That when the Saviour knew
The price of pardon was his blood,
His pity ne'er withdrew.

4 Now, though he reigns exalted high,
His love is still as great;
Well he remembers Calvary,
Nor lets his saints forget.

5 Here let our hearts begin to melt,
While we his death record;
And, with our joy for pardoned guilt,
Mourn that we pierced the Lord.

91 *Praise to the Redeemer.* C. M.

1 PLUNGED in a gulf of dark despair,
We wretched sinners lay,
Without one cheerful beam of hope,
Or spark of glimmering day.

2 With pitying eyes the Prince of grace
Beheld our helpless grief;
He saw—and oh, amazing love!
He ran to our relief.

3 Down from the shining seats above,
With joyful haste he fled,
Entered the grave in mortal flesh,
And dwelt among the dead.

4 Oh, for this love let rocks and hills
Their lasting silence break;

And all harmonious human tongues
The Saviour's praises speak.

5 Angels, assist our mighty joys;
Strike all your harps of gold;
But when you raise your highest notes,
His love can ne'er be told.

92 *The Redeemer's Commission.* C. M.

1 COME, happy souls, approach your God
With new melodious songs;
Come, render to almighty grace
The tribute of your tongues.

2 So strange, so boundless was the love
That pitied dying men,
The Father sent his equal Son
To give them life again.

3 Thy hands, dear Jesus, were not armed
With a revenging rod;
No hard commission to perform—
The vengeance of a God.

4 But all was mercy, all was mild,
And wrath forsook the throne,
When Christ on the kind errand came,
And brought salvation down.

5 Here, sinners, you may heal your wounds,
And wipe your sorrows dry;
Trust in the mighty Saviour's name,
And you shall never die.

93 *"Chief among Ten Thousand."* C. M

1 MAJESTIC sweetness sits enthroned
Upon the Saviour's brow;
His head with radiant glories crowned,
His lips with grace o'erflow.

2 He saw me plunged in deep distress,
And flew to my relief;
For me he bore the shameful cross,
And carried all my grief.

3 To him I owe my life and breath,
And all the joys I have:
He makes me triumph over death,
And saves me from the grave.

4 To heaven, the place of his abode,
He brings my weary feet;
Shows me the glories of my God;
And makes my joys complete.

5 Since from his bounty I receive
Such proofs of love divine,
Had I a thousand hearts to give,
Lord, they should all be thine.

94 *Condescension of Christ.* C. M

1 AND did the Holy and the Just,
The sovereign of the skies,
Stoop down to wretchedness and dust,
That guilty man might rise?

2 Yes—the Redeemer left his throne—
His radiant throne on high—

Surprising mercy!—love unknown!
  To suffer—bleed—and die.

3 To dwell with misery here below,
  The Saviour left the skies,
And sunk to wretchedness and wo,
  That worthless man might rise.

4 Jesus, my soul adoring bends
  To love so full, so free;
And may I hope that love extends
  Its saving power to me?

5 What glad returns can I impart
  For favors so divine?
Oh take my all—this worthless heart,
  And make it wholly thine.

95 *Gratitude.* L. M.

1 THE Lord of life, the Saviour, dies,
  For mortal crimes a sacrifice:
What love, what mercy—how divine!
Jesus, and can I call thee mine?

2 Be all my heart and all my days
Devoted to my Saviour's praise;
And let my glad obedience prove
How much I owe, how much I love.

3 Let humble, penitential wo,
With painful, pleasing anguish flow:
And thy forgiving smiles impart
Life, hope, and joy to every heart.

96 *The Resurrection and Ascension.* 7s.

1 ANGELS, roll the rock away;
  Death, yield up thy mighty prey;

See, he rises from the tomb,
Glowing with immortal bloom.

2 'Tis the Saviour; angels, raise
Your eternal songs of praise;
Let the earth's remotest bound
Hear the joy-inspiring sound.

3 Now, ye saints, lift up your eyes,
Now to glory see him rise;
Hosts of angels on the road
Hail and sing th' incarnate God.

4 Heaven unfolds its portals wide!
Glorious conqueror, through them ride;
King of Glory, mount the throne—
Boundless empire is thine own.

5 Praise him, all ye heavenly choirs;
Praise, and sweep your golden lyres;
Shout, O earth, in rapturous songs,
From ten thousand thousand tongues.

97 *The Resurrection of Christ.* 7s

1 MORNING breaks upon the tomb,
Jesus scatters all its gloom;
Day of triumph through the skies—
See the glorious Saviour rise!

2 Ye who are of death afraid,
Triumph in the scattered shade;
Drive your anxious cares away;
See the place where Jesus lay.

3 Christian, dry your flowing tears,
Chase your unbelieving fears;

Look on his deserted grave;
Doubt no more his power to save.

98 *The Ascension of Christ.* 7s.

1 HAIL the day that sees him rise,
Glorious, to his native skies!
Christ, awhile to mortals given,
Enters now the gates of heaven.

2 There the glorious triumph waits;
Lift your heads, eternal gates!
Christ hath vanquished death and sin;
Take the King of Glory in.

3 See, the heaven its Lord receives!
Yet he loves the earth he leaves:
Though returning to his throne,
Still he calls mankind his own.

4 Still for us he intercedes;
His prevailing death he pleads;
Near himself prepares our place,
Great Precursor of our race.

5 What though parted from our sight,
Far above yon starry height;
Thither our affections rise,
Following him beyond the skies.

99 *Jesus Glorified.*—John vii. 41, 52. 8. 7.

1 HAIL, thou once despised Jesus!
Hail, thou "Galilean" King!
Thou didst suffer to release us;
Thou didst free salvation bring;

Hail, thou agonizing Saviour,
  Bearer of our sin and shame;
By thy merits we find favor;
  Life is given through thy name.

2 Jesus, hail—enthroned in glory,
  There for ever to abide:
All the heavenly hosts adore thee,
  Seated at thy Father's side:
There for sinners thou art pleading,
  There thou dost our place prepare,
Ever for us interceding—
  Friend and Mediator there.

3 Worship, honor, power, and blessing,
  Thou art worthy to receive;
Loudest praises, without ceasing,
  Meet it is for us to give;
Help, ye bright, angelic spirits;
  Bring your sweetest, noblest lays;
Help to sing our Saviour's merits,
  Help to chant Immanuel's praise.

100 *Christ our Intercessor.*—Heb. vii. 25. L. M.

1 HE lives—the great Redeemer lives!
What joy the bless'd assurance gives!
And now, before his Father God,
Pleads the full merit of his blood.

2 Repeated crimes awake our fears,
And justice armed with frowns appears;
But in the Saviour's lovely face
Sweet mercy smiles, and all is peace.

3 Hence then, ye black despairing thoughts;
Above our fears, above our faults,
His powerful intercessions rise;
And guilt recedes, and terror dies.

4 In every dark, distressful hour,
When sin and Satan join their power,
Let this dear hope repel the dart—
That Jesus bears us on his heart.

5 Great Advocate, almighty Friend,
On thee our humble hopes depend;
Our cause can never, never fail,
For Jesus pleads, and must prevail.

101 *Confidence in the Intercessor.* H. M.

1 ARISE, my soul, arise,
Shake off thy guilty fears;
The bleeding Sacrifice
In my behalf appears;
Before the throne my Surety stands.
My name is written on his hands.

2 He ever lives above,
For me to intercede,
His all-redeeming love,
His precious blood to plead;
His blood atoned for all our race,
And sprinkles now the throne of grace.

3 My God is reconciled;
His pardoning voice I hear:
He owns me for his child—
I can no longer fear;

With confidence I now draw nigh,
And Father, Abba, Father, cry.

102 *Christ our High Priest.* C. M.

1 NOW let our cheerful eyes survey
Our great High Priest above;
And celebrate his constant care,
And sympathizing love.

2 Though raised to a superior throne,
Where angels bow around,
And high o'er all the shining train,
With matchless honors crowned;

3 The names of all his saints he bears,
Deep graven on his heart;
Nor shall the meanest Christian say
That he hath lost his part.

4 Those characters shall fair abide—
Our everlasting trust,
When gems, and monuments, and crowns,
Are mouldered down to dust.

5 So, gracious Saviour, on my breast
May thy dear name be worn;
A sacred ornament and guard,
To endless ages borne.

103 *Temptation.*—Heb. iv. 16. C. M.

1 WITH joy we meditate the grace
Of our High Priest above;
His heart is made of tenderness,
And overflows with love.

2 Touched with a sympathy within,
He knows our feeble frame;
He knows what sore temptations mean,
For he has felt the same.

3 But spotless, innocent, and pure,
The great Redeemer stood,
While Satan's fiery darts he bore,
And did resist to blood.

4 He, in the days of feeble flesh,
Poured out his cries and tears,
And, in his measure, feels afresh
What every member bears.

5 He'll never quench the smoking flax,
But raise it to a flame;
The bruised reed he never breaks,
Nor scorns the meanest name.

6 Then let our humble faith address
His mercy and his power;
We shall obtain delivering grace
In the distressing hour.

104 *The weeping Saviour.*—Luke xix. 41. S. M.

1 DID Christ o'er sinners weep,
And shall our cheeks be dry?
Let floods of penitential grief
Burst forth from every eye.

2 The Son of God in tears
The wondering angels see;
Be thou astonished, O my soul—
He shed those tears for thee.

3 He wept, that we might weep;
Each sin demands a tear;
In heaven alone no sin is found,
And there's no weeping there.

105 *Learn of me.*—Matt. xi. 29. 7s.

1 "LEARN of me," the Saviour said,
"I'm of meek and lowly heart;"
See! the feast of love is spread,
Peace and blessing I impart:
Come, ye weary, ye shall rest,
And from bondage shall be free,
When, with mild, submissive breast,
Ye will come and learn of me.

2 Learn of me on earth to dwell,
With thy hopes and home on high;
Every earthly treasure sell,
Heaven's precious pearl to buy;
Then the crown thou shalt obtain,
Where I am thou too shalt be,
King and priest for ever reign,
Endless praises learn of me.

106 *Christ the Guardian of his People.* L. M.

1 WHERE high the heavenly temple stands,
The house of God not made with hands,
A great High Priest our nature wears,
And on his heart his people bears.

2 He who for us a surety stood,
And made the offering of his blood,

Pursues in heaven his mighty plan,
The Saviour and the Friend of man.

3 Our fellow-sufferer still retains
The knowledge of our fears and pains;
And still remembers, in the skies,
His tears and agonies and cries.

4 With boldness, therefore, at his throne
We come to make our sorrows known;
And ask the aids of heavenly power,
To help us in the evil hour.

107 *Christ the Rock of Ages.* 7s. 6 lines.

1 ROCK of ages, cleft for me,
Let me hide myself in thee;
Let the water and the blood,
From thy wounded side which flowed,
Be of sin the double cure;
Save from wrath, and make me pure.

2 Should my tears for ever flow,
Should my zeal no languor know,
This for sin could not atone;
Thou must save, and thou alone:
In my hand no price I bring,
Simply to thy cross I cling.

3 While I draw this fleeting breath,
When my eye-lids close in death,
When I rise to worlds unknown,
And behold thee on thy throne,
Rock of ages, cleft for me,
Let me hide myself in thee.

108 *The Star of Bethlehem.* L. M.

1 WHEN, marshalled on the nightly plain,
The glitt'ring host bestud the sky,
One star alone, of all the train,
Can fix the sinner's wandering eye.

2 Hark! hark! to God the chorus breaks,
From every host, from every gem;
But one alone the Saviour speaks,
It is the Star of Bethlehem.

3 Once on the raging seas I rode—
The storm was loud, the night was dark,
The ocean yawned—and rudely blowed
The wind that tossed my foundering bark.

4 Deep horror then my vitals froze;
Death-struck, I ceased the tide to stem,
When suddenly a star arose,
It was the Star of Bethlehem.

5 It was my guide, my light, my all;
It bade my dark forebodings cease;
And, through the storm, and danger's thrall,
It led me to the port of peace.

6 Now safely moored—my perils o'er,
I'll sing, first in night's diadem,
For ever and for evermore,
The Star—the Star of Bethlehem!

109 *The Wounds of Sin.* 8. 7

1 JESUS, still will I adore thee;
Well thou know'st a sinner's heart;

All my wounds are fresh before thee,
Thou alone canst heal their smart.

2 Thou, of all-sufficient merit,
May the blood that from thee flowed,
May thy purifying Spirit
Be upon my heart bestowed.

3 Ah, how deeply am I wounded,
Spoiled by Satan, pierced by sin!
And hath love for me abounded?
Hark, a Saviour speaks within.

4 "Sinner, yes, my love is towards thee
Everlasting and divine—
Endless hope it yet affords thee,
Seal it—take it—I am thine."

5 And wilt thou be mine for ever?
Shall I live with thee, and reign?
Come, these mouldering chains to sever,
Come, for death to me is gain.

110 *Earnest Supplication.* 7s. Double.

1 SAVIOUR, when, in dust, to thee
Low we bow th' adoring knee;
When, repentant, to the skies
Scarce we lift our streaming eyes;
Oh, by all thy pains and wo,
Suffered once for man below,
Bending from thy throne on high,
Hear thy people when they cry.

2 By thine hour of dark despair,
By thine agony of prayer,

By the purple robe of scorn,
By thy wounds—the crown of thorns—
By thy cross—thy pangs and cries,
By thy perfect sacrifice,
Jesus, look with pitying eye;
Hear thy people when they cry.

3 By thy deep expiring groan,
By thy sealed sepulchral stone,
By thy triumphs o'er the grave,
By thy power from death to save,
Mighty God, ascended Lord,
To thy throne in heaven restored,
Saviour, Prince, exalted high,
Hear thy people when they cry.

111 *Christ our Righteousness.*—Phil. iii. 9. L. M.

1 JESUS, thy blood and righteousness
My beauty are, my glorious dress:
'Midst flaming worlds, in these arrayed,
With joy shall I lift up my head.

2 Bold shall I stand in that great day;
For who aught to my charge shall lay,
While, through thy blood, absolved I am
From sin's tremendous curse and shame?

3 When from the dust of death I rise,
To take my mansion in the skies,
E'en then shall this be all my plea—
"Jesus hath lived and died for me."

112 *Christ the Refuge.* 7s. Double.

1 JESUS, lover of my soul,
Let me to thy bosom fly,

While the raging billows roll,
  While the tempest still is high:
Hide me, O my Saviour, hide,
  Till the storm of life be past;
Safe into the haven guide;
  Oh receive my soul at last.

2 Other refuge have I none—
  Hangs my helpless soul on thee;
Leave, ah, leave me not alone,
  Still support and comfort me;
All my trust on thee is stayed,
  All my help from thee I bring;
Cover my defenceless head
  With the shadow of thy wing.

3 Thou, O Christ, art all I want;
  More than all in thee I find;
Raise the fallen, cheer the faint,
  Heal the sick, and lead the blind:
Just and holy is thy name,
  I am all unrighteousness;
Vile and full of sin I am,
  Thou art full of truth and grace.

4 Plenteous grace with thee is found—
  Grace to pardon all my sin;
Let the healing streams abound,
  Make and keep me pure within;
Thou of life the fountain art,
  Freely let me take of thee:
Spring thou up within my heart,
  Rise to all eternity.

113 *Excellence of Christ.* C. M.

1 INFINITE excellence is thine,
Thou lovely Prince of grace;
Thine uncreated beauties shine
With never fading rays.

2 Sinners, from earth's remotest end,
Come bending at thy feet;
To thee their prayers and praise ascend,
In thee their wishes meet.

3 Millions of happy spirits live
On thine exhaustless store;
From thee they all their bliss receive,
And still thou givest more.

4 Thou art their triumph and their joy;
They find their all in thee;
Thy glories will their tongues employ,
Through all eternity.

114 *Sinners directed to Calvary.* 7s. 6 lines.

1 WEARY souls, that wander wide
From the central point of bliss,
Turn to Jesus crucified,
Fly to those dear wounds of his;
Sink into the purple flood;
Rise into the life of God.

2 Oh believe the record true;
God to you his Son hath given;
Ye may now be happy too—
Find on earth the life of heaven,
Live the life of heaven above,
All the life of glorious love.

115 *Healing Mercy implored.* C. M.

1 HEAL us, Immanuel, here we are,
Waiting to feel thy touch;
Deep wounded souls to thee repair,
And Saviour, we are such.

2 Remember him who once applied,
With trembling, for relief;
"Lord, I believe," with tears he cried,
"Oh help my unbelief."

3 She too, who touched thee in the press,
And healing virtue stole,
Was answered, "Daughter, go in peace,
Thy faith hath made thee whole."

4 Like her, with hopes and fears we come,
To touch thee if we may;
Oh send us not despairing home,
Send none unhealed away.

116 *Union with Christ.* S. M.

1 DEAR Saviour, we are thine
By everlasting bands:
Our names, our hearts, we would resign
And souls, into thy hands.

2 Accepted for thy sake,
And justified by faith,
We of thy righteousness partake,
And find in thee our life.

3 Thy Spirit shall unite
Our souls to thee, our head;

Shall form us to thine image bright,
 That we thy paths may tread.

4 Death may our souls divide
 From these abodes of clay;
But love shall keep us near thy side,
 Through all the gloomy way.

5 Since Christ and we are one,
 Why should we doubt or fear?
Since he in heaven hath fixed his throne,
 He'll bring his people there.

117 *Christ the Way, the Truth, and the Life.* C. M.

1 THOU art the Way—to thee alone
 From sin and death we flee;
And he who would the Father seek,
 Must seek him, Lord, in thee.

2 Thou art the Truth—thy word alone
 True wisdom can impart;
Thou only canst instruct the mind,
 And purify the heart.

3 Thou art the Life—the rending tomb
 Proclaims thy conquering arm;
And those who put their trust in thee
 Nor death nor hell shall harm.

118 *The Great Physician.* 7. 6. Iambic

1 HOW lost was my condition,
 Till Jesus made me whole!
There is but one physician
 Can cure a sin-sick soul.

The worst of all diseases
  Is light, compared with sin;
On every part it seizes,
  But rages most within.

2 From men great skill professing,
  I thought a cure to gain;
But this proved more distressing,
  And added to my pain.
Some said that nothing ailed me;
  Some gave me up for lost;
Thus every refuge failed me,
  And all my hopes were crossed.

3 At length this great Physician—
  (How matchless is his grace!)
Accepted my petition,
  And undertook my case;
Next door to death he found me,
  And snatched me from the grave,
To tell to all around me
  His wondrous power to save.

4 A dying, risen Jesus,
  Seen by the eye of faith,
At once from danger frees us,
  And saves the soul from death:
Come then to this Physician,
  His help he'll freely give;
He makes no hard condition,
  'Tis only—look, and live.

119 *Christ crucified.* 7. 6.

1 VAIN, delusive world, adieu—
  With all of creature good;

Only Jesus I pursue,
  Who bought me with his blood.
All thy pleasures I forego,
  All thy wealth and all thy pride;
Only Jesus will I know,
  And Jesus crucified.

2 Turning to my rest again,
  The Saviour I adore;
He relieves my grief and pain,
  And bids me weep no more:
Rivers of salvation flow
  From his head, his hands, his side;
Only Jesus will I know,
  And Jesus crucified.

3 Him to know is life and peace
  And pleasure without end;
This is all my happiness—
  On Jesus to depend,
Daily in his grace to grow,
  Ever in his love abide:
Only Jesus will I know,
  And Jesus crucified.

120 *Praise to the Redeemer.* C. P. M.

1 OH, could I speak the matchless worth,
Oh, could I sound the glories forth
    Which in my Saviour shine—
I'd soar and touch the heavenly strings,
And vie with Gabriel, while he sings
    In notes almost divine.

2 I'd sing the precious blood he spilt—
My ransom from the dreadful guilt
Of sin, and wrath divine:
I'd sing his glorious righteousness,
In which all-perfect, heavenly dress,
My soul shall ever shine.

3 I'd sing the characters he bears,
And all the forms of love he wears,
Exalted on his throne:
In loftiest songs of sweetest praise,
I would, to everlasting days,
Make all his glories known.

4 Well, the delightful day will come,
When my dear Lord will call me home,
And I shall see his face;
Then, with my Saviour, brother, friend,
A bless'd eternity I'll spend,
Triumphant in his grace.

121 *The name of Jesus precious.*—1 Pet. ii. 7. C. M.

1 JESUS, I love thy charming name;
'Tis music to my ear;
Fain would I sound it out so loud
That earth and heaven might hear.

2 Yes—thou art precious to my soul,
My transport and my trust;
Jewels to thee are gaudy toys,
And gold is sordid dust.

3 All my capacious powers can wish,
In thee doth richly meet;

Nor to my eyes is light so dear,
Nor friendship half so sweet.

4 Thy grace shall dwell upon my heart,
And shed its fragrance there;
The noblest balm of all its wounds,
The cordial of its care.

5 I'll speak the honors of thy name
With my last laboring breath;
Then, speechless, clasp thee in my arms—
The antidote of death.

122 *Characters of Christ.* H. M.

1 JOIN all the glorious names
Of wisdom, love, and power,
That ever mortals knew,
That angels ever bore:
All are too mean to speak his worth,—
Too mean to set my Saviour forth.

2 Jesus, my great *High Priest*,
Offered his blood, and died;
My guilty conscience seeks
No sacrifice beside:
His powerful blood did once atone,
And now it pleads before the throne.

3 My *Advocate* appears
For my defence on high;
The Father bows his ears,
And lays his thunder by;
Not all that hell or sin can say
Shall turn his heart, his love away.

4 My dear Almighty *Lord*,
My *Conqueror* and my *King*,
Thy sceptre and thy sword—
Thy reigning grace I sing:
Thine is the power; behold I sit,
In willing bonds, beneath thy feet.

5 Should all the hosts of death,
And powers of hell unknown,
Put their most dreadful forms
Of rage and mischief on,
I shall be safe—for Christ displays
Superior power, and guardian grace.

123 *The name of Jesus.* C. M.

1 JESUS—the name high over all,
In hell, or earth, or sky—
Angels and men before it fall,
And devils fear and fly.

2 Jesus—the name to sinners dear,
The name to sinners given—
It scatters all their guilt and fear;
It turns their hell to heaven.

3 Oh that a dying world might know
The glory of his name;
My voice shall his salvation show,
And cry—"Behold the Lamb!"

4 Happy, if with my latest breath
I may but gasp his name;
Proclaim his love, and cry in death—
"Behold, behold the Lamb!"

124 *The Sinner's Friend.*—Prov. xviii. 24. 8. 7.

1 ONE there is, above all others
Well deserves the name of Friend;
His is love beyond a brother's,
Costly, free, and knows no end.

2 Which of all our friends, to save us,
Could or would have shed his blood?
But this Saviour died to have us
Reconciled in him to God.

3 When he lived on earth abased,
Friend of sinners was his name;
Now, above all glory raised,
He rejoices in the same.

4 Oh for grace our hearts to soften;
Teach us, Lord, at length to love;
We, alas, forget too often
What a Friend we have above.

125 *Preciousness of the Saviour.* C. M

1 HOW sweet the name of Jesus sounds
In a believer's ear!
It soothes his sorrows, heals his wounds,
And drives away his fear.

2 It makes the wounded spirit whole,
And calms the troubled breast;
'Tis manna to the hungry soul,
And to the weary rest.

3 By him my prayers acceptance gain,
Although with sin defiled;

Satan accuses me in vain,
  And I am owned a child.

4 Weak is the effort of my heart,
  And cold my warmest thought;
But when I see thee as thou art,
  I'll praise thee as I ought.

Till then I would thy love proclaim
  With every fleeting breath;
And may the music of thy name
  Refresh my soul in death.

126 *Not ashamed of Christ.*—Mark viii. 38. L. M.

1 JESUS—and shall it ever be—
  A mortal man ashamed of thee?
Ashamed of thee, whom angels praise,
Whose glories shine through endless days?

2 Ashamed of Jesus?—sooner far
Let evening blush to own a star;
He sheds the beams of light divine
O'er this benighted soul of mine.

3 Ashamed of Jesus—that dear friend
On whom my hopes of heaven depend?
No; when I blush, be this my shame—
That I no more revere his name.

4 Ashamed of Jesus?—yes, I may,
When I've no guilt to wash away;
No tear to wipe—no good to crave—
No fear to quell—no soul to save.

5 Till then—nor is my boasting vain—
Till then I boast a Saviour slain;

And oh, may this my glory be—
That Christ is not ashamed of me.

127 *Gratitude to the Saviour.* H. M.

1 COME, every pious heart
That loves the Saviour's name,
Your noblest powers exert
To celebrate his fame;
Tell all above, and all below,
The debt of love to him you owe.

2 He left his starry crown,
And laid his robes aside;
On wings of love came down,
And wept, and bled, and died;
What he endured no tongue can tell,
To save our souls from death and hell.

3 From the dark grave he rose,
The mansion of the dead;
And thence his mighty foes
In glorious triumph led:
Up through the sky the conqueror rode,
And reigns on high, the Saviour—God.

4 Jesus, we ne'er can pay
The debt we owe thy love;
Yet tell us how we may
Our gratitude approve:
Our hearts—our all to thee we give:
The gift, though small, do thou receive.

128 *The Love of Christ.* C. M.

1 TO our Redeemer's glorious name
Awake the sacred song;

Oh may his love—immortal flame—
Tune every heart and tongue.

2 He left his radiant throne on high,
Left the bright realms of bliss,
And came to earth to bleed and die—
Was ever love like this?

3 Dear Lord, while we adoring pay
Our humble thanks to thee,
May every heart with rapture say—
"The Saviour died for me."

4 Oh may the sweet, the blissful theme,
Fill every heart and tongue,
Till strangers love thy charming name,
And join the sacred song

129 *Loving-kindness.* L. M.

1 AWAKE, my soul, in joyful lays,
And sing thy great Redeemer's praise;
He justly claims a song from me,
His loving-kindness—oh, how free!

2 He saw me ruined in the fall,
Yet loved me notwithstanding all;
He saved me from my lost estate,
His loving-kindness—oh, how great!

3 When trouble, like a gloomy cloud,
Has gathered thick, and thundered loud,
He near my soul has always stood,
His loving-kindness—oh, how good!

4 Often I feel my sinful heart
Prone from my Saviour to depart;

But though I have him oft forgot,
His loving-kindness changes not.

5 Soon shall I pass the gloomy vale,
Soon all my mortal powers must fail;
Oh may my last expiring breath
His loving-kindness sing in death.

6 Then let me mount and soar away
To the bright world of endless day;
And sing, with rapture and surprise,
His loving-kindness in the skies.

130 *The name of Jesus.* H. M.

1 LET earth and heaven combine,
And one high anthem raise,
To sing of love divine,
And shout the Saviour's praise;
T' adore the all-atoning Lamb,
And bless the sound of Jesus' name.

2 Jesus—transporting name!
It charms the hosts above;
They evermore proclaim,
And wonder at his love;
They look upon his heavenly face,
And study his mysterious grace.

3 His name the sinner hears,
And is from sin set free;
'Tis music in his ears;
'Tis life and victory;
New songs do now his lips employ
And dances his glad heart for joy.

4 Stung by the scorpion sin,
My poor expiring soul
The balmy sound drinks in,
And is at once made whole:
I see my Lord upon the tree,
I know, I feel he died for me.

5 Oh for a trumpet voice,
On all the world to call;
To bid their hearts rejoice
In him who died for all;
Inspire with praise each human tongue,
And wake a universal song.

131 *Christ the Joy of his People.* 11. 8.

1 O THOU in whose presence my soul takes delight,
On whom in affliction I call;
My comfort by day, and my song in the night,
My hope, my salvation, my all;

2 Oh why should I wander an alien from thee,
And cry in the desert for bread?
Thy foes will rejoice when my sorrows they see,
And smile at the tears I have shed.

3 Ye daughters of Zion, declare—have you seen
The Star that on Israel shone?
Say if in your tents my Beloved has been,
And where with his flock he has gone.

4 His voice, as the sound of the dulcimer sweet,
Is heard through the shadows of death;

The cedars of Lebanon bow at his feet,
The air is perfumed with his breath.

5 His lips as a fountain of righteousness flow,
To water the gardens of grace;
From which their salvation the Gentiles shall know,
And bask in the smiles of his face.

6 He looks, and ten thousands of angels rejoice,
And myriads wait for his word;
He speaks, and eternity, filled with his voice,
Re-echoes the praise of the Lord.

132 *Christ crowned as Lord of all.* C. M.

1 ALL hail, the power of Jesus' name!
Let angels prostrate fall;
Bring forth the royal diadem,
And crown him Lord of all.

2 Crown him, ye martyrs of our God,
Who from his altar call;
Extol the stem of Jesse's rod,
And crown him Lord of all.

3 Ye chosen seed of Israel's race,
Ye ransomed from the fall—
Hail him who saves you by his grace,
And crown him Lord of all.

4 Ye Gentile sinners, ne'er forget
The wormwood and the gall;
Go spread your trophies at his feet,
And crown him Lord of all.

5 Let every kindred, every tribe
On this terrestrial ball,
To him all majesty ascribe,
And crown him Lord of all.

6 Oh that, with yonder sacred throng,
We at his feet may fall;
We'll join the everlasting song,
And crown him Lord of all.

133 *Universal Praise to the Redeemer.* C. M.

1 COME, let us join our cheerful songs
With angels round the throne;
Ten thousand thousand are their tongues,
But all their joys are one.

2 "Worthy the Lamb that died," they cry,
"To be exalted thus:"
"Worthy the Lamb," our lips reply,
"For he was slain for us."

3 Jesus is worthy to receive
Honor and power divine;
And blessings more than we can give,
Be, Lord, for ever thine.

4 Let all that dwell above the sky,
And air, and earth, and seas,
Conspire to lift thy glories high,
And speak thine endless praise.

5 The whole creation join in one,
To bless the sacred name
Of him who sits upon the throne,
And to adore the Lamb.

134 *Jesus is King.* 6. 4.

1 LET us awake our joys;
Strike up with cheerful voice—
Each creature, sing;
Angels—begin the song;
Mortals, the strains prolong,
In accents sweet and strong—
"Jesus is King."

2 He vanquished sin and hell,
And the last foe will quell;
Mourners, rejoice:
His dying love adore,
Praise him, now raised in power,
And triumph evermore,
With a glad voice.

135 *The Glory and Grace of Christ.* L. M.

1 NOW to the Lord a noble song;
Awake, my soul—awake, my tongue;
Hosanna to th' Eternal Name,
And all his boundless love proclaim.

2 See where it shines in Jesus' face,
The brightest image of his grace;
God, in the person of his Son,
Has all his mightiest works outdone.

3 Grace!—'tis a sweet, a charming theme;
My thoughts rejoice at Jesus' name:
Ye angels, dwell upon the sound;
Ye heavens, reflect it to the ground.

4 Oh may I reach that happy place
Where he unvails his lovely face;
Where all his beauties you behold,
And sing his name to harps of gold.

136 *The Mediation of Christ.* S. M.

1 RAISE your triumphant songs
To an immortal tune;
Let the wide earth resound the deeds
Celestial grace has done.

2 Sing how Eternal Love
Its Chief Beloved chose,
And bade him raise our wretched race
From their abyss of woes.

3 His hand no thunder bears,
Nor terror clothes his brow;
No bolts to drive our guilty souls
To fiercer flames below.

4 'Twas mercy filled the throne,
And wrath stood silent by,
When Christ was sent with pardons down
To rebels doomed to die.

5 Now, sinners, dry your tears,
Let hopeless sorrow cease;
Bow to the sceptre of his love,
And take the offered peace.

6 Lord, we obey thy call;
We lay a humble claim
To the salvation thou hast brought,
And love and praise thy name.

137 *Praise to the Redeemer.* C. M.

1 OH for a thousand tongues to sing
My dear Redeemer's praise;
The glories of my God and King,
The triumphs of his grace.

2 My gracious Master and my God,
Assist me to proclaim,
And spread through all the earth abroad,
The honors of thy name.

3 Jesus—the name that calms our fears,
That bids our sorrows cease;
'Tis music in the sinner's ears,
'Tis life, and health, and peace.

4 He breaks the sinner's heavy chain;
He sets the prisoner free;
His blood removes the guilty stain—
His blood availed for me.

5 Believe—and ye his grace shall know,
Shall feel your sins forgiven;
Anticipate your heaven below,
And own that love is heaven.

138 *Pardon and Peace.*—Matt. ix. 2. C. M.

1 MY Saviour, let me hear thy voice
Pronounce the word of peace,
And all my warmest powers shall join
To celebrate thy grace.

2 With gentle smiles call me thy child,
And speak my sins forgiven;

The accents mild shall charm my ear
Like the sweet harps of heaven.

3 Cheerful, where'er thy hand shall lead,
The darkest path I'll tread;
Cheerful I'll quit these mortal shores,
And mingle with the dead.

4 When dreadful guilt is done away,
No other fears we know;
That hand which scatters pardons down,
Shall crowns of life bestow.

139 *The Saviour.* C. M.

1 THE Saviour—oh, what endless charms
Dwell in the blissful sound!
Its influence every fear disarms,
And spreads sweet peace around.

2 Here pardon, life, and joys divine,
In rich effusion flow,
For guilty rebels, lost in sin,
And doomed to endless wo.

3 Th' almighty Former of the skies
Stooped to our vile abode;
While angels viewed with wondering eyes,
And hailed th' incarnate God!

4 Oh the rich depths of love divine,
Of bliss a boundless store!
Dear Saviour, let me call thee mine,
I cannot wish for more.

5 On thee alone my hope relies;
Beneath thy cross I fall;
My Lord, my Life, my Sacrifice,
My Saviour, and my All.

140 *God reconciled in Christ.* C. M.

1 DEAREST of all the names above,
My Jesus and my God—
Who can resist thy heavenly love,
Or trifle with thy blood?

2 'Tis by the merits of thy death
The Father smiles again;
'Tis by thine interceding breath
The Spirit dwells with men.

3 'Till God in human flesh I see,
My thoughts no comfort find;
The holy, just, and sacred Three
Are terrors to my mind.

4 But if Immanuel's face appear,
My hope, my joy begins;
His name forbids my slavish fear,
His grace removes my sins.

5 While Jews on their own law rely,
And Greeks of wisdom boast,
I love th' incarnate mystery,
And there I fix my trust.

THE HOLY SPIRIT.

141 *Invocation of the Holy Spirit.* C. M

1 COME, Holy Spirit, heavenly Dove,
With all thy quickening powers;
Kindle a flame of sacred love
In these cold hearts of ours.

2 Look how we grovel here below,
Fond of these trifling toys;
Our souls can neither fly nor go,
To reach eternal joys.

3 In vain we tune our formal songs,
In vain we strive to rise;
Hosannas languish on our tongues,
And our devotion dies.

4 Dear Lord—and shall we ever live
At this poor dying rate,
Our love so faint, so cold to thee,
And thine to us so great?

5 Come, Holy Spirit, heavenly Dove,
With all thy quickening powers;
Come, shed abroad a Saviour's love,
And that shall kindle ours.

142 *Reviving Influence implored.* S. M.

1 COME, Holy Spirit, come;
Let thy bright beams divine
Rise on our sorrow and our gloom,
And in our darkness shine.

2 Convince us all of sin,
Then lead to Jesus' blood;
And to our wondering view reveal
The mercy of our God.

3 Revive our drooping faith;
Our doubts and fears remove;
And kindle in our breasts the flame
Of never-dying love.

4 'Tis thine to cleanse the heart,
To sanctify the soul,
To pour fresh life in every part,
And new create the whole.

143 *Divine Illumination.* 8. 7.

1 HOLY Ghost—dispel our sadness,
Pierce the clouds of nature's night;
Come, thou source of joy and gladness,
Breathe thy life and spread thy light.

2 Hear, oh hear our supplication,
Blessed Spirit, God of Peace;
Rest upon this congregation,
With th' abundance of thy grace.

3 Author of our new creation—
Bid us all thine influence prove;
Make our souls thy habitation;
Shed abroad the Saviour's love.

144 *Regeneration.*—John i. 13. C. M.

1 NOT all the outward forms on earth,
Nor rites that God has given,

Nor will of man, nor blood, nor birth,
  Can raise a soul to heaven.

2 The sovereign will of God alone
  Creates us heirs of grace;
Born in the image of his Son,
  A new, peculiar race.

3 The Spirit, like some heavenly wind,
  Breathes on the sons of flesh;
New models all the carnal mind,
  And forms the man afresh.

4 Our quickened souls awake and rise
  From the long sleep of death;
On heavenly things we fix our eyes,
  And praise employs our breath.

145 *Renewing Grace.* C. M

1 HOW helpless guilty nature lies,
  Unconscious of its load!
The heart, unchanged, can never rise
  To happiness and God.

2 Can aught, beneath a power divine,
  The stubborn will subdue?
'Tis thine, almighty Saviour, thine
  To form the heart anew.

3 'Tis thine the passions to recall,
  And upward bid them rise,
And make the scales of error fall
  From reason's darkened eyes.

4 To chase the shades of death away,
  And bid the sinner live;

A beam of heaven, a vital ray
'Tis thine alone to give.

5 Oh change these wretched hearts of ours,
And give them life divine;
Then shall our passions and our powers,
Almighty Lord, be thine.

146 *The Dry Bones.*—Ezek. xxxvii. 3. L. M.

1 LOOK down, O Lord, with pitying eye,
See Adam's race in ruin lie;
Sin spreads its trophies o'er the ground,
And scatters slaughtered heaps around.

2 Thy ministers are sent in vain,
To prophesy upon the slain;
In vain they call, in vain they cry,
Till thine almighty aid is nigh.

3 But if thy Spirit deign to breathe,
Life spreads through all the realms of death;
Dry bones obey thy powerful voice;
They move—they waken—they rejoice.

147 *Divine Love.*—Rom. v. 5. 8. 7.

1 LOVE divine, all love excelling,
Joy of heaven, to earth come down;
Fix in us thy humble dwelling,
All thy faithful mercies crown;
Jesus—thou art all compassion;
Pure, unbounded love thou art;
Visit us with thy salvation,
Enter every longing heart.

2 Come, almighty to deliver,
  Let us now thy life receive:
Suddenly return, and never—
  Never more thy temples leave:
Thee we would be always blessing,
  Serve thee as thy hosts above,
Pray, and praise thee without ceasing,
  Glory in thy precious love.

3 Carry on thy new creation;
  Pure and spotless may we be;
Let us see our whole salvation
  Perfectly secured by thee;
Changed from glory into glory,
  Till in heaven we take our place;
Till we cast our crowns before thee,
  Lost in wonder, love, and praise.

148 *Prayer for Sanctification.*—Gen. xxxii. 26. 7s.

1 GRACIOUS Father, hear thy child,
Now in Jesus reconciled;
Let me now behold thy face—
Triumph in thy saving grace;
Pour thy graces from above,
Hope and joy and peace and love.

2 Lord, I will not let thee go,
Till the blessing thou bestow:
Hear my Advocate divine;
Lo, his powerful plea is mine;
Can his intercession fail?
Shall I not in him prevail?

3 Holy Spirit—Life Divine,
Come and make this temple thine;

Shed thy light throughout my soul,
Move and actuate the whole;
Spring of life—thyself impart,
Rise eternal in my heart.

149 *Praise for Recovering Grace.* 8. 7.

1 COME, thou fount of every blessing,
Tune my heart to sing thy grace;
Streams of mercy, never ceasing,
Call for songs of loudest praise.

2 Teach me some melodious measure,
Sung by flaming hosts above;
I would chant, with heavenly pleasure,
Praises to thy boundless love.

3 Jesus sought me when a stranger,
Wand'ring from the fold of God;
He, to save my soul from danger,
Interposed his precious blood.

4 Oh, to grace how great a debtor
Daily I'm constrained to be:
Let thy grace, Lord, like a fetter,
Bind my wand'ring heart to thee.

5 Prone to wander, Lord, I feel it—
Prone to leave the God I love;
Here's my heart, oh take and seal it,
Seal it from thy courts above.

150 *A good Conscience.* L. M

1 SWEET peace of conscience, heavenly guest—
Come, fix thy mansion in my breast;

Dispel my doubts, my fears control,
And heal the anguish of my soul.

2 Come, smiling hope, and joy sincere—
Come, make your constant dwelling here;
Still let your presence cheer my heart,
Nor sin compel you to depart.

3 Thou God of hope and peace divine,
Oh make these sacred pleasures mine;
Forgive my sins, my fears remove,
And send the tokens of thy love.

4 Then should my eyes, without a tear,
See death, with all its terrors, near;
My heart should then in death rejoice,
And raptures tune my faltering voice.

151 *Prayer for Reviving Grace.* 7s. Double.

1 LIGHT of life, seraphic fire,
Love divine—thyself impart;
Every fainting soul inspire,
Shine in every drooping heart;
Every mournful sinner cheer,
Scatter all our guilty gloom;
Son of God, appear, appear;
To thy human temples come.

2 Come in this accepted hour;
Bring thy heavenly kingdom in;
Fill us with thy glorious power,
Rooting out the love of sin:
Nothing more can we require,
We will covet nothing less;

Be thou all our heart's desire,
All our joy, and all our peace.

152 *Divine Guidance implored.* L. M.

1 COME, gracious Spirit, heavenly Dove,
With light and comfort from above;
Be thou our guardian, thou our guide,
O'er every thought and step preside.

2 The light of truth to us display,
And make us know and choose thy way;
Plant holy fear in every heart,
That we from God may ne'er depart.

3 Lead us to holiness, the road
That we must take to dwell with God:
Lead us to Christ, the living way,
Nor let us from his precepts stray.

4 Lead us to God, our final rest,
In his enjoyment to be bless'd;
Lead us to heaven, the seat of bliss,
Where pleasure in perfection is.

153 *Prayer for Sanctification.* S. M.

1 COME, Holy Spirit, come,
With energy divine,
And on this poor, benighted soul,
With beams of mercy shine.

2 Oh melt this frozen heart;
This stubborn will subdue;
Each evil passion overcome,
And form me all anew.

3 Mine will the profit be,
But thine shall be the praise;

And unto thee will I devote
The remnant of my days.

154 *Submission.* 7s.

1 WHEN, my Saviour, shall I be
Perfectly resigned to thee;
Poor and vile in my own eyes,
Only in thy wisdom wise?

2 Only thee content to know,
Ignorant of all below;
Only guided by thy light,
Only mighty in thy might?

3 So I may thy Spirit know—
Let him as he listeth blow;
Let the manner be unknown,
So I may with thee be one;

4 Fully in my life express
All the heights of holiness;
Sweetly let my spirit prove
All the depths of humble love.

155 *The Promise of the Spirit.* H. M.

1 O THOU who hearest prayer,
Attend our humble cry;
And let thy servants share
Thy blessing from on high:
We plead the promise of thy word;
Grant us thy Holy Spirit, Lord.

2 If earthly parents hear
Their children when they cry;

If they, with love sincere,
Their varied wants supply,
Much more wilt thou thy love display,
And answer when thy children pray.

3 Our Heavenly Father thou,
We children of thy grace—
Oh let thy Spirit now
Descend, and fill the place:
That all may feel the heavenly flame,
And all unite to praise thy name.

4 And send thy Spirit down
On all the nations, Lord,
With great success to crown
The preaching of thy word,
Till heathen lands shall own thy sway,
And cast their idol gods away.

5 Then shall thy kingdom come
Among our fallen race,
And the whole earth become
The temple of thy grace,
Whence pure devotion shall ascend,
And songs of praise, till time shall end.

156 *Prayer for spiritual Guidance.* 7s.

1 HOLY Spirit, from on high,
Bend on us a pitying eye;
Animate the drooping heart,
Bid the power of sin depart.

2 Teach us, with repentant grief,
Humbly to implore relief;

Then the Saviour's blood reveal,
All our deep disease to heal.

3 Other ground-work should we lay,
Sweep those empty hopes away;
Make us feel that Christ alone
Can for human guilt atone.

4 May we daily grow in grace,
And pursue the heavenly race,
Trained in wisdom, led by love,
Till we reach our rest above.

157 *Prayer for Sanctification.* 7s.

1 GRACIOUS Spirit—Love divine,
Let thy light within me shine;
All my guilty fears remove,
Fill me with thy heavenly love.

2 Speak thy pardoning grace to me,
Set the burdened sinner free;
Lead me to the Lamb of God,
Wash me in his precious blood.

3 Life and peace to me impart;
Seal salvation on my heart:
Breathe thyself into my breast,
Earnest of immortal rest.

4 Let me never from thee stray,
Keep me in the narrow way;
Fill my soul with joy divine;
Keep me, Lord, for ever thine.

158 *Assurance.*—Rom. viii. 14. 16. C. M.

1 WHY should the children of a King
Go mourning all their days?
Great Comforter, descend, and bring
Some tokens of thy grace.

2 Dost thou not dwell in all the saints,
And seal the heirs of heaven?
When wilt thou banish my complaints,
And show my sins forgiven?

3 Assure my conscience of her part
In the Redeemer's blood;
And bear thy witness with my heart
That I am born of God.

4 Thou art the earnest of his love,
The pledge of joys to come;
And thy soft wings, celestial Dove,
Will safe convey me home.

159 *The Holy Spirit addressed under Darkness.* 8s.

1 DESCEND, Holy Spirit, the Dove,
And visit a sorrowful breast;
My burden of guilt to remove,
And bring me assurance and rest:
Thou only hast power to relieve
A sinner o'erwhelmed with his load;
The sense of redemption to give,
And sprinkle his conscience with blood.

2 If, when I have put thee to grief,
And madly to folly returned,

Thy goodness has been my relief,
 And lifted me up as I mourned—
O Spirit of pity and grace,
 Relieve me again and restore;
My spirit in holiness raise,
 To fall and to grieve thee no more.

160 *The Spirit entreated not to depart.* L. M.

1 STAY, thou insulted Spirit, stay,
 Though I have done thee such despite;
Nor cast the sinner quite away,
 Nor take thine everlasting flight.

2 Though I have most unfaithful been
 Of all who e'er thy grace received;
Ten thousand times thy goodness seen,
 Ten thousand times thy goodness grieved;

3 Yet, oh, the chief of sinners spare,
 In honor of my great High Priest;
Nor, in thy righteous anger, swear
 I shall not see thy people's rest.

4 Now, Lord, my weary soul release,
 And raise me by thy gracious hand;
Guide me into thy perfect peace,
 And bring me to the promised land.

161 *Fear of grieving the Spirit.* S. M.

1 FORBID it, Lord, that we,
 Who from thy hand receive
The Spirit's power to make us free,
 Should e'er that Spirit grieve.

2 Oh keep our faith alive;
Help us to watch and pray;
Lest by our carelessness we drive
The sacred Guest away.

3 How can we bear to lose
Our best and kindest friend;
Life, health, and happiness refuse,
And joys that never end?

4 Lord, make us wholly thine;
Subdue these hearts of stone;
Let beams of saving mercy shine,
And mark us as thine own.

162 *Fear of grieving the Spirit.* C. M.

1 AND shall I still the Spirit grieve,
And still reject his call?
Oh, will he not the rebel leave
In sin's dark way to fall?

2 Shall I the heavenly Friend refuse,
And drive him from my heart?
His warnings and his love abuse,
And bid him hence depart?

3 Will he not justly give me o'er,
Though ready now to save?
Will he not bar the heavenly door,
When I his pity crave?

4 "Depart"—will he at last reply?
Oh, may I now attend;
Now to the cross for mercy fly,
And make my God my friend.

THE GOSPEL.

163 *The Gospel Invitation.* C. M.

1 LET every mortal ear attend,
And every heart rejoice;
The trumpet of the gospel sounds,
With an inviting voice.

2 Ho, all ye hungry, starving souls,
That feed upon the wind,
And vainly strive with earthly toys
To fill an empty mind;—

3 Eternal wisdom has prepared
A soul-reviving feast,
And bids your longing appetites
The rich provision taste.

4 Ho, ye that pant for living streams,
And pine away and die;—
Here you may quench your raging thirst,
With springs that never dry.

5 The happy gates of gospel grace
Stand open, night and day;
Lord, we are come to seek supplies,
And drive our wants away.

164 *Sinners invited to Christ.*—Matt. xi. 28. 8. 7. 4.

1 COME, ye weary, heavy-laden,
Lost and ruined by the fall;

If you tarry till you're better,
You will never come at all:
Not the righteous—
Sinners Jesus came to call.

2 Come, ye needy, come and welcome;
God's free bounty glorify:
True belief, and true repentance,
Every grace that brings us nigh—
Without money,
Come to Jesus Christ, and buy.

3 Let not conscience make you linger,
Nor of fitness fondly dream;
All the fitness he requireth,
Is to feel your need of him:
This he gives you;
'Tis the Spirit's rising beam.

4 Lo! th' incarnate God, ascended,
Pleads the merit of his blood;
Venture on him, venture wholly,
Let no other trust intrude;
None but Jesus
Can do helpless sinners good.

5 Saints and angels, joined in concert,
Sing the praises of the Lamb;
While the blissful seats of heaven
Sweetly echo with his name;
Hallelujah!
Sinners here may sing the same.

165 *The Gospel Feast.* C. M.

1 YE wretched, hungry, starving poor,
Behold a royal feast,

Where mercy spreads her bounteous store
For every humble guest.

2 See, Jesus stands with open arms:
He calls, he bids you come;
Guilt holds you back, and fear alarms,
But see, there yet is room.

3 Room in the Saviour's bleeding heart;
There love and pity meet;
Nor will he bid the soul depart,
That trembles at his feet.

4 In him the Father, reconciled,
Invites your souls to come;
The rebel shall be called a child,
And kindly welcomed home.

166 *The accepted Time.*--2 Cor. vi. 2. S. M.

1 NOW is th' accepted time,
Now is the day of grace;
Now, sinners, come without delay,
And seek the Saviour's face.

2 Now is th' accepted time,
The Saviour calls to-day;
To-morrow it may be too late—
Then why should you delay?

3 Now is th' accepted time,
The gospel bids you come;
And every promise in his word
Declares there yet is room.

167 *The Saviour's Invitation.*--John vii. 37. C. M.

1 THE Saviour calls—let every ear
Attend the heavenly sound:

Ye doubting souls, dismiss your fear,
Hope smiles reviving round.

2 For every thirsty, longing heart,
Here streams of bounty flow;
And life and health and bliss impart,
To banish mortal wo.

3 Ye sinners, come—'tis mercy's voice;
The gracious call obey;
Mercy invites to heavenly joys,
And can you yet delay?

4 Dear Saviour, draw reluctant hearts;
To thee let sinners fly,
And take the bliss thy love imparts,
And drink, and never die.

168 "*Yet there is room.*"—Luke xiv. 22. H. M

1 YE dying sons of men,
Sunk deep in sin and wo,
The gospel's voice attend,
While Jesus sends to you;
Ye perishing and guilty, come;
In Jesus' arms there yet is room.

2 No longer now delay;
No vain excuses frame;
He bids you come to-day,
Though poor, and blind, and lame:
All things are ready, sinners, come;
For every trembling soul there's room.

3 Compelled by bleeding love,
Ye wandering souls, draw near;

Christ calls you from above—
His charming accents hear;
Let whosoever will, now come;
In mercy's arms there still is room.

169 " *The word is nigh thee.*"—Rom. x. 6–8. 7. 6.

1 SAY not, sinner, in thy heart—
" Who shall ascend on high,
Call on Christ to take my part,
And bring him from the sky?"
Say not, in thine unbelief—
" Who will to the depths descend,
Tell the burdened sinner's grief,
And bring the sinner's Friend?"

2 No, the gracious word of faith
Hath taught thee better things;
" Inward turn thine eye," it saith;
While Christ to thee it brings:
Christ is ready to impart
Light and life to those who sigh;
" In thy mouth and in thy heart
The word is ever nigh."

170 *The Heavy-laden invited.*—Matt. xi. 28. L. M.

1 " COME hither, all ye weary souls,
Ye heavy-laden sinners, come;
I'll give you rest from all your toils,
And raise you to my heavenly home.

2 " They shall find rest, who learn of me;
I'm of a meek and lowly mind;

But passion rages like the sea,
And pride is restless as the wind.

3 "Bless'd is the man whose shoulders take
My yoke, and bear it with delight;
My yoke is easy to his neck,
My grace shall make the burden light."

4 Jesus, we come at thy command;
With faith, and hope, and humble zeal,
Resign our spirits to thy hand,
To mould and guide us at thy will.

171 *The Weary invited.* 7s.

1 COME, ye weary souls oppress'd,
Find in Christ the promised rest;
On him all your burdens roll,
He can wound, and he make whole.

2 Ye who dread the wrath of God,
Come and wash in Jesus' blood:
To the Son of David cry;
In his word he's passing by.

3 Naked, guilty, poor, and blind,
All your wants in Jesus find;
This the day of mercy is,
Now accept the proffered bliss.

172 *The Voice of Free Grace.* 12s.

1 THE voice of free grace cries, "Escape
to the mountain;
For Adam's lost race Christ hath opened a
fountain;

For sin and uncleanness and every transgression,
His blood flows most freely in streams of salvation."

CHORUS.

Hallelujah to the Lamb, who hath bought us our pardon;
We'll praise him again when we pass over Jordan.

2 Ye souls that are wounded, to Jesus repair;
He calls you in mercy—and can you forbear?
Though your sins have arisen as high as a mountain,
His blood can remove them—it flows from the fountain.

3 Bless'd Jesus, thou reignest exalted and glorious;
O'er sin, death, and hell, thou art ever victorious;
Thy name will we praise in the great congregation,
And triumph, ascribing to thee our salvation.

4 With joy shall we stand, when escaped to the shore;
With harps in our hands, we'll praise thee the more;
We'll range the sweet plains on the bank of the river,
And sing of salvation for ever and ever.

173 *The Sinner called.* S. M

1 RETURN and come to God;
Cast all your sins away;
Seek ye the Saviour's cleansing blood;
Repent, believe, obey.

2 Say not ye cannot come;
For Jesus bled and died,
That none who ask in humble faith
Should ever be denied.

3 Say not ye will not come;
'Tis God vouchsafes to call;
And fearful shall their end be found,
On whom his wrath shall fall.

4 Come, then, whoever will,
Come while 'tis called to-day;
Flee to the Saviour's cleansing blood;
Repent, believe, obey.

174 "*Behold I stand at the door.*"—Rev. iii. 20. L. M

1 BEHOLD a stranger at the door!
He gently knocks—has knocked before;
Has waited long—is waiting still:
You treat no other friend so ill.

2 Oh, lovely attitude, he stands
With melting heart and open hands!
Oh, matchless kindness! and he shows
This matchless kindness to his foes!

3 But will he prove a friend indeed?
He will—the very friend you need;

The friend of sinners—yes, 'tis He,
With garments dyed on Calvary.

4 Rise, touched with gratitude divine;
Turn out his enemy and thine;
Turn out that hateful monster, sin,
And let the heavenly stranger in.

5 Admit him, ere his anger burn,
Lest he depart, and ne'er return;
Admit him, or the hour's at hand,
When at his door denied you'll stand.

175 *The Backslider.*—Jer. xxxi. 18—20. L. M.

1 RETURN, O wand'rer, now return,
And seek an injured Father's face;
Those warm desires that in thee burn,
Were kindled by reclaiming grace.

2 Return, O wand'rer, now return,
And seek a Father's melting heart;
His pitying eyes thy grief discern,
His hand shall heal thine inward smart.

3 Return, O wand'rer, now return;
Thy Saviour bids thy spirit live;
Go to his bleeding feet, and learn
How freely Jesus can forgive.

4 Return, O wand'rer, now return,
And wipe away the falling tear;
'Tis God who says, "No longer mourn,"
'Tis mercy's voice invites thee near.

176 *Pardon and Peace offered.* 7s. 6 lines.

1 YE who in his courts are found,
Listening to the joyful sound,
Lost and helpless as ye are,
Full of sorrow, sin, and care,
Glorify the King of kings;
Take the peace the gospel brings.

2 Turn to Christ your longing eyes,
View his bleeding sacrifice;
See in him your sins forgiven,
Pardon, holiness, and heaven:
Glorify the King of kings,
Take the peace the gospel brings.

177 *The Invitation.*—Rev. xxii. 17, 20. S. M.

1 THE Spirit, in our hearts,
Is whispering, "Sinner, come;"
The bride, the church of Christ, proclaims
To all his children, "Come."

2 Let him that heareth say
To all about him, "Come;"
Let him that thirsts for righteousness,
To Christ, the fountain, come.

3 Yes, whosoever will,
Oh let him freely come,
And freely drink the stream of life;
'Tis Jesus bids him come.

4 Lo, Jesus, who invites,
Declares, "I quickly come:"
Lord, even so; we wait thy hour;
Jesus, our Saviour, come.

178 *The Weary invited.* L. M.

1 COME, weary souls, with sin distressed,
Come, and accept the promised rest;
The Saviour's gracious call obey,
And cast your gloomy fears away.

2 Oppressed with sin, a painful load,
Oh come, and spread your woes abroad:
Divine compassion, mighty love,
Will all the painful load remove.

3 Here mercy's boundless ocean flows,
To cleanse your guilt and heal your woes:
Pardon and life and endless peace,
How rich the gift, how free the grace!

4 Lord, we accept, with thankful heart,
The hope thy gracious words impart:
We come with trembling, yet rejoice,
And bless the kind inviting voice.

179 *The Gospel invitation.*—Isaiah lv. 1. L. M.

1 HO, every one that thirsts, draw nigh;
'Tis God invites the fallen race;
Mercy and free salvation buy,
Buy wine and milk and gospel grace.

2 Ye nothing in exchange can give;
Leave all ye have and are, behind;
Freely the gift of God receive,
Pardon and peace in Jesus find.

3 Come to the living waters, come;
Sinners, obey your Maker's call,

Return, ye weary wanderers, home.
And find my grace is free for all.

180 *The Saviour's Call.*—Matt. xi. 28. 7s

1 COME, ye weary sinners, come,
All who groan beneath your load;
Jesus calls the wanderers home;
Hasten to your pardoning God:
Come, ye guilty souls oppressed,
Answer to the Saviour's call—
"Come, and I will give you rest;
Come, and I will save you all."

2 Burdened with a world of grief,
Burdened with our sinful load,
Burdened with this unbelief,
Burdened with the wrath of God,
Lo, we come to thee for ease—
True and gracious as thou art;
Now our weary souls release,
Write forgiveness on our heart.

181 *The Gospel Message.* 8. 7. 4

1 SINNERS, will you scorn the message
Sent in mercy from above?
Every sentence—oh how tender!
Every line is full of love;
Listen to it—
Every line is full of love.

2 Hear the heralds of the gospel
News from Zion's King proclaim—

"Pardon to each rebel sinner,
  Free forgiveness in his name:"
    How important!—
"Free forgiveness in his name."

Tempted souls, they bring you succor;
  Fearful hearts, they quell your fears;
And, with news of consolation,
  Chase away the falling tears;
    Tender heralds
  Chase away the falling tears.

False professors, groveling worldlings,
  Callous hearers of the word—
While the messengers address you,
  Take the warnings they afford;
    We entreat you—
  Take the warnings they afford.

182 *Peace to the troubled Soul.* L. M. 6 lines.

1 PEACE, troubled soul, whose plaintive moan
  Has taught each scene the note of wo;
Cease thy complaint, suppress thy groan,
  And let thy tears forget to flow;
Behold, the precious balm is found,
To lull thy pain, to heal thy wound.

2 Come, freely come, by sin oppressed,
  Unburthen here thy weighty load;
Here find thy refuge and thy rest,
  And trust the mercy of thy God;
Thy God's thy Saviour—glorious word!
Oh hear, believe, and bless the Lord.

183 *Life the Day of Salvation.* L. M.

1 LIFE is the time to serve the Lord,
The time t' insure the great reward;
And while the lamp holds out to burn,
The vilest sinner may return.

2 Life is the hour that God has given
To 'scape from hell, and fly to heaven;
The day of grace, and mortals may
Secure the blessings of the day.

3 Then what my thoughts design to do,
My hands, with all your might pursue;
Since no device nor work is found,
Nor faith nor hope, beneath the ground.

4 There are no acts of pardon passed
In the cold grave to which we haste;
But darkness, death, and long despair,
Reign in eternal silence there.

184 *The Alarm.* 7. 6.

1 STOP, poor sinner, stop and think,
Before you farther go;
Will you sport upon the brink
Of everlasting wo?
Once again we charge you—stop;
For unless you warning take,
Ere you are aware, you drop
Into the burning lake.

2 Say, have you an arm like God,
That you his will oppose?

Fear you not that iron rod
With which he breaks his foes?
Can you stand in that dread day,
When he judgment shall proclaim,
And the earth shall melt away,
Like wax before the flame?

3 Soon relentless death will come,
To drag you to his bar;
Then, to hear your awful doom
Will fill you with despair;
All your sins will round you crowd,
Sins of a blood-crimson dye,
Each for vengeance crying loud;
And what can you reply?

4 Though your heart be made of steel,
Your forehead lined with brass,
God at length will make you feel;
He will not let you pass.
Sinners then in vain will call,
(Though they now despise his grace,)
"Rocks and mountains, on us fall,
And hide us from his face."

185

Few saved.—Luke xiii. 23. S. M.

1 DESTRUCTION'S dangerous road
What multitudes pursue!
While that which leads the soul to God
Is known or sought by few.

2 Believers enter in
By Christ, the living gate:

But those who will not leave their sin,
Complain it is too strait.

3 If self must be denied,
And sin forsaken quite,
They rather choose the way that's wide,
And strive to think it right.

4 Encompassed by a throng,
On numbers they depend;
They say, "so many can't be wrong,
And miss a happy end."

5 But hear the Saviour's word,
"Strive for the heavenly gate;
Many will call upon the Lord,
And find their cries too late."

6 Oh hear the gospel call,
And enter while you may;
The flock of Christ is always small,
Yet none are safe but they.

7 Lord, open sinners' eyes,
Their awful state to see;
And make them, ere the storm arise,
To thee for safety flee.

186 *"Why will ye die."* 7s. Double

1 SINNERS, turn, why will ye die?
God your Maker asks you why?
God who did you being give,
Made you with himself to live;
He the fatal cause demands,
Asks the work of his own hands;

Why, ye thankless creatures, why
Will ye cross his love, and die?

2 Sinners, turn, why will ye die?
God your Saviour asks you why;
He who did your souls retrieve—
Died himself that ye might live.
Will ye let him die in vain?
Crucify your Lord again?
Why, ye ransomed sinners, why
Will ye slight his grace, and die?

3 Sinners, turn, why will ye die?
God the Spirit asks you why;
Now his influence from above,
Moves you to embrace his love:
Will ye not his grace receive?
Will ye still refuse to live?
Why, ye long-sought sinners, why
Will ye grieve your God, and die?

187 *The Time is short.* C. M

1 THE time is short—ye sinners, fear
To trifle time away;
The word of great salvation hear,
While it is called to-day.

2 The time is short—ye rebels, now
To Christ the Lord submit;
To mercy's golden sceptre bow,
And fall at Jesus' feet.

3 The time is short—ye saints, rejoice;
The Lord will quickly come;
Soon shall you hear the Bridegroom's voice,
To call you to your home.

4 The time is short, the moment near,
When we shall dwell above,
And be for ever happy there,
With Jesus, whom we love.

188 *The Danger of Delay.* 7s.

1 HASTEN, sinner, to be wise;
Stay not for the morrow's sun:
Wisdom if you still despise,
Harder is it to be won.

2 Hasten mercy to implore;
Stay not for the morrow's sun;
Lest thy season should be o'er,
Ere this evening's course be run.

3 Hasten, sinner, to return;
Stay not for the morrow's sun;
Lest thy lamp should cease to burn,
Ere salvation's work is done.

4 Hasten, sinner, to be bless'd;
Stay not for the morrow's sun;
Lest perdition thee arrest,
Ere the morrow is begun.

5 Lord, do thou the sinner turn;
Rouse him from his senseless state;
Let him not thy counsel spurn,
And lament his choice too late.

189 *The Uncertainty of Life.* S. M.

1 TO-MORROW, Lord, is thine,
Lodged in thy sovereign hand;

And if its sun arise and shine,
It shines by thy command.

2 The present moment flies,
And bears our life away;
Oh make thy servants truly wise,
That they may live to-day.

3 Since on this winged hour
Eternity is hung,
Awaken, by thy mighty power,
The aged and the young.

4 One thing demands our care—
Oh, be it now pursued;
Lest, slighted once, the season fair
Should never be renewed.

5 To Jesus may we fly,
Swift as the morning light,
Lest life's young golden beams should die
In sudden, endless night.

190 *Repentance commanded.*—Acts xvii. 30. C. M.

1 REPENT, (the voice celestial cries,)
No longer dare delay;
The wretch that scorns the mandate dies,
And meets a fiery day.

2 Ye sinners, in his presence bow,
And all your guilt confess;
Accept the offered Saviour now,
Nor trifle with his grace.

3 Bow ere the awful trumpet sound,
And call you to his bar;

For mercy knows th' appointed bound,
And turns to vengeance there.

4 Amazing love, that yet will call,
And yet prolong our days!
Our hearts, subdued by goodness, fall,
And weep, and love, and praise.

191 *The Sinner warned.* 7s.

1 SINNER, rouse thee from thy sleep;
Wake, and o'er thy folly weep;
Raise thy spirit dark and dead;
Jesus waits his light to shed.

2 Wake from sleep, arise from death;
See the bright and living path:
Watchful tread that path—be wise;
Leave thy folly, seek the skies.

3 Leave thy folly, cease from crime,
From this hour redeem thy time;
Life secure, without delay;
Evil is the mortal day.

4 Rouse thee, sinner, from thy sleep;
Wake, and o'er thy folly weep;
Jesus calls from death and night,
Jesus waits to shed his light.

192 *Life the accepted Time.* L. M

1 WHILE life prolongs its precious light,
Mercy is found, and peace is given;
But soon, ah soon, approaching night
Shall blot out every hope of heaven.

2 While God invites, how bless'd the day!
How sweet the gospel's charming sound!
Come, sinners, haste, oh haste away,
While yet a pardoning God he's found.

3 Soon, borne on time's most rapid wing,
Shall death command you to the grave;
Before his bar your spirits bring,
And none be found to hear or save.

4 In that lone land of deep despair,
No sabbath's heavenly light shall rise;
No God regard your bitter prayer,
Nor Saviour call you to the skies.

193 *Sinners warned and entreated.* C. M.

1 SINNERS, the voice of God regard;
His mercy speaks to-day;
He calls you, by his sovereign word,
From sin's destructive way.

2 Like the rough sea that cannot rest,
You live devoid of peace;
A thousand stings within your breast
Deprive your souls of ease.

3 Your way is dark, and leads to hell;
Why will you persevere?
Can you in endless torments dwell,
Shut up in black despair?

4 Why will you in the crooked ways
Of sin and folly go?
In pain you travel all your days,
To reap eternal wo!

5 But he that turns to God shall live,
Through his abounding grace;
His mercy will the guilt forgive
Of those that seek his face.

6 His love exceeds your highest thoughts;
He pardons like a God;
He will forgive your numerous faults,
Through a Redeemer's blood.

194 *The Scoffer's Mistake.* C. M

1 YE scoffers, your expiring breath
Consigns your souls to chains;
By the last agonies of death
Sent down to fiercer pains.

2 When iron slumbers bind your flesh,
With strange surprise you'll find
Immortal vigor spring afresh,
And tortures wake the mind.

3 Then you'll confess the frightful names
Of plagues you scorned before,
No more appear like idle dreams,
Like foolish tales no more.

4 Then will you curse that fatal day,
(With flames upon your tongues,)
When you exchanged your souls away
For vanity and songs.

195 *Warning to the Sinner.*—Ezek. xxii. 14. 7s

1 SINNER, art thou still secure?
Wilt thou still refuse to pray?

Can thy heart or hand endure,
In the Lord's avenging day?

2 See, his mighty arm is bared;
Awful terrors clothe his brow!
For his judgments stand prepared;
Thou must either break or bow.

3 At his presence, nature shakes;
Earth, affrighted, hastes to flee;
Solid mountains melt like wax—
What will then become of thee?

4 Who his coming may abide?
You that glory in your shame,
Will you find a place to hide
When the world is wrapped in flame?

5 Lord, prepare us, by thy grace,
For that day when thou shalt come;
Be our shield and hiding-place,
And receive us, ransomed, home.

196 *The Judgment hastening.* C. M.

1 NOW is the time, th' accepted hour,
O sinners, come away;
The Saviour's knocking at your door—
Arise without delay.

2 Oh don't refuse to give him room,
Lest mercy should withdraw;
He'll then in robes of vengeance come,
To execute his law.

3 Then where, poor mortals, will you be,
If destitute of grace,

When you your injured Judge shall see,
And stand before his face?

4 Oh, could you shun that dreadful sight,
How would you wish to fly
To the dark shades of endless night,
From that all-searching eye!

5 Let not these warnings be in vain,
But lend a listening ear;
Lest you should meet them all again,
When wrapped in keen despair.

197 *"Where their worm dieth not."* 8. 7.

1 SINNER, can you slight the Saviour,
Press your downward way to hell,
Sink your priceless soul for ever,
Where the lost in anguish dwell?

2 Conscience is a worm undying,
Guilt an everlasting fire;
Hope, its blessed beam denying,
Must from that dark world retire.

3 In that prison, endless moanings,
Blasphemies, and madness dwell;
Chains of darkness, shrieks and groanings—
This, O sinner, this is hell.

198 *Power of the Gospel.*—Rom. i. 16. L. M.

1 WHAT shall the dying sinner do,
That seeks relief from all his wo?
Where shall the guilty conscience find
Ease for the torment of the mind?

2 How shall we have our crimes forgiven,
Or form our natures fit for heaven?
Can souls all o'er defiled with sin
Make their own powers and passions clean?

3 In vain we search, in vain we try,
Till Jesus brings his gospel nigh;
'Tis there that power and glory dwell,
Which save rebellious souls from hell.

4 This is the pillar of our hope,
That bears our fainting spirits up;
We read the grace—we trust the word,
And find salvation in the Lord.

199 *Restoration by Christ.* C. M.

1 HOW sad our state by nature is!
Our sin—how deep it stains!
And Satan holds our captive minds
Fast in his slavish chains.

2 But the inviting voice of grace
Sounds from the sacred word—
"Ho, ye despairing sinners, come,
And trust upon the Lord."

3 My soul obeys th' almighty call,
And runs to this relief;
I would believe thy promise, Lord,
Oh help my unbelief.

4 To the dear fountain of thy blood,
Incarnate God, I fly;
Here let me wash my spotted soul
From crimes of deepest dye.

5 A guilty, weak, and helpless worm,
 On thy kind arms I fall;
Be thou my strength and righteousness,
 My Jesus, and my all.

200 *Redeeming Love.* 7s.

1 NOW begin the heavenly theme—
 Sing aloud in Jesus' name;
Ye who his salvation prove,
Triumph in redeeming love.

2 Mourning souls, dry up your tears;
Banish all your guilty fears;
See your guilt and curse remove,
Cancelled by redeeming love.

3 Ye, alas, who long have been
Willing slaves to death and sin—
Now from bliss no longer rove;
Stop, and taste redeeming love.

4 Welcome, all by sin oppressed,
Welcome to his sacred rest;
Nothing brought him from above—
Nothing but redeeming love.

5 Hither, then, your music bring,
Strike aloud each joyful string;
Mortals, join the hosts above—
Join to praise redeeming love.

201 *God made known in the Gospel.* L. M.

1 GOD, in the gospel of his Son,
 Makes his eternal counsels known;

Where love in all its glory shines,
And truth is drawn in fairest lines.

2 Here sinners of a humble frame
May taste his grace, and learn his name;
May read, in characters of blood,
The wisdom, power, and grace of God.

3 The prisoner here may break his chains,
The weary rest from all his pains,
The captive feel his bondage cease,
The mourner find the way of peace.

4 Here faith reveals to mortal eyes
A brighter world beyond the skies;
Here shines the light which guides our way
From earth to realms of endless day.

5 Oh grant us grace, almighty Lord,
To read and mark thy holy word;
Its truths with meekness to receive,
And by its holy precepts live.

202 *The Mercy of God.*—Ps. lxxxix. 1. 11s.

1 THY mercy, my God, is the theme of my song,
The joy of my heart, and the boast of my tongue;
Thy free grace alone, from the first to the last,
Hath won my affections, and bound my soul fast.

2 The door of thy mercy stands open all day
To the poor and the needy who knock by the way;

No sinner shall ever be empty sent back,
Who comes the free gift of salvation to take.

3 Thy mercy in Jesus exempts me from hell;
Its glories I'll sing, and its wonders I'll tell;
'Twas Jesus, my friend, when he hung on the tree,
Who opened the channel of mercy for me.

4 Great Father of mercies, thy goodness I own,
And the covenant love of thy crucified Son:
All praise to the Spirit, whose whisper divine
Seals mercy and pardon and righteousness mine.

203 *The Ark.* S. M.

1 OH cease, my wandering soul,
On restless wing to roam;
All the wide world, to either pole,
Has not for thee a home.

2 Behold the ark of God,
Behold the open door;
Oh haste to gain that dear abode,
And rove, my soul, no more.

3 There safe thou shalt abide,
There sweet shall be thy rest;
Thy every longing satisfied—
With full salvation bless'd.

204 *The Faithfulness of God.* C. M.

1 BEGIN, my tongue, some heavenly [theme,
Awake, my voice, and sing

The mighty works, or mightier name,
Of our eternal King.

2 Tell of his wondrous faithfulness,
And sound his power abroad;
Sing the sweet promise of his grace,
And the performing God.

3 Proclaim salvation from the Lord,
To wretched, dying men;
His hand has writ the sacred word
With an immortal pen.

4 Engraved as in eternal brass,
The mighty promise shines;
Nor can the powers of darkness rase
Those everlasting lines.

5 Oh, might I hear his heavenly tongue
But whisper, "Thou art mine,"
Those gentle words should raise my song
To notes almost divine.

205 *Salvation by Grace.* S. M.

1 GRACE! 'tis a charming sound,
Harmonious to the ear;
Heaven with the echo shall resound,
And all the earth shall hear.

2 Grace first contrived a way
To save rebellious man;
And all the steps that grace display,
Which drew the wondrous plan.

3 Grace led my roving feet
To tread the heavenly road;

And new supplies each hour I meet,
While pressing on to God.

4 Grace all the work shall crown,
Through everlasting days;
It lays in heaven the topmost stone,
And well deserves the praise.

206 *The Glory of Redemption.*—Isa. xliv. 23. C. M.

1 FATHER, how wide thy glory shines!
How high thy wonders rise!
Known through the earth by thousand signs,
By thousands through the skies.

2 But when we view thy strange design
To save rebellious worms,
Where vengeance and compassion join
In their divinest forms;—

3 Here the whole Deity is known;
Nor dares a creature guess
Which of the glories brightest shone—
The justice or the grace.

4 Now the full glories of the Lamb
Adorn the heavenly plains;
Bright seraphs learn Immanuel's name,
And try their choicest strains.

5 Oh, may I bear some humble part
In that immortal song!
Wonder and joy shall tune my heart,
And love command my tongue.

207 *The three Mounts.* 7s.

1 WHEN on Sinai's top I see
God descend in majesty,

To proclaim his holy law,
All my spirit sinks with awe.

2 When, in ecstasy sublime,
Tabor's glorious steep I climb,
At the too transporting light,
Darkness rushes o'er my sight.

3 When on Calvary I rest—
God, in flesh made manifest,
Shines in my Redeemer's face,
Full of beauty, truth, and grace.

4 Here I would for ever stay,
Weep and gaze my soul away;
Thou art heaven on earth to me,
Lovely, mournful Calvary.

208 *The Blood of Christ.*—Rev. i. 5. C. M.

1 THERE is a fountain filled with blood
Drawn from Immanuel's veins;
And sinners plunged beneath that flood,
Lose all their guilty stains.

2 The dying thief rejoiced to see
That fountain in his day;
And there may I, though vile as he,
Wash all my sins away.

3 Dear, dying Lamb, thy precious blood
Shall never lose its power,
Till all the ransomed church of God
Be saved, to sin no more.

4 E'er since, by faith, I saw the stream
Thy flowing wounds supply,

Redeeming love has been my theme,
   And shall be till I die.

5 Then, in a nobler, sweeter song,
   I'll sing thy power to save,
When this poor lisping, faltering tongue
   Lies silent in the grave.

209 *Christ our Light and Salvation.* S. M.

1 HOW heavy is the night
   That hangs upon our eyes,
Till Christ, with his reviving light,
   Over our souls arise!

2 Our guilty spirits dread
   To meet the wrath of heaven;
But, in his righteousness arrayed,
   We see our sins forgiven.

3 Unholy and impure
   Are all our thoughts and ways;
His hands infected nature cure,
   With sanctifying grace.

4 The powers of hell agree
   To hold our souls in vain:
He sets the sons of bondage free,
   And breaks the cursed chain.

5 Lord, we adore thy ways
   To bring us near to God;
Thy sovereign power, thy healing grace,
   And thine atoning blood.

210 *The Gospel proclaimed.* H. M.

1 PRAISE to the Lord on high,
Who spreads his triumphs wide;
While Jesus' fragrant name
Is breathed on every side;
Balmy and rich the odors rise,
And fill the earth, and reach the skies.

2 Ten thousand dying souls
Its influence feel, and live;
Sweeter than vital air
The incense they receive;
They breathe anew, and rise, and sing
Jesus the Lord, their conquering King.

3 But sinners scorn the grace
That brings salvation nigh;
They turn away their face,
And faint, and fall, and die.
So sad a doom ye saints deplore,
For oh, they fall to rise no more.

211 *Praise for Salvation.* C. M.

1 SALVATION! oh, the joyful sound;
'Tis pleasure to our ears;
A sovereign balm for every wound,
A cordial for our fears.

2 Buried in sorrow and in sin,
At hell's dark door we lay;
But we arise by grace divine,
To see a heavenly day.

3 Salvation—let the echo fly
The spacious earth around;
While all the armies of the sky
Conspire to raise the sound.

212 *Come and welcome.* 7s. 6 lines

1 FROM the cross uplifted high,
Where the Saviour deigns to die,
What melodious sounds we hear,
Bursting on the ravished ear!—
"Love's redeeming work is done;
Come and welcome, sinner, come.

2 "Sprinkled now with blood the throne,
Why beneath thy burdens groan?
On my pierced body laid,
Justice owns the ransom paid:
Bow the knee, and kiss the Son—
Come and welcome, sinner, come.

3 "Spread for thee, the festal board
See with richest dainties stored;
To thy Father's bosom pressed,
Yet again a child confessed,
Never from his house to roam—
Come and welcome, sinner, come.

4 "Soon the days of life shall end;
Lo, I come—your Saviour, Friend,
Safe your spirits to convey
To the realms of endless day,
Up to my eternal home—
Come and welcome, sinner, come!"

213 *The Fountain of Life.* C. M.

1 OH, what amazing words of grace
Are in the gospel found!
Suited to every sinner's case,
Who hears the joyful sound.

2 Come, then, with all your wants and
Your every burden bring; [wounds,
Here love, unchanging love, abounds,
A deep celestial spring.

3 Millions of sinners, vile as you,
Have here found life and peace;
Come, then, and prove its virtues too,
And drink, adore, and bless.

214 *Reception of the Gospel.*—1 Cor. i. 23, 24. C. M.

1 CHRIST and his cross are all our theme;
The mysteries that we speak
Are scandal in the Jew's esteem,
And folly to the Greek.

2 But souls enlightened from above
With joy receive the word;
They see what wisdom, power, and love
Shine in their dying Lord.

3 The vital savor of his name
Restores their fainting breath;
But unbelief perverts the same
To guilt, despair, and death.

4 Till God diffuse his graces down
Like showers of heavenly rain,

In vain Apollos sows the ground,
And Paul may plant in vain.

215

The Soul.—Mark viii. 36. C. M

1 WHAT is the thing of greatest price
The whole creation round—
That which was lost in Paradise,
That which in Christ is found?

2 The soul of man—Jehovah's breath—
That keeps two worlds at strife;
Hell moves beneath to work its death,
Heaven stoops to give it life.

3 God, to redeem it, did not spare
His well beloved Son;
Jesus, to save it, deigned to bear
The sins of all in one.

4 And is this treasure borne below,
In earthen vessels frail?
Can none its utmost value know,
Till flesh and spirit fail?

5 Then let us gather round the cross,
That knowledge to obtain—
Not by the soul's eternal loss,
But everlasting gain.

216

The One Thing needful. C. M.

1 RELIGION is the chief concern
Of mortals here below;
May I its great importance learn,
Its sovereign virtue know.

2 More needful this than glittering wealth,
Or aught the world bestows;
Nor reputation, food, or health,
Can give us such repose.

3 Religion should our thoughts engage,
Amidst our youthful bloom;
'Twill fit us for declining age,
And for the awful tomb.

4 Oh may my heart, by grace renewed,
Be my Redeemer's throne;
And be my stubborn will subdued,
His government to own.

5 Let deep repentance, faith, and love,
Be joined with godly fear;
And all my conversation prove
My heart to be sincere.

217 *Sowing the Seed.* S. M.

1 SOW in the morn the seed,
At eve hold not thy hand;
To doubt and fear give thou no heed
Broad-cast it round the land.

2 Beside all waters sow,
The highway furrows stock;
Drop it where thorns and thistles grow,
Scatter it on the rock.

3 Thou know'st not which may thrive,
The late or early sown;
Grace keeps the precious germ alive,
When and wherever strown.

4 Thou canst not toil in vain;
  Cold, heat, and moist, and dry,
Shall foster and mature the grain
  For garners in the sky.

5 Then, when the glorious end,
  The day of God, is come,
The angel-reapers shall descend,
  And heaven shout—"harvest home."

218 *After Sermon.* C. M

1 NOW, Lord, the gospel seed is sown,
  Be it thy servants' care
Thy heavenly blessing to bring down,
  By humble, fervent prayer.

2 In vain we plant, without thine aid,
  And water, too, in vain;
Lord of the harvest, God of grace,
  Send down thy heavenly rain.

3 Then shall our cheerful hearts and tongues
  Begin this song divine—
"Thou, Lord, hast given the rich increase,
  And be the glory thine."

219 *The same.* C. M.

1 O GOD, by whom the seed is given,
  By whom the harvest blessed,
Whose word, like manna showered from heaven,
  Is planted in our breast;

2 Preserve it from the passing feet,
And plund'rers of the air,
The sultry sun's intenser heat,
And weeds of worldly care.

3 Though buried deep, or thinly strown,
Do thou thy grace supply;
The hope in earthly furrows sown,
Shall ripen in the sky.

220 *The same.* H. M.

ON what has now been sown,
Thy blessing, Lord, bestow;
The power is thine alone
To make it spring and grow:
Do thou the gracious harvest raise,
And thou alone shalt have the praise.

221 *The same.* 8. 7

1 OF thy love some gracious token
Grant us, Lord, before we go;
Bless the word which has been spoken,
And thy saving grace bestow.

2 Give us hearts resolved, believing;
Plant in us thy holy fear;
That, with joy thy word receiving,
We may do, as well as hear.

THE SINNER AWAKENED.

222

Time and Eternity C. P. M.

1 LO, on a narrow neck of land,
'Twixt two unbounded seas I stand,
Yet how insensible!
A point of time, a moment's space,
Removes me to yon heavenly place,
Or—shuts me up in hell.

2 O God, my inmost soul convert,
And deeply on my thoughtless heart
Eternal things impress;
Give me to feel their solemn weight,
And save me ere it be too late—
Wake me to righteousness.

3 Before me place, in dread array,
The pomp of that tremendous day,
When thou with clouds shalt come,
To judge the nations at thy bar;
And tell me, Lord, shall I be there,
To meet a joyful doom?

4 Be this my one great business here—
With holy trembling, holy fear,
To make my calling sure;
Thine utmost counsel to fulfill,
And suffer all thy righteous will,
And to the end endure.

5 Then, Saviour, then my soul receive,
Transported from this vale, to live
And reign with thee above;

Where faith is sweetly lost in sight,
And hope in full, supreme delight,
And everlasting love.

223 *Conviction by the Law.*—Rom. vii. 8, 9. C. M.

1 LORD, how secure my conscience was,
And felt no inward dread!
I was alive without the law,
And thought my sins were dead.

2 My hopes of heaven were firm and bright;
But since the precept came
With a convincing power and light,
I find how vile I am.

3 My guilt appeared but small before,
Till terribly I saw
How perfect, holy, just, and pure,
Is thine eternal law.

4 Then felt my soul the heavy load—
My sins revived again;
I had provoked a dreadful God,
And all my hopes were slain.

5 My God, I cry with every breath
For some kind power to save;
To break the bonds of sin and death,
And thus redeem the slave.

224 *The evil Heart.*—Matt. xv. 19. S. M.

1 ASTONISHED and distressed,
I turn my eyes within;
My heart with loads of guilt oppressed,
The seat of every sin.

2 What crowds of evil thoughts,
  What vile affections there!
Distrust, presumption, artful guile,
  Pride, envy, slavish fear.

3 Almighty King of saints,
  These inward foes subdue;
Dispel the darkness of my mind,
  And all my powers renew.

4 This done, my cheerful voice
  Shall loud hosannas raise;
My soul shall glow with gratitude,
  My lips proclaim thy praise.

225 *The Heart of Stone.*—Ezek. xxxvi. 26. L. M.

1 OH for a glance of heavenly day,
To take this stubborn stone away,
And thaw, with beams of love divine,
This heart, this frozen heart of mine.

2 The rocks can rend, the earth can quake,
The seas can roar, the mountains shake;
Of feeling, all things show some sign,
But this unfeeling heart of mine.

3 To hear the sorrows thou hast felt,
Dear Lord, an adamant would melt;
But I can read each moving line,
And nothing move this heart of mine.

4 But power divine the heart can move,
And melt to penitence and love:
Spirit of Grace, the work is thine;
Oh move and melt this heart of mine.

226 *Seeking Rest.* S. M.

1 AH, whither should I go,
Burdened, and sick, and faint?
To whom should I my troubles show,
And pour out my complaint?

2 My Saviour bids me come,
Ah, why do I delay?
He calls the weary sinner home,
And yet from him I stay!

3 What worldly tie must break?
What idol yet depart,
Which will not let the Saviour take
Possession of my heart?

4 Jesus, the hind'rance show,
Which I have feared to see;
And let me now consent to know
What keeps me back from thee.

5 Oh break the fatal chain,
And all my bonds remove;
Nor let one bosom-sin remain,
To keep me from thy love.

227 *Light dawning on the convicted Soul.* S. M.

1 MY former hopes are fled,
My terror now begins;
I feel, alas, that I am dead
In trespasses and sins.

2 Ah, whither shall I fly?
I hear the thunder roar;

The law proclaims destruction nigh,
And vengeance at the door.

3 When I review my ways,
I dread impending doom;
But sure a friendly whisper says,
"Flee from the wrath to come."

4 I see, or think I see,
A glimmering from afar;
A beam of day that shines for me,
To save me from despair.

5 Forerunner of the sun,
It marks the pilgrim's way;
I'll gaze upon it while I run,
And watch the rising day.

228 *Confession.* 7s.

1 SOVEREIGN Ruler, Lord of all,
Prostrate at thy feet I fall;
Hear, oh hear the sinner's cry,
Frown not, lest I faint and die.

2 Vilest of the sons of men,
Worst of rebels I have been;
Oft abused thee to thy face,
Trampled on thy richest grace.

3 Justly might thy vengeful dart
Pierce this bleeding, broken heart;
Justly might thy kindled ire
Blast me in eternal fire.

4 But with thee there's mercy found,
Balm to heal my every wound;

Soothe, oh soothe the troubled breast,
Give the weary wanderer rest.

229 *Lost State of Man.* S M.

1 AH, how shall fallen man,
Be just before his God?
If he contend in righteousness,
We fall beneath his rod.

2 If he our ways should mark
With strict inquiring eyes,
Could we for one of thousand faults
A just excuse devise?

3 All-seeing, powerful God,
Who can with thee contend?
Or who that tries th' unequal strife,
Shall prosper in the end?

4 The mountains, in thy wrath,
Their ancient seats forsake;
The trembling earth deserts her place,
Her rooted pillars shake.

5 Ah, how shall guilty man
Contend with such a God?
None, none can meet him and escape,
But through the Saviour's blood.

230 "*Behold, I am vile.*"—Job xl. 4. S. M.

1 O LORD, how vile am I,
Unholy and unclean!
How can I dare to venture nigh
With such a load of sin?

2 Is this polluted heart
A dwelling fit for thee?
Swarming, alas, in every part,
What evils do I see!

3 If I attempt to pray,
And lisp thy holy name,
My thoughts are hurried soon away,
My soul is put to shame.

4 If in thy word I look,
Such darkness fills my mind,
I only read a sealed book,
But no relief can find.

5 And must I then indeed
Sink in despair, and die?
Lord, I believe that thou didst bleed
For such a wretch as I.

6 Low at thy feet I bow;
Oh pity and forgive;
Here will I lie and wait till thou
Shalt bid me rise and live.

THE SUPPLIANT.

231 *The Suppliant.* 8. 7.

1 JESUS, full of all compassion,
Hear thy humble suppliant's cry;
Let me know thy great salvation;
See, I languish, faint, and die.

2 Guilty, but with heart relenting,
Overwhelmed with helpless grief,
Prostrate at thy feet repenting—
Send, oh send me quick relief.

3 Whither should a wretch be flying,
But to him who comfort gives?
Whither, from the dread of dying,
But to him who ever lives?

4 On the word thy blood hath sealed
Hangs my everlasting all;
Let thine arm be now revealed,
Stay, oh stay me, lest I fall.

5 Saved—the deed shall spread new glory
Through the shining realms above;
Angels sing the pleasing story,
All enraptured with thy love.

232 *Ingratitude of the sinful Heart.* C. M

1 AND will the Lord thus condescend
To visit sinful worms?
Thus at the door shall mercy stand,
In all her winning forms?

2 Surprising grace!—and shall my heart
Unmoved and cold remain?
Has this hard rock no tender part?
Must mercy plead in vain?

3 Shall Jesus for admittance sue,
His charming voice unheard?
And this vile heart, his rightful due,
Remain for ever barred?

4 'Tis sin, alas, with tyrant power,
The lodging has possessed;
And crowds of traitors bar the door
Against the heavenly guest.

5 Ye dangerous inmates, hence depart;
Dear Saviour, enter in;
And guard the passage to my heart,
And keep out every sin.

233 *Ingratitude lamented.* S. M.

1 IS this the kind return,
Are these the thanks we owe—
Thus to abuse eternal love,
Whence all our blessings flow?

2 To what a stubborn frame
Has sin reduced our mind;
What strange, rebellious wretches we,
And God as strangely kind!

3 Turn, turn us, mighty God,
And mould our souls afresh;
Break, sovereign grace, these hearts of [stone,
And give us hearts of flesh.

4 Let past ingratitude
Provoke our weeping eyes;
And hourly, as new mercies fall,
Let hourly thanks arise.

234 *The Divine Patience.* C. M.

1 AND are we, wretches, yet alive?
And do we yet rebel?

'Tis boundless, 'tis amazing love
That bears us up from hell!

2 The burden of our weighty guilt
Would sink us down to flames;
And threatening vengeance rolls above,
To crush our feeble frames.

3 Almighty goodness cries—"Forbear"—
And straight the thunder stays;
And dare we now provoke his wrath,
And weary out his grace?

4 No more, ye lusts, shall ye command;
No more will we obey:
Stretch out, O God, thy conquering hand,
And drive thy foes away.

235 *Review of the Past.* C. M

1 AS o'er the past my memory strays,
Why heaves the secret sigh?
'Tis that I mourn departed days,
Still unprepared to die.

2 The world and worldly things beloved,
My anxious thoughts employed;
And time unhallowed, unimproved,
Presents a fearful void.

3 Yet, O my Saviour, wild despair
Chase from my laboring breast;
Thy grace it is which prompts the prayer,
That grace can do the rest.

4 My life's brief remnant all be thine;
And when thy sure decree

Bids me this fleeting breath resign,
Oh speed my soul to thee.

236 *In-dwelling Sin lamented.* C. M.

1 WITH tears of anguish I lament,
Here at thy feet, my God,
My passion, pride, and discontent,
And vile ingratitude.

2 Sure there was ne'er a heart so base,
So false as mine has been;
So faithless to its promises,
So prone to every sin.

3 How long, dear Saviour, shall I feel
These struggles in my breast?
When wilt thou bow my stubborn will,
And give my conscience rest?

4 Break, sovereign grace, oh break the charm,
And set the captive free:
Reveal, Almighty God, thine arm
And haste to rescue me.

237 *The Contrite Heart.* S. M.

1 LORD, I would now repent—
With all my idols part,
And to thy gracious eye present
A humble, contrite heart;

2 A heart with grief oppressed,
For having grieved my God;
A troubled heart that cannot rest
Till washed in Jesus' blood.

3 Jesus, on me bestow
  The penitent desire;
With true sincerity of wo
  My aching breast inspire.

4 With softening pity look,
  And melt my hardness down;
Strike with thy love's resistless stroke,
  And break this heart of stone.

238 *The Penitent.* C. M.

1 PROSTRATE, dear Jesus, at thy feet,
  A guilty rebel lies,
And upward to thy mercy-seat
  Presumes to lift his eyes.

2 If tears of sorrow would suffice
  To pay the debt I owe,
Tears should from both my weeping eyes
  In ceaseless torrents flow.

3 But no such sacrifice I plead
  To expiate my guilt;
No tears but those which thou hast shed,
  No blood but thou hast spilt.

4 Think of thy sorrows, dearest Lord,
  And all my sins forgive;
Then Justice will approve the word
  That bids the sinner live.

239 *Hatefulness of Sin.* C. M.

1 OH, if my soul were formed for wo,
  How would I vent my sighs!

Repentance should like rivers flow
From both my streaming eyes.

2 'Twas for my sins my dearest Lord
Hung on the cursed tree,
And groaned away a dying life,
For thee, my soul, for thee.

3 Oh, how I hate those lusts of mine,
That crucified my Lord;
Those sins, that pierced and nailed his flesh
Fast to the fatal wood!

4 Yes, my Redeemer—they shall die;
My heart has so decreed;
Nor will I spare the guilty things
That made my Saviour bleed.

5 While with a melting, broken heart,
My murdered Lord I view,
I'll raise revenge against my sins,
And slay the murderers too.

240 *Confession and Pardon.* S. M.

1 MY sorrows, like a flood,
Impatient of restraint,
Into thy bosom, O my God,
Pour out a long complaint.

2 How often I have stood
A rebel to the skies!
And yet, and yet, oh, matchless grace,
Thy thunder silent lies.

3 O'ercome by dying love,
Here at thy cross I lie,

Submit my soul, my all, to thee,
And weep, and love, and die,

4 "Rise," says the Saviour, "rise;
Behold my wounded veins!
Here flows a sacred crimson flood
To wash away thy stains."

5 See, God is reconciled!
Behold his smiling face!
Let sinners in his love rejoice,
And sound aloud his grace.

241 *Prayer of the Penitent.* 7. 6. Iambic.

1 WE stand, in deep repentance,
Before thy throne of grace;
Thou God of love, forgive us,
The stain of guilt efface:
Behold us in our weeping,
Our sighs ascend to thee;
Touch thou our hearts—subdue them—
O Father, set us free.

2 Our souls—on thee we cast them—
Our dearest treasure thou:
Enrich us with thy favor,
While at thy feet we bow;
Reveal thy wondrous mercy,
Display thy saving love,
And give us, with the holy,
A sinless rest above.

242 *The Contrite Prayer.* S. M. Double.

1 FATHER, a weary heart
Hath come to thee for peace;
The world hath not the healing art
To bid its troubles cease;
It brings before thy throne
Its weight of wo and care;
Do thou accept its pleading tone—
The contrite sinner's prayer.

2 Father—it hath rebelled,
Hath wandered from thy path,
Nor heeded when the thunder swelled,
The tempest of thy wrath;
But now, a bruised thing,
Neglected, pale, and bare,
Lo, at thy footstool it doth bring
The contrite sinner's prayer.

3 Father, it bends before
Thy throne among the bless'd;
Peace to the wretched heart restore,
Give to the weary rest:
Through Christ's atonement given,
It trusteth yet to share
The glorious heritage of heaven,
By lowly, contrite prayer.

243 *The Rebel subdued by Mercy.* C. P. M.

1 LORD, to thy mercy now I yield;
My heart, by mighty grace compelled,
Surrenders all to thee·

Against thy terrors long I strove,
But who can stand against thy love?
Love conquers even me.

2 Now, Lord, I would be thine alone;
Come take possession of thine own,
For thou hast set me free;
Released from Satan's hard command,
See all my powers in waiting stand,
To be employed by thee.

3 My will conformed to thine would move,
On thee my hope, desire, and love,
In fixed attention join:
My hands, my eyes, my ears, my tongue,
Have Satan's servants been too long,
But now they shall be thine.

244 *Mercy implored.* C. M.

1 MERCY alone can meet my case;
For mercy, Lord, I cry:
Jesus, Redeemer, show thy face
In mercy, or I die.

2 Save me, for none beside can save;
At thy command I tread,
With failing step, life's stormy wave;
The wave goes o'er my head.

3 I perish, and my doom were just;
But wilt thou leave me? No:
I hold thee fast, my hope, my trust;
I will not let thee go.

4 Still sure to me thy promise stands,
And ever must abide;
Behold it written on thy hands,
And graven on thy side.

5 To this, this only, will I cleave;
Thy word is all my plea;
That word is truth, and I believe:
Have mercy, Lord, on me.

245 *Prayer for spiritual Healing.* C. M.

1 PHYSICIAN of the sin-sick soul,
To thee I bring my case;
My raging malady control,
And heal me by thy grace.

2 I would disclose my whole complaint,
But where shall I begin?
No words of mine can fully paint
That worst distemper—sin.

3 Pity the anguish I endure,
And save by power divine;
For never can I find a cure
From any hand but thine.

4 Thou great Physician, hear my cry,
And set my spirit free;
Thou wilt not let the sinner die,
Who longs to live to thee.

246 *The Burden of Sin.* L. M

1 OH that my load of sin were gone!
Oh that I could at last submit,

At Jesus' feet to lay me down—
To lay my soul at Jesus' feet.

2 Rest for my soul I long to find;
Saviour of all, if mine thou art,
Give me thy meek and lowly mind,
And stamp thine image on my heart.

3 Break off the yoke of inbred sin,
And fully set my spirit free;
I cannot rest till pure within,
Till I am wholly lost in thee.

247 *Pleading in the name of Jesus.* L. M. 6 lines.

1 FATHER of mercies, God of love,
Oh hear a humble suppliant's cry;
Bend from thy lofty seat above,
Thy throne of glorious majesty;
Oh deign to hear my mournful voice,
And bid my drooping heart rejoice.

2 I urge no merit of my own,
No worth to claim thy gracious smile;
No—when I bow before thy throne,
And dare converse with God awhile,
Thy name, bless'd Jesus, is my plea,
The dearest, sweetest name to me.

3 Within this heart of mine I feel
The weight of sin's oppressive load:
Oh help me, or I sink to hell,
Crushed by thine arm, avenging God;
Where not a ray of hope appears,
Or beam of joy the bosom cheers.

4 Yet, mighty God, thy powerful arm
Can snatch me from that dread abode;
Can shield me from th' impending harm,
And ease me of my heavy load:
One pardoning word can make me whole,
And soothe the anguish of my soul.

5 Father of mercies, God of love,
Then hear thy humble suppliant's cry;
Bend from thy lofty seat above,
Thy throne of glorious majesty:
Oh listen to a sufferer's voice,
And make this bleeding heart rejoice.

248 *Pleading for Mercy.* C. M.

1 LORD, at thy feet we sinners lie,
And knock at mercy's door;
With heavy heart and downcast eye,
Thy favor we implore.

2 On us the vast extent display
Of thy forgiving love;
Take all our heinous guilt away,
This heavy load remove,

3 'Tis mercy—mercy we implore,
Oh may thy pity move;
Thy grace is an exhaustless store,
And thou thyself art love.

4 Oh, for thine own, for Jesus' sake,
Our many sins forgive;
Thy grace our rocky hearts can break,
And breaking, soon relieve.

5 Thus melt us down, thus make us bend,
And thy dominion own;
Nor let a rival more pretend
To re-possess thy throne.

249 *The Resolve.*—Esth. iv. 16. C. M.

1 COME, trembling sinner, in whose breast
A thousand thoughts revolve—
Come, with your guilt and fear oppressed,
And make this last resolve:

2 I'll go to Jesus, though my sin
Hath like a mountain rose;
I know his courts, I'll enter in,
Whatever may oppose.

3 Prostrate I'll lie before his throne,
And there my guilt confess;
I'll tell him I'm a wretch undone,
Without his sovereign grace.

4 I'll to the gracious King approach,
Whose sceptre pardon gives;
Perhaps he will command my touch—
And then the suppliant lives.

5 Perhaps he will admit my plea,
Perhaps will hear my prayer;
But if I perish, I will pray,
And perish only there.

6 I can but perish if I go;
I am resolved to try;
For if I stay away, I know
I must for ever die.

CHRISTIAN EXPERIENCE.

250 *The New Birth.*—John iii. 7. C. P. M

1 AWAKED by Sinai's awful sound,
My soul in bonds of guilt I found,
And knew not where to go:
My hopes were by that precept slain—
The sinner must be born again,
Or sink to endless wo.

2 When to the law I trembling fled,
It poured its curses on my head,
I no relief could find;
This fearful truth increased my pain—
The sinner must be born again—
And terror filled my mind.

3 Again did Sinai's thunders roll,
And guilt lay heavy on my soul
A vast, oppressive load;
Alas, I read, and saw it plain—
The sinner must be born again,
Or drink the wrath of God.

4 The saints I heard with rapture tell
How Jesus vanquished death and hell,
And broke the fowler's snare;
Yet, when I found this truth remain—
The sinner must be born again—
I sunk in deep despair.

5 But while I thus in anguish lay,
The gracious Saviour passed that way,
And felt his pity move;
The sinner by his justice slain,
Now by his grace is born again,
And sings redeeming love.

251 *Faith victorious.* 8s.

1 THE moment a sinner believes,
And trusts in his crucified God,
His pardon at once he receives—
Redemption in full through his blood.
The faith that unites to the Lamb,
And brings such salvation as this,
Is more than mere fancy, or name—
The work of God's Spirit it is.

2 It treads on the world and on hell,
It vanquishes death and despair;
And, what is still stranger to tell—
It overcomes heaven by prayer;
Permits a vile worm of the dust
With God to commune as a friend;
His promise of mercy to trust,
And look for his love to the end.

3 It says to the mountains, "Depart,"
That stand between God and the soul;
It binds up the broken in heart,
The wounded in spirit makes whole;
Bids sins of a crimson-like dye
Be spotless as snow, and as white;

And raises the sinner on high,
To dwell with the angels of light.

252 *Happiness of the Believer.* 5. 9.

1 HOW happy are they
Who the Saviour obey,
And have laid up their treasure above!
Oh, what tongue can express
The sweet comfort and peace
Of a soul in its earliest love!

2 That comfort was mine,
When compassion divine
To my soul in its misery came;
When first I believed,
And salvation received,
And rejoiced in Immanuel's name.

3 My remnant of days
Would I spend to his praise,
Who hath died my lost soul to redeem;
Whether many or few,
All my years are his due—
May they all be devoted to him.

253 *Self-righteousness renounced.* C. M.

1 HOW long beneath the law I lay
In bondage and distress!
I toiled the precept to obey,
But toiled without success.

2 Then all my servile works were done
A righteousness to raise;

Now, freely chosen in the Son,
I freely choose his ways.

3 To see the law by Christ fulfilled,
And hear his pardoning voice,
Will change a slave into a child,
And duty into choice.

254 *Jesus our Fore-runner.*—John xiv. 6. L. M

1 JESUS, my all, to heaven is gone,
He whom I fix my hopes upon;
His track I see, and I'll pursue
The narrow way, till him I view.

2 This is the way I long have sought,
And mourned because I found it not;
My grief, my burden, long has been
Because I could not cease from sin.

3 The more I strove against its power,
I sinned and stumbled but the more;
Till late I heard my Saviour say—
"Come hither, soul, I am the way."

4 Lo, glad I come, and thou, bless'd Lamb,
Shalt take me to thee as I am;
Nothing but sin I thee can give,
Nothing but love shall I receive.

5 Then will I tell to sinners round
What a dear Saviour I have found;
I'll point to thy redeeming blood,
And say, "Behold the way to God."

255

Self-consecration. 6. 4

1 MY faith looks up to thee,
Thou Lamb of Calvary,
Saviour divine:
Now hear me while I pray;
Take all my guilt away;
Oh let me from this day
Be wholly thine.

2 May thy rich grace impart
Strength to my fainting heart,
My zeal inspire;
As thou hast died for me,
Oh may my love to thee
Pure, warm, and changeless be—
A living fire.

3 While life's dark maze I tread,
And griefs around me spread,
Be thou my guide;
Bid darkness turn to day,
Wipe sorrow's tears away,
Nor let me ever stray
From thee aside.

4 When ends life's transient dream,
When death's cold, sullen stream
Shall o'er me roll;
Bless'd Saviour, then, in love,
Fear and distress remove;
Oh bear me safe above—
A ransomed soul.

256 *Grace.* C. M.

1 AMAZING grace, (how sweet the sound,)
That saved a wretch like me!
I once was lost, but now am found;
Was blind, but now I see.

2 'Twas grace that taught my heart to fear,
And grace my fears relieved;
How precious did that grace appear,
The hour I first believed.

3 Through many dangers, toils, and snares,
I have already come;
But grace has brought me safe thus far,
And grace will lead me home.

4 Yes, when this flesh and heart shall fail,
And mortal life shall cease;
I shall possess, within the vail,
A life of joy and peace.

257 *Outward Forms vain.* C. M.

1 LONG did I seem to serve thee, Lord,
With unavailing pain;
Fasted, and prayed, and read thy word,
And heard it preached in vain.

2 Oft did I with th' assembly join,
Oft near thine altar drew;
A form of godliness was mine,
The power I never knew.

3 I rested in the outward law,
Nor knew its deep design:

The length and breadth I never saw,
And height of love divine.

4 To please thee thus, at length I see
I vainly toiled and strove;
For what are outward works to thee,
Unless they spring from love?

5 But I of means have made my boast,
Of means an idol made;
The spirit in the letter lost,
The substance in the shade.

6 Now on thy grace I build my hope,
What can my weakness do?
Jesus, to thee my soul looks up,
For thou must make it new.

258 *Fleeing to Christ as a Refuge.* C. P. M.

1 O THOU who hear'st the prayer of faith,
Wilt thou not save a soul from death,
That casts itself on thee?
I have no refuge of my own,
But fly to what my Lord hath done
And suffered once for me.

2 Slain in the guilty sinner's stead
Thy spotless righteousness I plead,
And thine atoning blood:
Thy righteousness my robe shall be,
Thy merit shall avail for me,
And bring me near to God.

3 Then snatch me from eternal death,
The Spirit of adoption breathe,
His consolation send:

By him some word of life impart,
And sweetly whisper to my heart—
"Thy Maker is thy friend."

4 Then will the king of terrors be
A welcome messenger to me,
To bid me come away:
Unclogged by earth, or earthly things,
I'll mount, I'll fly, with eager wings,
To everlasting day.

259 *Self-righteousness renounced.* L. M.

1 NO more, my God, I boast no more
Of all the duties I have done;
I quit the hopes I held before,
To trust the merits of thy Son.

2 Now, for the love I bear his name,
What was my gain I count my loss;
My former pride I call my shame,
And nail my glory to his cross.

3 Yes, and I must and will esteem
All things but loss for Jesus' sake;
Oh may my soul be found in him,
And of his righteousness partake.

4 The best obedience of my hands
Dares not appear before thy throne;
But faith can answer thy demands,
By pleading what my Lord has done.

260 *Need of a Saviour.* 7. 6.

1 WRETCHED, helpless, and distressed,
Ah, whither shall I fly?

Saviour, give my spirit rest;
  To thee would I draw nigh.
Naked, sick, and poor, and blind,
  Bound in sin and misery—
Friend of sinners, let me find
  My help, my all in thee.

2 Poor, alas, thou know'st I am,
  And would be poorer still—
See my wretchedness and shame,
  And all my vileness feel:
Jesus, Lord, restore my sight,
  Take, oh take the vail away;
Turn my darkness into light,
  My midnight into day.

3 Clothe me in thy righteousness,
  Endue my soul with thee;
Having on that glorious dress,
  I can my Maker see:
In thy name will I arise,
  Hastening to that bless'd abode
Where thou reignest in the skies,
  And pleadest with my God.

261 *Safety at the Cross.* L. M.

1 HERE, at thy cross, incarnate God,
  I lay my soul beneath thy love;
Beneath the droppings of thy blood,
  Jesus—nor shall it e'er remove.

2 Should worlds conspire to drive me hence,
  Moveless and firm this heart should lie·

Resolved, for that's my last defence,
If I must perish, here to die.

3 But speak, my Lord, and calm my fear;
Am I not safe beneath thy shade?
Thy vengeance will not strike me here,
Nor Satan dare my soul invade.

4 Yes, I'm secure beneath thy blood,
And all my foes shall lose their aim;
Hosanna to th' incarnate God,
And my best honors to his name.

262 *The Disciple at the Cross.* 8. 7.

1 SWEET the moments, rich in blessing,
Which before the cross I spend;
Life, and health, and peace possessing,
From the sinner's dying Friend.

2 Truly blessed is this station—
Low before his cross to lie;
While I see divine compassion
Floating in his languid eye.

3 Love and grief my heart dividing,
With my tears his feet I bathe;
Constant still in faith abiding,
Life deriving from his death.

263 *Forsaking all for Christ.*—Mark x. 28. 8. 7.

1 JESUS, I my cross have taken,
All to leave, and follow thee;
Naked, poor, despised, forsaken,
Thou, from hence, my all shalt be:

Perish every fond ambition—
All I've sought, or hoped, or known—
Yet how rich is my condition,
God and heaven are still my own!

2 Let the world despise and leave me;
They have left my Saviour too;
Human hearts and looks deceive me—
Thou art not, like them, untrue;
And while thou shalt smile upon me,
God of wisdom, love, and might,
Foes may hate, and friends disown me—
Show thy face, and all is bright.

3 Go, then, earthly fame and treasure;
Come disaster, scorn, and pain;
In thy service pain is pleasure,
With thy favor loss is gain.
I have called thee Abba, Father,
I have set my heart on thee;
Storms may howl, and clouds may gather,
All must work for good to me.

4 Man may trouble and distress me,
'Twill but drive me to thy breast;
Life with trials hard may press me,
Heaven will bring me sweeter rest.
Oh, 'tis not in grief to harm me,
While thy love is left to me;
Oh, 'twere not in joy to charm me,
Were that joy unmixed with thee.

5 Soul, then know thy full salvation;
Rise o'er sin, and fear, and care;

Joy to find in every station
  Something still to do or bear.
Think what Spirit dwells within thee;
  Think what Father's smiles are thine;
Think that Jesus died to win thee:
  Child of heaven, canst thou repine?

6 Haste thee on from grace to glory,
  Armed by faith, and winged by prayer;
Heaven's eternal day's before thee,
  God's own hand shall guide thee there.
Soon shall close thy earthly mission,
  Soon shall pass thy pilgrim days,
Hope shall change to glad fruition,
  Faith to sight, and prayer to praise.

264 *Self-dedication.* L. M.

1 LORD, I am thine, entirely thine,
  Purchased and saved by blood divine;
With full consent thine I would be,
And own thy sovereign right in me.

2 Here, Lord, my flesh, my soul, my all,
I yield to thee beyond recall;
Accept thine own, so long withheld;
Accept what I so freely yield.

3 Grant one poor sinner more a place
Among the children of thy grace;
A wretched sinner, lost to God,
But ransomed by Immanuel's blood.

4 Thee my new Master now I call,
And consecrate to thee my all;

Thine would I live, thine would I die,
Be thine through all eternity.

5 Do thou assist a feeble worm
The great engagement to perform:
Thy grace can full assistance lend,
And on that grace I dare depend.

265 *Covenant with God.* L. M.

1 OH happy day that fixed my choice
On thee, my Saviour and my God;
Well may this glowing heart rejoice,
And tell its raptures all abroad.

2 Oh happy bond that seals my vows
To him who merits all my love;
Let cheerful anthems fill his house,
And echo through his courts above.

3 'Tis done—the great transaction's done;
I am my Lord's, and he is mine:
He drew me, and I followed on,
Glad to obey the call divine.

4 Now rest—my long-divided heart—
Fixed on this blissful centre, rest;
From all my idols now I part,
And welcome Jesus to my breast.

5 High Heaven, that hears the solemn vow,
That vow renewed shall daily hear,
Till in life's latest hour I bow,
And bless in death a bond so dear.

266 *Old things passed away.*—2 Cor. v. 17. C. M.

LET worldly minds the world pursue;
  It has no charms for me;
Once I admired its trifles too,
  But grace has set me free.

Its pleasures now no longer please,
  No more content afford:
Far from my heart be joys like these,
  Now I have seen the Lord.

As by the light of opening day
  The stars are all concealed,
So earthly pleasures fade away,
  When Jesus is revealed.

Creatures no more divide my choice;
  I bid them all depart;
His name, and love, and gracious voice,
  Have fixed my roving heart.

Now, Lord, I would be thine alone,
  And wholly live to thee;
But may I hope that thou wilt own
  A worthless worm like me?

Yes, though of sinners I'm the worst,
  I cannot doubt thy will;
For if thou hadst not loved me first,
  I had refused thee still.

267 *The New Covenant sealed.* C. M.

"THE promise of my Father's love
  Shall stand for ever good,"

He said—and gave his soul to death,
And sealed the grace with blood.

2 To this dear covenant of thy word
I set my worthless name;
I seal th' engagement to my Lord,
And make my humble claim.

3 The light, and strength, and pardonir [grac
And glory shall be mine:
My life and soul—my heart and flesh,
And all my powers are thine.

4 I call that legacy my own,
Which Jesus did bequeath;
'Twas purchased with a dying groan,
And ratified in death.

5 Sweet is the memory of his name,
Who blessed us in his will;
And to his testament of love
Made his own life the seal.

268 *Self-consecration.* L. I

1 OH sweetly breathe the lyres above,
When angels touch the quiverin string,
And wake, to chant Immanuel's love,
Such strains as angel lips can sing.

2 And sweet, on earth, the choral swell
From mortal tongues, of gladsome lays
When pardoned souls their raptures tell,
And, grateful, hymn Immanuel's prais

3 Jesus—thy name our souls adore;
We own the bond that makes us thine;
And carnal joys, that charmed before,
For thy dear sake we now resign.

4 Our hearts, by dying love subdued,
Accept thine offered grace to-day;
Beneath the cross, with blood bedewed,
We bow, and give ourselves away.

5 In thee we trust—on thee rely;
Though we are feeble, thou art strong;
Oh keep us till our spirits fly
To join the bright immortal throng.

269 *Renouncing the World.* H. M.

1 COME, my fond fluttering heart,
Come, struggle to be free;
Thou and the world must part,
However hard it be:
My trembling spirit owns it just,
But cleaves yet closer to the dust.

2 Ye tempting sweets forbear,
Ye dearest idols, fall;
My love ye must not share,
Jesus shall have it all:
'Tis bitter pain, 'tis cruel smart,
But oh, thou must consent, my heart.

3 Ye fair enchanting throng,
Ye golden dreams, farewell:
Earth has prevailed too long,
And now I break the spell:

Ye cherished joys of early years—
Jesus, forgive these parting tears.

4 Oh may I feel thy worth,
And let no idol dare,
No vanity of earth,
With thee, my Lord, compare;
Now bid all worldly joys depart,
And reign supremely in my heart.

270 "*Seek ye first,*" *&c.*—Matt. vi. 33. C. M

1 NOW let a true ambition rise,
And ardor fire our breast
To reign in worlds above the skies,
In heavenly glories dressed.

2 Behold Jehovah's royal hand
A radiant crown display,
Whose gems with vivid lustre shine,
While stars and suns decay.

3 Away, each groveling, anxious care,
Beneath a Christian's thought;
Oh spring to seize immortal joys,
Which your Redeemer bought.

4 Ye hearts with youthful vigor warm,
The glorious prize pursue;
Nor fear the want of earthly good,
While heaven is kept in view.

271 *Parting with earthly Joys.* L. M

1 I SEND the joys of earth away;
Away, ye tempters of the mind,

False as the smooth deceitful sea,
And empty as the whistling wind.

Your streams were floating me along,
Down to the gulf of black despair;
And while I listened to your song,
Your streams had e'en conveyed me there.

Lord, I adore thy matchless grace,
That warned me of that dark abyss;
That drew me from those treacherous seas,
And bade me seek superior bliss.

Now to the shining realms above
I stretch my hands, and glance my eyes;
Oh for the pinions of a dove,
To bear me to the upper skies.

272 *Self-denial.*—Luke ix. 23. C. M.

AND must I part with all I have,
My dearest Lord, for thee?
It is but right, since thou hast done
Much more than this for me.

Yes, let it go—one look from thee
Will more than make amends
For all the losses I sustain
Of credit, riches, friends.

Ten thousand worlds, ten thousand lives,
How worthless they appear,
Compared with thee, supremely good,
Divinely bright and fair.

Saviour of souls, could I from thee
A single smile obtain,

Though destitute of all things else,
I'd glory in my gain.

273 *The happy Choice.*—Ruth i. 16. 7s. Double

1 PEOPLE of the living God,
I have sought the world around,
Paths of sin and sorrow trod,
Peace and comfort no-where found:
Now to you my spirit turns—
Turns, a fugitive unbless'd;
Brethren, where your altar burns,
Oh receive me into rest.

2 Lonely I no longer roam,
Like the cloud, the wind, the wave;
Where you dwell shall be my home,
Where you die shall be my grave;
Mine the God whom you adore,
Your Redeemer shall be mine;
Earth can fill my soul no more,
Every idol I resign.

274 *The Pearl of great Price.* C. M.

1 YE glittering toys of earth, adieu,
A nobler choice be mine;
A real prize attracts my view,
A treasure all divine.

2 Jesus, to multitudes unknown,
Oh name divinely sweet!
Jesus, in thee, in thee alone,
Wealth, honor, pleasure meet.

Should earth's vain treasures all depart,
  Of this dear gift possessed,
I'd clasp it to my joyful heart,
  And be for ever bless'd.

Dear Sovereign of my soul's desires,
  Thy love is bliss divine;
Accept the gift that love inspires,
  And bid me call thee mine.

275 *Love to the Redeemer.* 8s.

MY gracious Redeemer I love,
  His praises aloud I'll proclaim,
And join with the armies above,
  To shout his adorable name:
To gaze on his glories divine
  Shall be my eternal employ;
To see them incessantly shine
  My boundless, ineffable joy.

2 He freely redeemed, with his blood,
  My soul from the confines of hell,
To live on the smiles of my God,
  And in his sweet presence to dwell;
To shine with the angels in light,
  With saints and with seraphs to sing,
To view, with eternal delight,
  My Jesus, my Saviour, my King.

3 Ye palaces, sceptres, and crowns,
  Your pride with disdain I survey;
Your pomps are but shadows and sounds,
  And pass in a moment away;

The crown that my Saviour bestows,
  Yon permanent sun shall outshine;
My joy everlastingly flows—
  My God, my Redeemer is mine.

276. *Sincerity*—John xxi. 15. C. M.

1 DO not I love thee, O my Lord?
  Behold my heart, and see;
And turn each hateful idol out,
  That dares to rival thee.

2 Do not I love thee from my soul?
  Then let me nothing love;
Dead be my heart to every joy,
  When Jesus cannot move.

3 Is not thy name melodious still
  To my attentive ear?
Doth not each pulse with pleasure bound,
  My Saviour's voice to hear?

4 Hast thou a lamb in all thy flock
  I would disdain to feed?
Hast thou a foe before whose face
  I fear thy cause to plead?

5 Thou know'st I love thee, gracious Lord;
  But oh, I long to soar
Far from the sphere of mortal joys,
  And learn to love thee more.

277 *The Presence of the Comforter.* L. M

1 SURE the bless'd Comforter is nigh;
  'Tis he sustains my fainting heart;

Else would my hope for ever die,
  And every cheering ray depart.
2 Whene'er to call the Saviour mine
  With ardent wish my heart aspires,
Can it be less than power divine,
  Which animates these strong desires?
3 And when my cheerful hope can say
  I love my God, and taste his grace,
Lord, is it not thy blissful ray,
  Which brings this dawn of sacred peace?
4 Let thy kind Spirit in my heart
  For ever dwell, O God of love,
And light, and heavenly peace impart,
  Sweet earnest of the joys above.

278 *Christ a King.* C. M.

1 COME, ye that love the Saviour's name,
  And joy to make it known;
The Sovereign of your heart proclaim,
  And bow before his throne.

2 Behold your King, your Saviour, crowned
  With glories all divine;
And tell the wondering nations round,
  How bright these glories shine.
3 Infinite power and boundless grace
  In him unite their rays;
Ye that have e'er beheld his face,
  Can ye forbear his praise?
4 When in his earthly courts we view
  The beauties of our King,

We long to love as angels do,
And wish like them to sing.

5 And shall we long and wish in vain?
Lord, teach our songs to rise;
Thy love can animate the strain,
And bid it reach the skies.

279 *Confidence in the Saviour.* C. M.

1 THOU lovely source of true delight,
Whom I unseen adore,
Unvail thy beauties to my sight,
That I may love thee more.

2 Thy glory o'er creation shines;
But in thy sacred word
I read, in fairer, brighter lines,
My bleeding, dying Lord.

3 'Tis here, whene'er my comforts droop,
And sin and sorrow rise,
Thy love, with cheerful beams of hope,
My fainting breast supplies.

4 But ah, too soon the pleasing scene
Is clouded o'er with pain;
My gloomy fears rise dark between,
And I again complain.

5 Jesus, my Lord, my life, my light,
Oh come with blissful ray,
Break radiant through the shades of night
And chase my fears away.

6 Then shall my soul with rapture trace
The wonders of thy love;

But the full glories of thy face
  Are only known above.

280 *Jesus precious.*—1 Pet. ii. 7. C. M.

1 BLESS'D Jesus, when my soaring
  O'er all thy graces rove, [thoughts
How is my soul in transport lost—
  In wonder, joy, and love!

2 Not softest strains can charm my ear,
  Like thy beloved name;
Nor aught beneath the skies inspire
  My heart with equal flame.

3 Where'er I look, my wondering eyes
  Unnumbered blessings see;
But what is life, with all its bliss,
  If once compared with thee?

4 Hast thou a rival in my breast?
  Search, Lord—for thou canst tell
If aught can raise my passions thus,
  Or please my soul so well.

5 No—thou art precious to my heart—
  My portion and my joy;
For ever let thy boundless grace
  My sweetest thoughts employ.

6 When nature faints, around my bed
  Let thy bright glories shine,
And death shall all his terrors lose,
  In raptures so divine.

281 *Love to God.* C. M.

1 HAPPY the heart where graces reign,
Where love inspires the breast;
Love is the brightest of the train,
And strengthens all the rest.

2 Knowledge, alas, 'tis all in vain,
And all in vain our fear;
Our stubborn sins will fight and reign,
If love be absent there.

3 This is the grace that lives and sings,
When faith and hope shall cease:
'Tis this shall strike our joyful strings,
In the sweet realms of bliss.

4 Before we quite forsake our clay,
Or leave this dark abode,
The wings of love bear us away,
To see our smiling God.

282 *"Patient in Tribulation."* 8. 6.

1 WHEN I can trust my all with God,
In trial's fearful hour,
Bow, all resigned, beneath his rod,
And bless his sparing power;
A joy springs up amid distress,
A fountain in the wilderness.

2 Oh, to be brought to Jesus' feet,
Though sorrows fix me there,
Is still a privilege most sweet—
'Tis sweet to plead in prayer,

Though sighs and tears its language be,
If Christ be near, and smile on me.

3 Then blessed be the hand that gave,
Still blessed when it takes;
Blessed be he who smites to save,
Who heals the heart he breaks:
Perfect and true are all his ways,
Whom heaven adores, and death obeys.

283 *Submission.* L. M.

1 WAIT, O my soul, thy Maker's will;
Tumultuous passions, all be still;
Nor let a murmuring thought arise;
His ways are just, his counsels wise.

2 He in the thickest darkness dwells,
Performs his work, the cause conceals;
But, though his methods are unknown,
Judgment and truth support his throne.

3 In heaven, and earth, and air, and seas,
He executes his firm decrees;
And by his saints it stands confessed
That what he does is ever best.

4 Wait, then, my soul, submissive wait,
Prostrate before his awful seat;
And 'midst the terrors of his rod,
Trust in a wise and gracious God.

284 *The Covenant of Mercy.* C. M.

1 MY God, the covenant of thy love
Abides for ever sure;

And in its matchless grace I feel
My happiness secure.

2 Since thou, the everlasting God,
My Father art become,
Jesus my guardian and my friend,
And heaven my final home;—

3 I welcome all thy sovereign will,
For all that will is love;
And when I know not what thou dost,
I wait the light above.

4 Thy covenant, in the darkest gloom,
Shall be my strength and stay;
Shall cheer my passage to the tomb,
And guide to endless day.

285 *Happiness in God.* C. M.

1 FATHER, whate'er of earthly bliss
Thy sovereign will denies,
Accepted at thy throne of grace
Let this petition rise:

2 "Give me a calm, a thankful heart,
From every murmur free;
The blessings of thy grace impart,
And make me live to thee.

3 "Let the sweet hope that I am thine
My life and death attend;
Thy presence through my journey shine,
And crown my journey's end."

286 "*It is the Lord.*"—1 Sam. iii. 18. C. M.

1 IT is the Lord—enthroned in light,
Whose claims are all divine,
Who has an undisputed right
To govern me and mine.

2 It is the Lord—who gives me all—
My wealth, my friends, my ease;
And of his bounties may recall
Whatever part he please.

3 It is the Lord—whose matchless skill
Can from afflictions raise
Blessings, eternity to fill
With ever-growing praise.

4 It is the Lord, my covenant God,
Thrice blessed be his name;
Whose gracious promise, sealed with blood,
Must ever be the same.

5 Can I, with hopes so firmly built,
Be sullen, or repine?
No—gracious God—take what thou wilt,
To thee I all resign.

287 *Submission to God.* C. M.

1 MY God, my Father, blissful name!
Oh, may I call thee mine?
May I with sweet assurance claim
A portion so divine?

2 This only can my fears control,
And bid my sorrows fly:

What harm can ever reach my soul,
Beneath my Father's eye?

3 Whate'er thy providence denies,
I calmly would resign;
For thou art good and just and wise;
Oh bend my will to thine.

4 Whate'er thy sacred will ordains,
Oh give me strength to bear:
And let me know my Father reigns,
And trust his tender care.

288 *Happiness in God.* C. M

1 MY times of sorrow and of joy,
Great God, are in thy hand;
My choicest comforts come from thee,
And go at thy command.

2 If thou shouldst take them all away,
Yet would I not repine;
Before they were possessed by me,
They were entirely thine.

3 Nor would I drop a murmuring word,
Though the whole world were gone,
But seek enduring happiness
In thee, and thee alone.

289 *Resignation.* C. M

1 ALL-WISE, all-mighty, and all-good,
In thee I firmly trust;
Thy ways, unknown, or understood,
Are merciful and just.

2 May I remember that to thee
Whate'er I have I owe,
And back in gratitude from me
May all thy bounties flow.

3 And though thy wisdom takes away,
Shall I arraign thy will?
No, let me bless thy name, and say—
"The Lord is gracious still."

4 A pilgrim, through the earth I roam,
Of nothing long possessed;
And all must fail when I go home,
For this is not my rest.

5 Write but my name upon the roll
Of thy redeemed above, [soul
Then with my heart and strength and
I'll love thee for thy love.

290 *Refuge in God.* C. M

1 DEAR refuge of my weary soul,
On thee, when sorrows rise—
On thee, when waves of trouble roll,
My fainting hope relies.

2 To thee I tell each rising grief,
For thou alone canst heal;
Thy word can bring a sweet relief
For every pain I feel.

3 B. t oh, when gloomy doubts prevail,
fear to call thee mine;
T ɐe springs of comfort seem to fail,
And all my hopes decline.

4 Yet, gracious God, where shall I flee?
Thou art my only trust;
And still my soul would cleave to thee,
Though prostrate in the dust.

5 Thy mercy-seat is open still;
Here let my soul retreat,
With humble hope attend thy will,
And wait beneath thy feet.

291 *Assurance.*—Jer. xxxi. 3. L. M. 6 lines.

1 JESUS, I know, hath died for me—
Here is my hope, my joy, my rest;
Hither, when hell assails, I flee,
And look into my Saviour's breast:
Away, sad doubts and anxious fear—
Mercy is all that's written there.

2 Though waves and storms go o'er my head,
Though strength and health and friends be gone;
Though joys be withered all, and dead,
And every comfort be withdrawn;
Steadfast on this my soul relies—
Father, thy mercy never dies.

3 Fixed on this rock will I remain,
When heart shall fail, and flesh decay;—
A rock which shall my soul sustain,
When earth's foundations melt away:
Mercy's full power I then shall prove,
Loved with an everlasting love.

292 *Divine Support and Guidance.* L. M.

1 O THOU to whose all-searching sight
The darkness shineth as the light,
Search, prove my heart, it pants for thee;
Oh burst these bonds, and set it free.

2 If in this darksome wild I stray,
Be thou my light, be thou my way;
No foes, no violence I fear,
No fraud, while thou, my God, art near.

3 When rising floods my soul o'erflow,
When sinks my heart in waves of wo,
Jesus, thy timely aid impart,
And raise my head, and cheer my heart.

4 Saviour, where'er thy steps I see,
Dauntless, untired, I follow thee;
Oh let thy hand support me still,
And lead me to thy holy hill.

5 If rough and thorny be the way,
My strength proportion to my day;
Till toil and grief and pain shall cease,
Where all is calm and joy and peace.

293 *Hope encouraged.*—Ps. xlii. 5. 8. 7. 4.

1 O MY soul, what means this sadness?
Wherefore art thou thus cast down?
Let thy grief be turned to gladness,
Bid thy restless fears begone;
Look to Jesus,
And confide in him alone.

2 Though ten thousand ills beset thee,
From without and from within,
Jesus never will forget thee,
But will break the power of sin:
He is faithful—
Thou the victory shalt win.

3 Though distresses now attend thee,
And thou tread'st the thorny road,
His right hand shall still defend thee—
Guide thee to his bless'd abode—
Bring thee, ransomed,
To thy home, thy heaven, thy God.

294 *Christian Confidence.*—2 Tim. i. 12. C. M.

1 I'M not ashamed to own my Lord,
Or to defend his cause—
Maintain the honor of his word,
The glory of his cross.

2 Jesus, my God—I know his name—
His name is all my trust;
Nor will he put my soul to shame,
Nor let my hope be lost.

3 Firm as his throne his promise stands;
And he can well secure
What I've committed to his hands,
Till the decisive hour.

4 Then will he own my worthless name
Before his Father's face;
And in the new Jerusalem
Appoint my soul a place.

295 *The Fearful encouraged.*

1 GIVE to the winds thy fears,
Hope, and be undismayed;
God hears thy sighs, and counts thy tears,
God shall lift up thy head.

2 Through waves and clouds and storms
He gently clears thy way;
Wait thou his time, so shall this night
Soon end in joyous day.

3 Still heavy is thy heart?
Still sink thy spirits down?
Cast off the weight, let fear depart,
And every care be gone.

4 What though thou rulest not;
Yet heaven and earth and hell
Proclaim God sitteth on the throne,
And ruleth all things well.

5 Leave to his sovereign sway
To choose and to command:
So shalt thou, wond'ring, own his way
How wise; how strong his hand.

296 *Looking to Jesus.* S. M. Double.

1 JESUS, my strength, my hope,
On thee I cast my care,
With humble confidence look up,
And know thou hear'st my prayer.
Give me on thee to wait,
Till I can all things do,

On thee, almighty to create,
 Almighty to renew.

2 Give me the godly fear,
 The quick discerning eye,
That looks to thee when sin is near,
 And sees the tempter fly;
A spirit still prepared,
 And armed with jealous care,
For ever standing on its guard,
 And watching unto prayer.

3 I rest upon thy word,
 The promise is for me;
My succor and salvation, Lord,
 Shall surely come from thee;
But let me still abide,
 Nor from my hope remove,
Till thou my patient spirit guide
 To know thy perfect love.

297 *Remember me.* C. M.

1 O THOU from whom all goodness flows,
 I lift my heart to thee;
In all my sorrows, conflicts, woes,
 Dear Lord, remember me.

2 When on my sad and burdened heart
 My sins lie heavily,
My pardon speak, new peace impart,
 In love remember me.

3 When trials sore obstruct my way,
 And ills I cannot flee,

Oh let my strength be as my day;
For good remember me.

4 If, for thy sake, upon my name
Shame and reproach shall be,
I'll hail reproach, and welcome shame,
If thou remember me.

5 When worn with pain, disease, and grief,
This feeble body see;
Grant patience, rest, and kind relief;
And, Lord, remember me.

6 When, in the solemn hour of death,
I wait thy just decree,
Be this the prayer of my last breath—
Dear Lord, remember me.

298 *Strength equal to the Day.* 7s.

1 WAIT, my soul, upon the Lord,
To his gracious promise flee,
Laying hold upon his word,
"As thy days thy strength shall be."

2 If the sorrows of my case
Seem peculiar still to me,
God has promised needful grace,
"As thy days thy strength shall be."

3 Days of trial, days of grief,
In succession I may see;
Daily this is my relief,
"As thy days thy strength shall be."

4 Rock of Ages, I'm secure,
With thy promise full and free—

Faithful, positive, and sure—
"As thy days thy strength shall be."

299 *"My Redeemer liveth."* C. M.

1 I KNOW that my Redeemer lives,
And ever pleads for me:
Salvation to his saints he gives,
And life and liberty.

2 I find him lifting up my head,
He brings salvation near;
His presence makes me free indeed,
And he will soon appear.

3 He will perform the work begun;
He will his own defend;
Will give me strength my course to run,
And love me to the end.

4 Lord, I believe, and rest secure
In confidence divine;
Thy promise stands for ever sure,
And all thou art is mine.

300 *Confidence in Preserving Grace.* 8s.

1 A DEBTOR to mercy alone,
Of covenant mercy I sing;
Nor fear, with thy righteousness on,
My person and off'rings to bring:
The terrors of law and of God
With me can have nothing to do;
My Saviour's obedience and blood
Hide all my transgressions from view.

2 The work which his goodness began,
The arm of his strength will complete;
His promise is Yea and Amen,
And never was forfeited yet:
Things future, nor things that are now,
Not all things below or above,
Can make him his purpose forego,
Or sever my soul from his love.

3 My name from the palms of his hands
Eternity will not erase;
Impressed on his heart it remains,
In marks of indelible grace:
Yes—I to the end shall endure,
As sure as the earnest is given;
More happy, but not more secure,
The glorified spirits in heaven.

301 *Delight in God.* C. M.

1 O LORD, I would delight in thee,
And on thy care depend;
To thee in every trouble flee,
My best, my only friend.

2 When all created streams are dried,
Thy fullness is the same;
May I with this be satisfied,
And glory in thy name.

3 Oh that I had a stronger faith
To look within the vail,
To credit what my Saviour saith,
Whose word can never fail.

4 O Lord, I cast my care on thee;
I triumph and adore;
Henceforth my great concern shall be
To love and praise thee more.

302 *Prayer for spiritual Strength.* 7. 6

1 NEAR me, O my Saviour, stand,
In sore temptation's hour;
Save me with thine outstretched hand,
And show forth all thy power;
Oh be mindful of thy word;
All-sufficient grace bestow;
Keep me, keep me, gracious Lord,
And never let me go.

2 Give me, Lord, a holy fear,
And fix it in my heart;
That I may from evil near
With timely care depart;
Sin be more than hell abhorred,
Faith resist the tyrant foe;
Keep me, keep me, gracious Lord,
And never let me go.

3 Never let me leave thy breast,
Or from my Saviour stray;
Thou art my support and rest,
My true and living way;
My exceeding great reward,
Mine above, and mine below;
Keep me, keep me, gracious Lord,
And never let me go.

4 Never let me go, till I,
Upborne on wings of love,
Gain the region of the sky,
And take my seat above;
See thee by all heaven adored,
And thy glorious fullness know;
Keep me, keep me, gracious Lord,
And never let me go.

303 *Fear not.* C. M

1 YE trembling souls, dismiss your fears;
Be mercy all your theme;
Mercy, which like a river flows
In one continued stream.

2 Fear not the powers of earth and hell;
God will these powers restrain;
His mighty arm their rage repel,
And make their efforts vain.

3 Fear not the want of outward good;
He will for his provide,
Grant them supplies of daily food,
And give them heaven beside.

4 Fear not that he will e'er forsake,
Or leave his work undone;
He's faithful to his promises,
And faithful to his Son.

5 Fear not the terrors of the grave,
Or death's tremendous sting:
He will from endless wrath preserve,
To endless glory bring.

6 You in his wisdom, power, and grace,
May confidently trust;
His wisdom guides, his power protects,
His grace rewards the just.

304 *"Casting all your care," &c.*—1 Pet. v. 7. S. M

1 HOW gentle God's commands!
How kind his precepts are!
Come, cast your burdens on the Lord,
And trust his constant care.

2 Beneath his powerful sway,
His saints securely dwell;
That hand which bears all nature up,
Will guide his children well.

3 Why should this anxious load
Press down your weary mind?
Haste to your heavenly Father's throne,
And sweet refreshment find.

4 His goodness stands approved,
Renewed from day to day;
I'll drop my burden at his feet,
And bear a song away.

305 *Prayer for Submission.* C. M

1 O LORD, my best desire fulfill,
And help me to resign
Life, health, and comfort to thy will,
And make thy pleasure mine.

2 Why should I shrink at thy command,
Whose love forbids my fears?

Or tremble at the gracious hand
That wipes away my tears?

3 No, rather let me freely yield
What most I prize to thee,
Who never hast a good withheld,
Or wilt withhold from me.

4 Wisdom and mercy guide my way;
Shall I resist them both—
A poor blind creature of a day,
And crushed before the moth?

5 But ah, my inward spirit cries—
Still bind me to thy sway;
Else the next cloud that vails my skies,
Will drive these thoughts away.

306 "*Trust ye in the Lord.*"—Isa. xxvi. 4. C. M.

1 WHEN grief and anguish press me down,
And hope and comfort flee,
I cling, bless'd Saviour, to thy throne,
And stay my heart on thee.

2 When clouds of dark temptation rise,
And pour their wrath on me,
To thee, for aid, I turn my eyes,
And fix my trust on thee.

3 When death invades my peaceful home,
The sundered ties shall be
A closer bond, in time to come,
To bind my heart to thee.

4 Lord—"not my will, but thine be done:"
My soul, from fear set free,

Her faith shall anchor at thy throne,
  And trust alone in thee.

307 "*What shall I render?*"—Ps. cxvi. 12. C. M

1 FOR mercies countless as the sands,
  Which daily I receive
From Jesus my Redeemer's hands,
  My soul, what canst thou give?

2 Alas, from such a heart as mine,
  What can I bring him forth?
My best is stained and dyed with sin,
  My all is nothing worth.

3 Yet this acknowledgment I'll make
  For all he has bestowed—
Salvation's sacred cup I'll take,
  And call upon my God.

4 The best return for one like me,
  So wretched and so poor,
Is from his gifts to draw a plea,
  And ask him still for more.

308 *Everlasting Praise.* C. M.

1 YES—I will bless thee, O my God,
  Through all my mortal days,
And to eternity prolong
  Thy vast, thy boundless praise.

2 Nor shall my tongue alone proclaim
  The honors of my God;
My life, with all its active powers,
  Shall spread thy praise abroad.

3 Not death itself shall stop my song,
Though death will close my eyes:
My thoughts shall then to nobler heights
And sweeter raptures rise.

4 There shall my lips in endless praise
Their grateful tribute pay;
The theme demands an angel's tongue,
And an eternal day.

309 "*The Good Shepherd.*" C. M.

1 TO thee, my Shepherd, and my Lord,
A grateful song I'll raise;
Oh let the feeblest of thy flock
Attempt to sing thy praise.

2 But oh, what mortal tongue can speak
A subject so divine,
Do justice to so vast a theme,
And praise a love like thine?

3 My life, my joy, my hope, I owe
To this amazing love;
Ten thousand thousand comforts here,
And nobler bliss above.

4 To thee my trembling spirit flies,
With sin and grief oppressed;
Thy gentle voice dispels my fears,
And lulls my cares to rest.

5 Nay, should I walk through death's dark [vale
With double horrors spread,
Thy rod would guide my doubtful steps,
And guard my drooping head.

6 Lead on, dear Shepherd—led by thee,
No evil shall I fear;
Soon shall I reach thy fold above,
And praise thee better there.

310 *Sickness and Recovery.* C. M.

1 MY God, thy service well demands
The remnant of my days;
Why was this fleeting breath renewed,
But to renew thy praise.

2 Thine arm of everlasting love
Did this weak frame sustain,
When life was hovering o'er the grave,
And nature sunk with pain.

3 Calmly I bowed my fainting head
On thy dear faithful breast;
Pleased to obey my Father's call
To his eternal rest.

4 Into thy hands, my Saviour God,
Did I my all resign,
In firm dependence on that truth
Which made salvation mine.

5 Back from the borders of the grave
At thy command I come;
Nor will I urge a speedier flight
To my celestial home.

6 Where thou appointest my abode,
There would I choose to be;
For in thy presence death is life,
And earth is heaven with thee.

311 *The Tribute of Gratitude.* C. M.

1 BRIGHT source of everlasting love,
To thee our souls we raise;
And to thy sovereign bounty rear
A monument of praise.

2 Thy mercy gilds the path of life
With every cheering ray,
And still restrains the rising tear,
Or wipes that tear away.

3 When, sunk in guilt, our souls approached
The borders of despair,
Thy grace, through Jesus' blood, pro-
A free salvation near. [claimed

4 What shall we render, bounteous Lord,
For all the grace we see?
Alas, the goodness we can yield
Extendeth not to thee.

5 To tents of wo, to beds of pain,
We cheerfully repair;
And, with the gift thy hand bestows,
Relieve the sufferer's care.

6 The widow's heart shall sing for joy;
The orphan's tear be dry;
The sinner hear the call of love,
And find a Saviour nigh.

312 *Sin and Darkness deplored.*—Ps. li. 12. C. M

1 OH for a closer walk with God,
A calm and heavenly frame;

A light to shine upon the road
  That leads me to the Lamb.

2 Where is the blessedness I knew
  When first I saw the Lord?
Where is the soul-refreshing view
  Of Jesus and his word?

3 What peaceful hours I once enjoyed;
  How sweet their memory still!
But they have left an aching void
  The world can never fill.

4 Return, O holy Dove, return,
  Sweet messenger of rest;
I hate the sins that made thee mourn,
  And drove thee from my breast.

5 The dearest idol I have known,
  Whate'er that idol be,
Help me to tear it from thy throne,
  And worship only thee.

6 So shall my walk be close with God—
  Calm and serene my frame;
So purer light shall mark the road
  That leads me to the Lamb.

313 *The Believer in darkness.* 7s. 6 lines

1 ONCE I thought my mountain strong,
  Firmly fixed, no more to move;
Then my Saviour was my song,
  Then my soul was filled with love:
Those were happy, golden days,
Sweetly spent in prayer and praise.

2 Little, then, myself I knew,
  Little thought of Satan's power;
Now I feel my sins anew,
  Now I feel the stormy hour.
Sin has put my joys to flight,
Sin has turned my day to night.

3 Saviour, shine, and cheer my soul;
  Bid my dying hopes revive;
Make my wounded spirit whole,
  Far away the tempter drive:
Speak the word, and set me free,
Let me live alone to thee.

314 *Prayer in Affliction.* 7. 6. Iambic.

1 GREAT author of my being,
  Who seest my inward care,
The ills of thy decreeing
  Enable me to bear;
The justice of thy sentence
  With meekest awe to own,
And spend in deep repentance
  My last expiring groan.

2 My sin to thee confessing,
  I ask thee to impart
That greatest, richest blessing—
  The humble, contrite heart:
The spirit of contrition
  Oh might I now receive,
For all my soul's ambition
  Is worthily to grieve.

3 Oh, for the Saviour's merit,
The forfeiture restore,
And land my fainting spirit
On yonder happy shore.
In safety waft me over,
To harbor in thy breast,
And let me there recover
My everlasting rest.

315 *Mourning over Declension.* C. M.

1 WHY is my heart so far from thee,
My God, my chief delight?
Why are my thoughts no more by day
With thee—no more by night.

2 Why should my foolish passions rove?
Where can such sweetness be
As I have tasted in thy love,
As I have found in thee?

3 When my forgetful soul renews
The savor of thy grace,
My heart presumes I cannot lose
The relish all my days.

4 But ere one fleeting hour is past,
The flattering world employs
Some sensual bait to seize my taste,
And to pollute my joys.

5 Wretch that I am, to wander thus,
In chase of false delight!
Let me be fastened to thy cross,
Rather than lose thy sight.

6 Make haste, my days, to reach the goal,
And bring my heart to rest
On the dear centre of my soul,
My God, my Saviour's breast.

316 "*Will ye also go away?*"—John vi. 67. C. M

1 WHEN any turn from Zion's way,
(Alas, what numbers do!)
Methinks I hear my Saviour say—
"Wilt thou forsake me too?"

2 Ah, Lord, with such a heart as mine,
Unless thou hold me fast,
I feel I must, I shall decline,
And prove like them at last.

3 Yet thou alone hast power, I know,
To save a wretch like me;
To whom, or whither could I go,
If I should turn from thee?

4 No voice but thine can give me rest,
And bid my fears depart;
No love but thine can make me bless'd,
And satisfy my heart.

5 What anguish has that question stirred—
"And wilt thou also go?"
Yet, Lord, relying on thy word,
I humbly answer—no.

317 *Prayer for Divine Light.* 7s. 6 lines.

1 OH reveal thy lovely face;
Quicken all my drooping powers;

Gasps my fainting soul for grace,
As a thirsty land for showers;
Haste, my Lord, no more delay;
Come, my Saviour, come away.

2 Dark and cheerless is the morn,
Unaccompanied by thee;
Joyless is the day's return,
Till thy mercy's beams I see;
Till thou inward light impart,
Glad my eyes, and warm my heart.

3 Visit, then, this soul of mine,
Pierce the gloom of sin and grief;
Fill me, Radiancy divine;
Scatter all my unbelief;
More and more thyself display,
Shining to the perfect day.

318 *The Smile of the Saviour withdrawn.* H. M.

1 WHERE is the Saviour now,
Whose smiles I once possessed?
Till he return, I bow,
By heaviest grief oppressed;
My days of happiness are gone,
And I am left to weep alone.

2 Where can the mourner go
And tell his tale of grief?
Ah, who can soothe his wo,
And give him sweet relief?
What balm can heal the wounded breast,
And give the troubled conscience rest?

3 Thou, Jesus, canst impart,
By thy long-wished return,
Ease to this wounded heart,
And bid me cease to mourn;
Then shall this night of sorrow flee,
And I rejoice, my Lord, in thee.

319 *Hope in God.*—Ps. lxxvii. 7. 8s.

1 ENCOMPASSED with clouds of dis-
Just ready all hope to resign, [tress,
I pant for the light of thy face,
And fear it will never be mine:
Disheartened with waiting so long,
I sink at thy feet with my load;
All plaintive I pour out my song,
And stretch forth my hands unto God.

2 Shine, Lord, and my terror shall cease;
The blood of atonement apply;
And lead me to Jesus for peace—
The rock that is higher than I.
Almighty to rescue thou art;
Thy grace is my shield and my tower:
Oh visit and gladden my heart;
Let this be the day of thy power.

320 *Supplication.* C. M.

1 HEAR, gracious God, my humble moan,
To thee I breathe my sighs;
When will the mournful night be gone,
And when my joys arise?

2 My God!—Oh could I make the claim—
My Father and my Friend—
And call thee mine by every name
On which thy saints depend—

3 By every name of power and love,
I would thy grace entreat:
Nor should my humble hope remove,
Nor leave thy mercy-seat.

4 Yet, though my soul in darkness mourns,
Thy word is all my stay;
Here would I rest till light returns;
Thy presence makes my day.

5 Speak, Lord, and bid celestial peace
Relieve my aching heart;
Oh smile, and bid my sorrows cease,
And all the gloom depart.

6 Then shall my drooping spirit rise,
And bless the healing rays;
And change these deep, complaining sighs
To songs of sacred praise.

321 *Spiritual Desertion.* 8s.

1 HOW tedious and tasteless the hours
When Jesus no longer I see!
Sweet prospects, sweet birds, and sweet flowers,
Have lost all their sweetness to me.

2 His name yields the richest perfume,
And sweeter than music his voice:

His presence disperses my gloom,
And makes all within me rejoice.

3 Dear Lord, if indeed I am thine,
And thou art my sun and my song,
Say, why do I languish and pine,
And why are my winters so long?

4 Oh drive these dark clouds from my sky,
Thy soul-cheering presence restore,
Or take me up to thee on high,
Where winter and clouds are no more.

322 *Prayer of the Penitent.* 7. 6.

1 JESUS, let thy pitying eye
Call back a wandering sheep;
False to thee, like Peter, I
Would fain like Peter weep;
Let me be by grace restored,
And to me thy mercy shown;
Turn and look upon me, Lord,
And break my heart of stone.

2 Saviour, Prince, enthroned above,
Repentance to impart,
Give me, through thy dying love,
The humble, contrite heart:
This I should have long implored,
For thou all my sin hast known;
Turn and look upon me, Lord,
And break my heart of stone.

3 See me, Saviour, from above,
Nor suffer me to die;

Life and happiness and love
  Fall from thy gracious eye:
Speak the reconciling word,
  Let thy mercy melt me down;
Turn and look upon me, Lord,
  And break my heart of stone.

323 *The Backslider penitent.* C. M.

1 O THOU whose tender mercy hears
  Contrition's humble sigh;
Whose hand, indulgent, wipes the tears
  From sorrow's weeping eye—

2 See, low before thy throne of grace,
  A wretched wanderer mourn;
Hast thou not bid me seek thy face?
  Hast thou not said—Return?

3 And shall my guilty fears prevail
  To drive me from thy feet?
Oh let not this dear refuge fail,
  This only safe retreat.

4 Oh shine on this benighted heart,
  With beams of mercy shine;
And let thy healing voice impart
  A taste of joys divine.

324 *Long-suffering of God.* 7s

1 DEPTH of mercy!—can there be
  Mercy still reserved for me?
Can my God his wrath forbear—
Me, the chief of sinners, spare?

2 I have long withstood his grace;
Long provoked him to his face;
Would not hear his gracious calls;
Grieved him by a thousand falls.

3 Lo, I cumber still the ground,
Lo, an advocate is found!
There for me the Saviour stands,
Shows his wounds, and spreads his hands.

4 Lord, incline me to repent;
Let me now my fall lament,
Deeply my revolt deplore,
Weep, believe, and sin no more.

325 *The Backslider restored.* C. M. Double.

1 JESUS, thou friend of sinners, hear,
Yet once again I pray;
Forgive my debt, and set me clear,
For I have nought to pay:
Speak now, oh speak the kind release,
My wandering soul restore;
Speak thou my pardon, seal my peace,
And bid me sin no more.

2 For my ingratitude and pride,
Thou hast withdrawn thy grace;
Hast left me long to wander wide,
An outcast from thy face:
But now my vileness I confess,
And mercy I implore;
Oh speak my pardon, seal my peace,
And bid me sin no more.

3 From the hard tyranny of sin
My struggling soul set free:
Thy perfect righteousness begin
And carry on in me;
Speak, and the war within will cease,
The tempter will give o'er:
Oh speak my pardon, seal my peace,
And bid me sin no more.

326 *Repentance.* C. M.

1 HOW oft, alas, this wretched heart
Has wandered from the Lord!
How oft my roving thoughts depart,
Forgetful of his word!

2 Yet sovereign mercy calls—"Return."
Dear Lord, and may I come?
My vile ingratitude I mourn;
Oh take the wanderer home.

3 And canst thou—wilt thou yet forgive,
And bid my crimes remove?
And shall a pardoned rebel live
To speak thy wondrous love?

4 Almighty grace, thy healing power
How glorious—how divine!
That can to life and bliss restore
A heart so vile as mine.

5 Thy pardoning love—so free, so sweet—
Dear Saviour, I adore;
Oh keep me at thy sacred feet,
And let me rove no more.

327 *The returning Backslider.* C. M

1 SINCE from thy feet I dared to roam,
My soul has found no rest;
Chastised and contrite, back I come,
To seek it in thy breast.

2 And dost thou say thou wilt receive
And call me still thine own?
My spirit, hear, accept, believe—
And melt, my heart of stone.

3 Again that gracious word to me,
Oh speak that word again;
'Twill set my soul from bondage free,
And loose my every chain.

4 No—blessed Lord, not every chain,
Not every bond remove;
Let one, at least, unloosed remain—
The bond of grateful love.

328 *Deliverance from Sin.* 7. 5

1 JESUS, make this heart thine own,
Make it wholly thine;
What to earth is sadly prone,
Now to heaven incline.

2 Let thy love my soul imbue
With a holy joy;
Let thy blessed will to do
Be my chief employ.

3 Wean me from the things of sense,
That must fade away;

Fix my earnest wishes hence,
'Mid a clearer day.

4 Bless me with thy heavenly peace,
Bid all darkness flee,
And when earthly things shall cease,
Let me rest with thee.

329 *Self-examination.* L. M

1 AND what am I?—My soul, awake,
And an impartial survey take:
Does no dark sign, no ground of fear,
In practice or in heart appear?

2 What image does my spirit bear?
Is Jesus formed and living there?
Say—do his lineaments divine
In thought, and word, and action shine?

3 Searcher of hearts, oh search me still;
The secrets of my soul reveal;
My fears remove—let me appear
To God and my own conscience clear.

4 May I at that bless'd world arrive,
Where Christ through all my soul shall
And give full proof that he is there, [live,
Without one gloomy doubt or fear.

330 *Self-examination.* 7s.

1 'TIS a point I long to know—
Oft it causes anxious thought—
Do I love the Lord, or no?
Am I his, or am I not?

2 Could my heart so hard remain,
Prayer a task and burden prove,
Every trifle give me pain,
If I knew a Saviour's love?

3 When I turn my eyes within,
All is dark and vain and wild;
Filled with unbelief and sin,
Can I deem myself a child?

4 If I pray, or hear, or read,
Sin is mixed with all I do;
You who love the Lord indeed,
Tell me—is it thus with you?

5 Yet, I mourn my stubborn will,
Find my sin a grief and thrall;
Should I grieve for what I feel,
If I did not love at all?

6 Could I joy his saints to meet,
Choose the ways I once abhorred,
Find at times the promise sweet,
If I did not love the Lord?

7 Lord, decide this doubtful case—
Thou who art thy people's Sun,
Shine upon thy work of grace,
If it be indeed begun.

8 Let me love thee more and more,
If I love at all, I pray;
If I have not loved before,
Help me to begin to-day.

331 *The Contrite Heart.*—Isa. lvii. 15. C. M.

1 THE Lord will happiness divine
On contrite hearts bestow;
Then tell me, gracious God, is mine
A contrite heart, or no?

2 My best desires are faint and few,
I fain would strive for more;
But when I cry—"My strength renew,"
Seem weaker than before.

3 Thy saints are comforted, I know,
And love thy house of prayer;
I therefore go where others go,
But find no comfort there.

4 Oh make this heart rejoice or ache;
Decide this doubt for me;
And if it be not broken, break—
And heal it if it be.

332 *Address to the Judge of all.* C. P. M.

1 WHEN thou, my righteous Judge, shalt come
To bring thy ransomed people home,
Shall I among them stand?
Shall such a worthless worm as I,
Who sometimes am afraid to die,
Be found at thy right hand?

2 I love to meet among them now,
Before thy gracious feet to bow,
Though vilest of them all:

But can I bear the piercing thought—
What if my name should be left out,
When thou for them shalt call!

3 Prevent, prevent it by thy grace;
Be thou, dear Lord, my hiding-place
In this accepted day:
Thy pardoning voice oh let me hear,
To still my unbelieving fear;
Nor let me fall, I pray.

4 Let me among thy saints be found,
Whene'er th' archangel's trump shall [sound,
To see thy smiling face;
Then loudest of the crowd I'll sing,
While heaven's resounding mansions ring
With shouts of sovereign grace.

333 *Hope and Solicitude.* C. M.

1 MY soul would fain indulge a hope
To reach the heavenly shore;
And, when I drop this dying flesh,
That I shall sin no more.

2 I hope to hear and join the song
That saints and angels raise;
And while eternal ages roll,
To sing eternal praise.

3 But oh—this dreadful heart of sin!
It may deceive me still;
And while I look for joys above,
May plunge me down to hell.

4 The scene must then for ever close,
Probation at an end;

No gospel grace can reach me there,
  No pardon there descend.

5 Come, then, O blessed Jesus, come,
  To me thy Spirit give;
Shine through a dark, benighted soul,
  And bid a sinner live.

334 *The Pilgrim's Song.* 7. 6.

1 RISE, my soul, and stretch thy wings,
  Thy better portion trace;
Rise from transitory things,
  Towards heaven, thy native place:
Sun and moon and stars decay;
  Time shall soon this earth remove;
Rise, my soul, and haste away
  To seats prepared above.

2 Rivers to the ocean run,
  Nor stay in all their course;
Fire ascending seeks the sun—
  Both speed them to their source;
So a soul that's born of God
  Pants to view his glorious face;
Upward tends to his abode,
  To rest in his embrace.

3 Cease, ye pilgrims, cease to mourn,
  Press onward to the prize;
Soon the Saviour will return,
  Triumphant in the skies:
Yet a season, and you know
  Happy entrance will be given;
All your sorrows left below,
  And earth exchanged for heaven.

335 *Support in the hope of Heaven.* C. M.

1 WHEN I can read my title clear
To mansions in the skies,
I bid farewell to every fear,
And wipe my weeping eyes.

2 Should earth against my soul engage,
And hellish darts be hurled,
Then I can smile at Satan's rage,
And face a frowning world.

3 Let cares like a wild deluge come,
And storms of sorrow fall,
May I but safely reach my home,
My God, my heaven, my all.

4 There shall I bathe my weary soul
In seas of heavenly rest;
And not a wave of trouble roll
Across my peaceful breast.

336 *Desiring to depart.* 7. 6.

1 HAPPY who in Jesus live;
But happier far are they
Who to God their spirits give,
And flee from earth away:
Yet, if so thy will ordain,
We'll pursue this toilsome road,
Cheerful in the flesh remain,
And meekly bear the load.

2 To thy wise and gracious will
We quietly submit;
Waiting for redemption still,
But waiting at thy feet:

When thou wilt the blessing give,
Call us up thy face to see;
Only let thy servants live,
And let us die—to thee.

337 *Consolation in the Thought of God.* C. M

1 THY gracious presence, O my God,
My every wish contains;
With this, beneath affliction's load,
My heart no more complains.

2 This can my every care control,
Gild each dark scene with light;
This is the sunshine of the soul;
Without it all is night.

3 Oh happy scenes of pure delight,
Where thy full beams impart
Unclouded beauty to the sight,
And rapture to the heart.

4 Her part in those fair realms of bliss
My spirit longs to know;
My wishes terminate in this,
Nor can they rest below.

5 Lord, shall these breathings of my hea..
Aspire in vain to thee?
Confirm my hope that where thou art,
I shall for ever be.

6 Then shall my cheerful spirit sing
The darksome hours away,
And rise, on faith's expanded wing,
To everlasting day.

338 *Longing to be with Christ.* 8s.

1 TO Jesus, the crown of my hope,
My soul is in haste to be gone;
Oh bear me, ye cherubim, up,
And waft me away to his throne.

2 My Saviour, whom absent I love;
Whom, not having seen, I adore;
Whose name is exalted above
All glory, dominion, and power—

3 Dissolve thou these bonds, that detain
My soul from her portion in thee;
Oh strike off this adamant chain,
And make me eternally free.

4 When that happy era begins,
Arrayed in thy glories I'll shine;
Nor grieve any more, by my sins,
The bosom on which I recline.

339 *Confidence in God.* C. M.

1 MY soul, triumphant in the Lord,
Shall tell its joys abroad,
And march with holy vigor on,
Supported by its God.

2 Through all the winding maze of life
His hand has been my guide;
And in that long experienced care
My heart shall still confide.

3 His grace through all the desert flows,
An unexhausted stream;

That grace, on Zion's sacred mount,
Shall be my endless theme.

4 Beyond the choicest joys of time
These distant courts I love;
But oh, I burn with strong desire
To view thy house above.

5 Amid the shining, glorious band,
My soul would there adore;
A pillar in thy temple fixed,
To be removed no more.

340 *Longing for Heaven.* 8s

1 YE angels who stand round the throne,
And view my Immanuel's face,
In rapturous songs make him known;
Tune, tune your soft harps to his praise.
Ye saints, who stand nearer than they,
And cast your bright crowns at his feet,
His grace and his glory display,
And all his rich mercy repeat.

2 Oh, when will the period appear,
When I shall unite in your song?
I'm weary of lingering here,
And I to your Saviour belong:
I'm fettered and chained up in clay;
I struggle and pant to be free;
I long to be soaring away,
My God and my Saviour to see.

3 I long to put on my attire,
Washed white in the blood of the Lamb;

I long to be one of your choir,
And tune my sweet harp to his name.
I long—oh, I long to be there,
Where sorrow and sin bid adieu;
Your joy and your friendship to share,
To wonder and worship with you.

PRAYER.

341 *Coming to the Mercy-seat.* C. M

1 APPROACH, my soul, the mercy-seat,
Where Jesus answers prayer;
There humbly fall before his feet,
For none can perish there.

2 Thy promise is my only plea—
With this I venture nigh;
Thou callest burdened souls to thee,
And such, O Lord, am I.

3 Bowed down beneath a load of sin,
By Satan sorely pressed,
By war without, and fears within,
I come to thee for rest.

4 Be thou my shield and hiding-place,
That, sheltered near thy side,
I may my fierce accuser face,
And tell him thou hast died.

5 Oh wondrous love! to bleed and die,
To bear the cross and shame,

That guilty sinners, such as I,
  Might plead thy gracious name.

342 *Persevering Prayer.*—Luke xviii. 7. S. M

1 OUR Lord, who knows full well
  The heart of every saint,
Invites us all our wants to tell,
  To pray, and never faint.

2 He bows his gracious ear—
  We never plead in vain;
Yet we must wait till he appear,
  And pray, and pray again.

3 'Twas thus a widow poor,
  Without support or friend,
Beset the unjust judge's door,
  And gained, at last, her end.

4 And will not Jesus hear
  His chosen when they cry?
Yes, though he may a while forbear,
  He'll help them from on high.

5 Then let us earnest be,
  And never faint in prayer;
He loves our humble faith to see,
  And makes our cause his care.

343 *The Mercy-seat.* L. M.

1 FROM every stormy wind that blows,
  From every swelling tide of woes,
There is a calm, a sure retreat—
'Tis found beneath the mercy-seat.

2 There is a place where Jesus sheds
The oil of gladness on our heads;
A place, than all besides more sweet—
It is the blood-bought mercy-seat.

3 There is a scene where spirits blend,
Where friend holds fellowship with friend;
Though sundered far, by faith they meet,
Around one common mercy-seat.

4 There, there on eagle-wings we soar,
And sense and sin becloud no more,
And heaven comes down, our souls to greet,
And glory crowns the mercy-seat.

344 *Waiting for God.*—Ps. cxxx. 5. S. M.

1 OUT of the depths of wo,
To thee, O Lord, I cry;
Darkness surrounds me, but I know
That thou art ever nigh.

2 Then hearken to my voice,
Give ear to my complaint;
Thou bid'st the mourning soul rejoice,
Thou comfortest the faint.

3 I cast my hope on thee,
Thou canst, thou wilt forgive:
Wert thou to mark iniquity,
Who in thy sight could live?

4 Humbly on thee I wait,
Confessing all my sin;
Lord, I am knocking at thy gate,
Open and take me in.

345 *The Mercy-seat.* C. M.

1 NO, never shall my heart despond,
Long as my lips can pray;
My latest breath, with effort fond,
Shall pass in prayer away.

2 There is a heavenly mercy-seat
To calm the sinner's fears;
There is a Saviour at whose feet
The mourner dries his tears.

3 When friends depart, and hopes are riven,
And gathering storms I see,
My soul is but the sooner driven,
Eternal Rock, to thee.

4 Oh for a voice of sweeter sound,
For every wind to bear—
To teach the listening world around
The blessedness of prayer!

346 *Seeking after God.*—Job xxiii. 3. C. M.

1 OH that I knew the secret place
Where I might find my God;
I'd spread my wants before his face,
And pour my woes abroad.

2 I'd tell him how my sins arise,
What sorrows I sustain;
How grace decays, and comfort dies,
And leaves my heart in pain.

3 He knows what arguments I'd take
To wrestle with my God;

I'd plead for his own mercy's sake,
And for my Saviour's blood.

4 My God will pity my complaints,
And heal my broken bones;
He knows the meaning of his saints,
The language of their groans.

5 Arise, my soul, from deep distress,
And banish every fear;
He calls thee to his throne of grace,
To spread thy sorrows there.

347 *Exhortation to Prayer.* L. M

1 WHAT various hind'rances we meet,
In coming to a mercy-seat!
Yet, who that knows the worth of prayer,
But wishes to be often there?

2 Prayer makes the darkened cloud with-
Prayer climbs the ladder Jacob saw; [draw;
Gives exercise to faith and love,
Brings every blessing from above.

3 Restraining prayer, we cease to fight;
Prayer makes the Christian's armor bright;
And Satan trembles when he sees
The weakest saint upon his knees.

4 Have you no words? Ah, think again;
Words flow apace when you complain,
And fill your fellow-creature's ear
With the sad tale of all your care.

5 Were half the breath thus vainly spent,
To heaven in supplication sent,

Your cheerful song would oftener be—
"Hear what the Lord has done for me."

348 *What is Prayer?* C. M.

1 PRAYER is the soul's sincere desire,
Uttered or unexpressed;
The motion of a hidden fire
That trembles in the breast.

2 Prayer is the burden of a sigh,
The falling of a tear,
The upward glancing of an eye,
When none but God is near.

3 Prayer is the simplest form of speech
That infant lips can try;
Prayer the sublimest strains that reach
The Majesty on high.

4 Prayer is the Christian's vital breath,
The Christian's native air;
His watch-word at the gates of death;
He enters heaven with prayer.

5 Prayer is the contrite sinner's voice,
Returning from his ways;
While angels in their songs rejoice,
And cry—"Behold he prays."

6 O thou by whom we come to God—
The life, the truth, the way—
The path of prayer thyself hast trod;
Lord, teach us how to pray.

349 *Prayer for Sanctification.* 7s.

1 COME, my soul, thy suit prepare,
Jesus loves to answer prayer;
He himself has bid thee pray,
Thou wilt not be thrust away.

2 With my burden I begin;
Lord, remove this load of sin;
Let thy blood, for sinners spilt,
Set my conscience free from guilt.

3 Lord, I come to thee for rest,
Take possession of my breast;
There thy blood-bought right maintain,
And without a rival reign.

4 While I am a pilgrim here,
Let thy love my spirit cheer;
Be my guide, my guard, my friend;
Lead me to my journey's end.

5 Show me what I have to do,
Every hour my strength renew;
Let me live a life of faith,
Let me die thy people's death.

350 *Watchfulness and Prayer.* S. M. Double.

1 AH, when shall I awake
From sin's soft soothing power;
The slumber from my spirit shake,
And rise to fall no more?
Awake, no more to sleep,
But stand with constant care,

Look up to God my soul to keep,
 And ever watch in prayer.

2 Oh, could I always pray,
 And never, never faint—
Freely to God might I convey
 Each wo and each complaint;
Before him might I lie,
 And tell him all my care;
And Father, Abba, Father, cry,
 And pour a ceaseless prayer.

3 My Saviour, I would wait,
 Till thou shalt make me whole;
Till thou shalt all things new create
 In my believing soul;
Till thou my sins subdue,
 Till thou my sins destroy,
My spirit after God renew,
 And fill with peace and joy.

351 *Help from God.*—Ps. cxxi. 7. 6.

1 TO the hills I lift my eyes,
 The everlasting hills;
Thence I draw divine supplies,
 My soul new vigor fills:
Faithful is his promised word;
 Help, while yet I ask, is given—
Given by the sovereign Lord,
 Who made both earth and heaven.

2 Faithful soul, pray always—pray,
 And still in God confide;

He thy feeble steps shall stay,
Nor suffer thee to slide;
Lean on thy Redeemer's breast;
He thy trusting spirit keeps;
Rest in him, securely rest;
Thy watchman never sleeps.

3 Not the powers of earth or hell
Thy Guardian can surprise;
Careless slumber cannot steal
On his all-seeing eyes;
To his saints a sure defence,
They his faithful care shall prove;
Kept by watchful providence,
And ever-waking love.

352 "*To whom shall we go.*"—John vi. 68. C. M.

1 LORD, teach us how to pray aright,
With rev'rence and with fear:
Though dust and ashes in thy sight,
We may, we must draw near.

2 We perish if we cease from prayer;
Oh grant us power to pray;
And when to meet thee we prepare,
Lord, meet us by the way.

3 Burdened with guilt, convinced of sin,
In weakness, want, and wo,
Beset by foes without, within,
Lord, whither shall we go?

4 In patience would we wait and weep,
Though mercy long delay;

Our hold upon thy footstool keep,
And trust thee, though thou slay.

5 Give us to say—"Thy will be done;"
Thus, strengthened by thy might,
We, by thy Spirit, through thy Son,
Shall pray, and pray aright.

353 *Invitation to Prayer.* 7. 6. Iambic.

1 GO when the morning shineth,
Go when the noon is bright,
Go when the eve declineth,
Go in the hush of night;
Go with pure mind and feeling,
Cast earthly thought away,
And, in thy chamber kneeling,
Do thou in secret pray.

2 Remember all who love thee,
All who are loved by thee;
Pray too for those who hate thee,
If any such there be;
Then, for thyself, in meekness,
A blessing humbly claim,
And link with each petition,
The dear Redeemer's name.

3 Oh, not a joy or blessing
With this can we compare,
The power that he hath giv'n us
To pour our souls in prayer:
Whene'er thou pin'st in sadness,
Before his footstool fall;
Remember in thy gladness,
His grace who gave thee all.

354 *The Morning Prayer meeting.* S. M.

1 HOW sweet the melting lay
Which breaks upon the ear,
When, at the hour of rising day,
Christians unite in prayer.

2 The breezes waft their cries
Up to Jehovah's throne;
He listens to their heaving sighs,
And sends his blessings down.

3 So Jesus rose to pray,
Before the morning light;
Once on the chilling mount did stay
And wrestle all the night.

4 Glory to God on high,
Who sends his blessings down,
To rescue souls condemned to die,
And make his people one.

CHRISTIAN LIFE.

355 *Holy Fortitude.*—1 Cor. xvi. 13. C. M.

1 AM I a soldier of the cross,
A follower of the Lamb—
And shall I fear to own his cause,
Or blush to speak his name?

2 Must I be carried to the skies
On flowery beds of ease,

While others fought to win the prize,
And sailed through bloody seas?

3 Are there no foes for me to face?
Must I not stem the flood?
Is this vile world a friend to grace,
To help me on to God?

4 Sure I must fight, if I would reign;
Increase my courage, Lord;
I'll bear the toil, endure the pain,
Supported by thy word.

5 Thy saints, in all this glorious war
Shall conquer, though they die;
They see the triumph from afar,
And faith accounts it nigh.

6 When that illustrious day shall rise,
And all thine armies shine
In robes of victory through the skies,
The glory shall be thine.

356 "*Strong in the Lord.*"—Eph. vi. 10. S. M

1 SOLDIERS of Christ, arise,
And put your armor on;
Strong in the strength which God supplies
Through his eternal Son—

2 Strong in the Lord of Hosts,
And in his mighty power;
Who in the strength of Jesus trusts,
Is more than conqueror.

3 Stand then, in his great might,
With all his strength endued;

And take, to arm you for the fight,
The panoply of God.

4 That having all things done,
And all your conflicts passed,
Ye may o'ercome through Christ alone,
And stand entire at last.

5 From strength to strength go on,
Wrestle, and fight, and pray:
Tread all the powers of darkness down,
And win the well-fought day.

357 *Christian Warfare and Victory.* L. M.

1 STAND up, my soul—shake off thy fears,
And gird the gospel armor on;
March to the gates of endless joy,
Where Jesus, thy great Captain's gone.

2 Hell and thy sins resist thy course;
But hell and sin are vanquished foes;
Thy Jesus nailed them to the cross,
And sung the triumph when he rose.

3 Then let my soul march boldly on,
Press forward to the heavenly gate;
There peace and joy eternal reign,
And glittering robes for conquerors wait.

4 There shall I wear a starry crown,
And triumph in almighty grace;
While all the armies of the skies
Join in my glorious Leader's praise.

358 *Bearing the Cross,*—Mark viii. 38. C. M

1 DIDST thou, dear Jesus, suffer shame,
And bear the cross for me?
And shall I fear to own thy name,
Or thy disciple be?

2 Forbid it, Lord, that I should dread
To suffer shame or loss;
Oh let me in thy footsteps tread,
And glory in thy cross.

3 Inspire my soul with life divine,
And make me truly bold;
Let knowledge, faith, and meekness shine
Nor love nor zeal grow cold.

4 Let mockers scoff—the world defame,
And treat me with disdain;
Still may I glory in thy name,
And count reproach my gain.

359 *Spiritual Sloth.* C. M

1 MY drowsy powers, why sleep ye so?
Awake, my sluggish soul;
Nothing has half thy work to do,
Yet nothing's half so dull.

2 The little ants for one poor grain
Labor, and toil, and strive;
Yet we, who have a heaven t' obtain,
How negligent we live!

3 We for whose sake all nature stands,
And stars their courses move—

We for whose guard the angel bands
Come flying from above—

4 We for whom God the Son came down
And labored for our good—
How careless to secure that crown
He purchased with his blood!

5 Lord, shall we lie so sluggish still,
And never act our parts?
Come, Holy Spirit, come and fill,
And wake, and warm our hearts.

6 Then shall our active spirits move;
Upward our souls shall rise:
With hands of faith and wings of love,
We'll fly and take the prize.

360 *Benevolence of Jesus.*—Acts x. 38. L. M.

1 WHEN Jesus dwelt in mortal clay,
What were his works, from day to day,
But miracles of power and grace,
That spread salvation through our race?

2 Teach us, O Lord, to keep in view
Thy pattern, and thy steps pursue;
Let alms bestowed, let kindness done
Be witnessed by each rolling sun.

3 That man may *last*, but never *lives*,
Who much receives, but nothing gives,
Whom none can love, whom none can [thank—
Creation's blot, creation's blank.

4 But he who marks, from day to day,
With generous acts his radiant way,

Treads the same path his Saviour trod,
The path to glory and to God.

361 *Charity.*—Matt. xxv. 40. C. M.

1 JESUS, my Lord, how rich thy grace!
Thy bounties how complete!
How shall I count the matchless sum?
How pay the mighty debt?

2 High on a throne of radiant light
Dost thou, exalted, shine;
What can my poverty bestow,
When all the worlds are thine?

3 But thou hast brethren here below,
The partners of thy grace,
And wilt confess their humble names
Before thy Father's face.

4 In them thou may'st be clothed and fed,
And visited and cheered;
And in their accents of distress,
My Saviour's voice is heard.

5 Thy face, with reverence and with love,
I in the poor would see;
Oh rather let me beg my bread,
Than hold it back from thee.

362 *Pity for the Distressed.* C. M.

1 FATHER of mercies, send thy grace
All powerful from above,
To form in our obedient souls
The image of thy love.

2 Oh may our sympathizing breasts
 That generous pleasure know,
Kindly to share in others' joy,
 And weep for others' wo.

3 When the most helpless sons of grief
 In low distress are laid,
Soft be our hearts their pains to feel,
 And swift our hands to aid.

4 So Jesus looked on dying men,
 When throned above the skies;
And, 'midst th' embraces of thy love,
 He felt compassion rise.

5 On wings of love the Saviour flew,
 To raise us from the ground;
And gave the richest of his blood,
 A balm for every wound.

363 "*To whom shall we go?*"—John vi. 68. L. M.

1 THOU only Sovereign of my heart,
 My refuge, my almighty Friend—
And can my soul from thee depart,
 On whom alone my hopes depend?

2 Whither, ah whither shall I go,
 A wretched wanderer from my Lord?
Can this dark world of sin and wo
 One glimpse of happiness afford?

3 Eternal life thy words impart;
 On these my fainting spirit lives;
Here sweeter comforts cheer my heart,
 Than all the round of nature gives.

4 Let earth's alluring joys combine—
While thou art near, in vain they call
One smile, one blissful smile of thine,
My dearest Lord, outweighs them all.

5 Thy name my inmost powers adore,
Thou art my life, my joy, my care;
Depart from thee! 'tis death! 'tis more;
'Tis endless ruin, deep despair!

6 Low at thy feet my soul would lie;
Here safety dwells, and peace divine;
Still let me live beneath thine eye,
For life, eternal life is thine.

364 *Adoption.* S. M.

1 BEHOLD what wondrous grace
The Father hath bestowed
On sinners of a mortal race,
To call them sons of God!

2 'Tis no surprising thing
That we should be unknown;
The Jewish world knew not their King,
God's everlasting Son.

3 Nor doth it yet appear
How great we must be made;
But when we see our Saviour here,
We shall be like our Head.

4 A hope so much divine
May trials well endure;
May purge our souls from sense and sin,
As Christ, the Lord, is pure.

5 If in my Father's love
I share a filial part,
Send down thy Spirit, like a dove,
To rest upon my heart.

6 We would no longer lie
Like slaves beneath the throne;
Our faith shall Abba, Father, cry,
And thou the kindred own.

365 *Choosing the Service of God.*—Josh. xxiv. 15. L. M.

1 MAY I resolve, with all my heart,
With all my powers, to serve the
Nor from his precepts e'er depart, [Lord;
Whose service is a rich reward.

2 Oh, be his service all my joy;
Around let my example shine,
Till others love the bless'd employ,
And join in labors so divine.

3 Be this the purpose of my soul,
My solemn, my determined choice—
To yield to his supreme control,
And in his kind commands rejoice.

4 Oh may I never faint nor tire,
Nor, wandering, leave his sacred ways;
Great God, accept my soul's desire,
And give me strength to live thy praise.

366 *Nearness to God.* C. M.

1 OH, could I find, from day to day,
A nearness to my God,

Then should my hours glide sweet away,
  Nor sin nor fear intrude.

2 Lord, I desire with thee to live
  Anew from day to day;
In joys the world can never give,
  Nor ever take away.

3 O Jesus, come and rule my heart,
  And make me wholly thine,
That I may never more depart,
  Nor grieve thy love divine.

4 Thus, till my last expiring breath,
  Thy goodness I'll adore;
And when my flesh dissolves in death,
  My soul shall love thee more.

367 *Holy Life.*—Titus ii. 10, 13. L. M.

1 SO let our lips and lives express
  The holy gospel we profess;
So let our works and virtues shine,
To prove the doctrine all divine.

2 Thus shall we best proclaim abroad
The honors of our Saviour God;
When his salvation reigns within,
And grace subdues the power of sin.

3 Religion bears our spirits up,
While we expect that blessed hope—
The bright appearance of the Lord—
And faith stands leaning on his word.

368 *Christ our Pattern.* L. M.

1 AND is the gospel peace and love?
 Such let our conversation be;
The serpent blended with the dove—
 Wisdom and meek simplicity.

2 Whene'er the angry passions rise,
 And tempt our thoughts and tongues to strife,
To Jesus let us lift our eyes,
 Bright pattern of the Christian life.

3 Dispensing good where'er he came,
 The labors of his life were love;
Then, if we bear the Saviour's name,
 By his example let us move.

4 Oh, how benevolent and kind!
 How mild, how ready to forgive!
Be this the temper of our mind,
 And these the rules by which we live.

369 *Christ our Pattern.* L. M.

1 MY dear Redeemer and my Lord,
 I read my duty in thy word;
But in thy life the law appears,
Drawn out in living characters.

2 Such was thy truth, and such thy zeal,
Such deference to thy Father's will,
Such love, and meekness so divine—
I would transcribe and make them mine.

3 Cold mountains and the midnight air
Witnessed the fervor of thy prayer;

The desert thy temptations knew,
Thy conflict, and thy victory too.

4 Be thou my pattern; make me bear
More of thy gracious image here;
Then God, the Judge, shall own my name
Among the followers of the Lamb.

370 *Walking with God.* C. M.

1 THRICE happy souls, who, born of hea-
While yet they sojourn here, [ven,
Humbly begin their days with God,
And spend them in his fear.

2 So may our eyes, with holy zeal,
Prevent the dawning day;
And turn the sacred pages o'er,
And praise thy name, and pray.

3 'Midst hourly cares may love present
Its incense to thy throne;
And, while the world our hands employs,
Our hearts be thine alone.

4 At night we lean our weary heads
On thy paternal breast;
And, safely folded in thine arms,
Resign our powers to rest.

5 In solid, pure delights, like these,
Let all my days be passed;
Nor shall I then impatient wish,
Nor shall I fear the last.

371 *Rising to God.* L. M.

1 NOW let our souls, on wings sublime,
Rise from the vanities of time;
Draw back the parting vail, and see
The glories of eternity.

2 Born by a new, celestial birth,
Why should we grovel here on earth?
Why grasp at transitory toys,
So near to heaven's eternal joys?

3 Shall aught beguile us on the road,
When we are walking back to God?
For strangers into life we come,
And dying is but going home.

4 Welcome, sweet hour of full discharge,
That sets our longing souls at large;
Unbinds our chains, breaks up our cell,
And gives us with our God to dwell.

372 *The Broad and the Narrow Way.* L. M.

1 BROAD is the road that leads to death,
And thousands walk together there;
But wisdom shows a narrow path,
With here and there a traveller.

2 "Deny thyself, and take thy cross,"
Is the Redeemer's great command:
Nature must count her gold but dross,
If she would gain this heavenly land.

3 The fearful soul that tires and faints,
And walks the ways of God no more,

Is but esteemed almost a saint,
  And makes his own destruction sure.

4 Lord, let not all my hopes be vain;
  Create my heart entirely new;
Which hypocrites could ne'er attain,
  Which false apostates never knew.

373 *The Lord will provide.* 5. 6.

1 THOUGH troubles assail,
  And dangers affright;
Though friends should all fail,
  And foes all unite;
Yet one thing secures us,
  Whatever betide;
The Scripture assures us
  The Lord will provide.

2 We may, like the ships,
  By tempests be tossed
On perilous deeps,
  But cannot be lost;
Though Satan enrages
  The wind and the tide,
The promise engages
  The Lord will provide.

3 His call we obey,
  Like Abra'm of old,
Not knowing our way,
  But faith makes us bold;
For though we are strangers,
  We have a good guide,

And trust in all dangers
  The Lord will provide.

4 No strength of our own,
  Or goodness we claim;
Yet since we have known
  The Saviour's great name,
In this our strong tower
  For safety we hide—
The Lord is our power,
  The Lord will provide.

5 When life sinks apace,
  And death is in view,
This word of his grace
  Shall comfort us through:
No fearing or doubting
  With Christ on our side,
We hope to die shouting—
  The Lord will provide.

374 *Trust in God under Affliction.* C. M.

1 AFFLICTION is a stormy deep,
  Where wave responds to wave;
Though o'er my head the billows roll,
  I know the Lord can save.

2 The hand that now withholds my joys
  Can yet restore my peace;
And he who bade the tempest roar,
  Can bid the tempest cease.

3 In darkest watches of the night
  I'll count his mercies o'er;

I'll praise him for ten thousand past,
And humbly sue for more.

4 When darkness and when sorrow rose,
And pressed on every side,
The Lord has still sustained my steps,
And still has been my guide.

3 Here will I rest and build my hopes,
Nor murmur at his rod;
He's more than all the world to me—
My Saviour and my God.

375 *Gratitude and Praise.* L. M.

1 GOD of my life, through all my days
My grateful powers shall sound thy praise;
The song shall wake with opening light,
And warble to the silent night.

2 When anxious cares would break my rest,
And griefs would tear my throbbing breast,
Thy praises will I raise on high,
And check the murmur and the sigh.

3 When death o'er nature shall prevail,
And all the powers of language fail,
Joy through my swimming eyes shall break,
And mean the thanks I cannot speak.

4 But oh, when that last conflict's o'er,
And I am chained to earth no more,
With what glad accents shall I rise
To join the music of the skies!

5 Then shall I learn th' exalted strains
Which echo o'er the heavenly plains;
And emulate, with joy unknown,
The glowing seraphs round thy throne.

376 *The Promises.*—2 Pet. i. 4. 11s

1 HOW firm a foundation, ye saints of the Lord,
Is laid for your faith in his excellent word;
What more can he say than to you he hath said,
Who unto the Saviour for refuge have fled?

2 "Fear not, I am with thee, oh be not dismayed,
For I am thy God, and will still give thee aid;
I'll strengthen thee, help thee, and cause thee to stand,
Upheld by my righteous, omnipotent hand.

3 "When through the deep waters I call thee to go,
The rivers of sorrow shall not overflow;
For I will be with thee, thy troubles to bless,
And sanctify to thee thy deepest distress.

4 "When through fiery trials thy pathway shall lie,
My grace all-sufficient shall be thy supply;
The flame shall not hurt thee, I only design
Thy dross to consume, and thy gold to refine.

5 "E'en down to old age, all my people shall
prove
My sovereign, eternal, unchangeable love;
And when hoary hairs shall their temples
adorn, [borne.
Like lambs they shall still in my bosom be

6 "The soul that on Jesus hath leaned for
repose,
I will not, I will not desert to its foes;
That soul, though all hell should endeavor
to shake,
I'll never—no, never—no, never forsake."

377 *Confidence in the Mediator.*—Heb. iv. 15. L. M. 6l.

1 WHEN gathering clouds around I view,
And days are dark and friends are few,
On him I lean, who, not in vain,
Experienced every human pain;
He sees my wants, allays my fears,
And counts and treasures up my tears.

2 If aught should tempt my soul to stray
From heavenly virtue's narrow way,
To fly the good I would pursue,
Or do the sin I would not do,
Still, he who felt temptation's power
Shall guard me in that dangerous hour.

3 When sorrowing o'er some stone I bend,
Which covers all that was a friend;
And from his voice, his hand, his smile,
Divides me—for a little while,—

Thou, Saviour, seest the tears I shed,
For thou didst weep o'er Lazarus dead.

4 And oh, when I have safely passed
Through every conflict, but the last,
Still, still unchanging, watch beside
My painful bed—for thou hast died;
Then point to realms of cloudless day,
And wipe the latest tear away.

378 *"I will trust."*—Isa. xii. 2. 5. 6.

1 BEGONE, unbelief,
My Saviour is near,
And for my relief
Will surely appear:
By prayer let me wrestle,
And he will perform;
With Christ in the vessel,
I smile at the storm.

2 Though dark be my way,
Since he is my guide,
'Tis mine to obey,
'Tis his to provide;
His way was much rougher
And darker than mine;
Did Jesus thus suffer,
And shall I repine?

3 Determined to save,
He watched o'er my path,
When, Satan's blind slave,
I sported with death:

And can he have taught me
To trust in his name,
And thus far have brought me
To put me to shame?

4 Why should I complain
Of want or distress,
Temptation or pain?
He told me no less:
The heirs of salvation,
I know from his word,
Through much tribulation
Must follow their Lord.

5 His love, in time past,
Forbids me to think
He'll leave me at last
In trouble to sink:
Though painful at present,
'Twill cease before long,
And then oh how pleasant
The conqueror's song!

379 *Trials.* 7s

1 'TIS my happiness below,
Not to live without the cross;
But the Saviour's power to know,
Sanctifying every loss.

2 Trials must and will befall;
But with humble faith to see
Love inscribed upon them all—
This is happiness to me.

3 Did I meet no trials here,
Meet no chast'ning by the way,
Might I not with reason fear
I should prove a cast-away?

4 Trials make the promise sweet;
Trials give new life to prayer;
Trials bring me to his feet,
Lay me low, and keep me there.

380 *Jesus the Pilot.* H. M.

1 JESUS, at thy command
I launch into the deep;
And leave my native land,
Where sin lulls all asleep:
For thee I fain would all resign,
And sail to heaven with thee and thine.

2 Thou art my Pilot wise;
My compass is thy word;
My soul each storm defies,
While I have such a Lord:
I trust thy faithfulness and power,
To save me in the trying hour.

3 Though rocks and quicksands deep,
Through all my passage lie,
Yet thou wilt safely keep,
And guide me with thine eye:
My anchor, hope, shall firm abide,
And I each boisterous storm outride.

4 By faith I see the land,
The port of endless rest;

My soul, thy sails expand,
And fly to Jesus' breast.
Oh may I reach the heavenly shore,
Where winds and waves distress no more

5 Whene'er becalmed I lie,
And all my storms subside,
Then to my succor fly,
And keep me near thy side:
For more the treacherous calm I dread,
Than tempests bursting o'er my head.

6 Come, heavenly wind, and blow
A prosperous gale of grace,
To waft me from below,
To heaven, my destined place:
Then, in full sail, my port I'll find,
And leave the world and sin behind.

381 *"Who can be against us?"*--Rom. viii. 31. C. M

1 LET Christian faith and hope dispel
The fears of wrath and wo;
The Lord Almighty is our friend,
And who can prove a foe?

2 He gave his well-beloved Son
For sinful man to die;
And will he not all good bestow,
And all our wants supply?

3 Let troubles rise, and terrors frown,
And days of darkness fall;
Through him all dangers we'll defy,
And more than conquer all.

4 Nor death nor life, nor earth nor hell
His promise can remove;
Can e'er efface us from his heart,
Or quench his endless love.

382 *Joy and Peace in Believing.* 7. 6. Iambic.

1 SOMETIMES a light surprises
The Christian while he sings;
It is the Lord who rises
With healing on his wings:
When comforts are declining,
He grants the soul again
A season of clear shining,
To cheer it after rain.

2 In holy contemplation
We sweetly then pursue
The theme of God's salvation,
And find it ever new:
Set free from present sorrow,
We cheerfully can say—
Let the unknown to-morrow
Bring with it what it may.

3 It can bring with it nothing
But he will bear us through;
Who gives the lilies clothing,
Will clothe his people too:
Beneath the spreading heavens,
No creature but is fed;
And he who feeds the ravens,
Will give his children bread.

4 Though vine nor fig-tree neither
Their wonted fruit should bear,

Though all the fields should wither,
  Nor flocks nor herds be there;
Yet, God the same abiding,
  His praise shall tune my voice;
For while in him confiding,
  I cannot but rejoice.

383 *Spiritual Darkness.*—Job xxix. 2. C. M

1 SWEET was the time when first I felt
  The Saviour's pardoning blood
Applied to cleanse my soul from guilt,
  And bring me home to God.

2 Soon as the morn the light revealed,
  His praises tuned my tongue;
And when the evening shades prevailed,
  His love was all my song.

3 In vain the tempter spread his wiles—
  The world no more could charm;
I lived upon my Saviour's smiles,
  And leaned upon his arm.

4 In prayer my soul drew near the Lord,
  And saw his glory shine;
And when I read his holy word,
  I called each promise mine.

5 But now, when evening shade prevails,
  My soul in darkness mourns;
And when the morn the light reveals,
  No light to me returns.

6 Rise, Lord, now help me to prevail;
  Oh make my soul thy care;

I know thy mercy cannot fail,
  Let me that mercy share.

384 *Watchfulness.* S. M.

1 A CHARGE to keep I have;
    A God to glorify;
  A never-dying soul to save,
    And fit it for the sky;

2 To serve the present age,
    My calling to fulfill;
  Oh may it all my powers engage
    To do my Master's will.

3 Arm me with jealous care
    As in thy sight to live;
  And oh, thy servant, Lord, prepare
    A strict account to give.

4 Help me to watch and pray,
    And on thyself rely;
  Assured if I my trust betray,
    I shall for ever die.

385 *Prayer for spiritual Strength.* C. M.

1 ALAS, what hourly dangers rise,
    What snares beset my way!
  To heaven oh let me lift my eyes,
    And hourly watch and pray.

2 How oft my mournful thoughts complain,
    And melt in flowing tears!
  My weak resistance—ah, how vain!
    How strong my foes and fears!

3 O Lord, increase my faith and hope,
When foes and fears prevail;
And bear my fainting spirit up,
Or soon my strength will fail.

4 Oh keep me in thy heavenly way,
And bid the tempter flee;
And let me never—never stray
From happiness and thee.

386 *"Watch and Pray."*—Matt. xxvi. 41. S. M.

1 MY soul, be on thy guard;
Ten thousand foes arise,
And hosts of sins are pressing hard,
To draw thee from the skies.

2 Oh watch, and fight, and pray;
The battle ne'er give o'er;
Renew it boldly every day,
And help divine implore.

3 Ne'er think the victory won,
Nor once at ease sit down;
Thine arduous work will not be done,
Till thou receive thy crown.

4 Fight on, my soul, till death
Shall bring thee to thy God;
He'll take thee, at thy parting breath,
Up to his bless'd abode.

387 *The Christian Race.* C. M

1 AWAKE, my soul—stretch every nerve,
And press with vigor on;

A heavenly race demands thy zeal,
And an immortal crown.

2 A cloud of witnesses around
Hold thee in full survey;
Forget the steps already trod,
And onward urge thy way.

3 'Tis God's all-animating voice
That calls thee from on high;
'Tis his own hand presents the prize
To thine aspiring eye.

4 Bless'd Saviour, introduced by thee,
Have we our race begun;
And, crowned with victory, at thy feet
We'll lay our laurels down.

388 *Danger of Self-confidence.* S. M.

1 BEWARE of Peter's word,
Nor confidently say,
"I never *will* deny the Lord,"
But "grant I never may."

2 Man's wisdom is to seek
His strength in God alone;
And e'en an angel would be weak,
Who trusted in his own.

3 Retreat beneath his wings,
And in his grace confide;
This more exalts the King of kings
Than all your works beside.

4 In Jesus is our store;
Grace issues from his throne;

Whoever says, "I want no more,"
Confesses he has none.

389 *The Pilgrim's Guide.*—Ps. xlviii. 14. 8. 7 4.

1 GUIDE me, O thou great Jehovah,
Pilgrim through this barren land;
I am weak, but thou art mighty;
Hold me with thy powerful hand:
Bread of heaven,
Feed me till I want no more.

2 Open, Lord, the crystal fountain,
Whence the healing waters flow;
Let the fiery, cloudy pillar
Lead me all my journey through:
Strong Deliverer,
Be thou still my strength and shield.

3 When I tread the verge of Jordan,
Bid my anxious fears subside:
Bear me through the swelling torrent,
Land me safe on Canaan's side:
Songs of praises
I will ever give to thee.

390 *Christ our Defender.* C. M.

1 WE seek a rest beyond the skies,
In everlasting day;
Through floods and flames the passage lies,
But Jesus guards the way.

2 The swelling flood and raging flame
Hear and obey his word;
Then let us triumph in his name,
Our Saviour is the Lord.

391 *Walking by Faith.* L. M.

1 'TIS by the faith of joys to come
We walk through deserts dark as night;
Till we arrive at heaven, our home,
Faith is our guide, and faith our light.

2 The want of sight she well supplies;
She makes the pearly gates appear;
Far into distant worlds she pries,
And brings eternal glories near.

3 Cheerful we tread the desert through,
While faith inspires a heavenly ray,
Though lions roar, and tempests blow,
And rocks and dangers fill the way.

4 So Abra'm, by divine command,
Left his own house, to walk with God;
His faith beheld the promised land,
And fired his zeal along the road.

392 *Longing to be with Christ.* 7. 6. Iambic.

1 OH when shall I see Jesus,
And reign with him above,
And from the flowing fountain
Drink everlasting love?
When shall I be delivered
From this vain world of sin,

And with my blessed Jesus
  My heavenly life begin.

2 Through grace I am determined
  To conquer, though I die;
And then away to Jesus,
  On wings of love, I'll fly;
Farewell to sin and sorrow,
  I'll bid them both adieu—
And you, my friends, prove faithful,
  And on your way pursue.

3 Whene'er you meet with troubles
  And trials on the way,
Cast all your care on Jesus,
  And never cease to pray.
Gird on the heavenly armor
  Of faith and hope and love,
For short will be the warfare,
  And bright the crown above.

4 Our race will soon be ended,
  And we shall rise to God;
To reign with him for ever,
  Who bought us with his blood;
With saints we'll join to praise him,
  For grace divinely free,
And rise in glorious raptures,
  To all eternity.

393 *Believers encouraged.* S. M.

1 YOUR harps, ye trembling saints,
  Down from the willows take:

Loud to the praise of love divine
  Bid every string awake.

2 Though in a foreign land,
  We are not far from home,
And nearer to our house above
  We every moment come.

3 His grace will, to the end,
  Stronger and brighter shine;
Nor present things, nor things to come,
  Shall quench the spark divine.

4 When we in darkness walk,
  Nor feel the heavenly flame—
Then is the time to trust our God,
  And rest upon his name.

5 Soon shall our doubts and fears
  Subside at his control;
His loving kindness shall break through
  The midnight of the soul.

6 Bless'd is the man, O God,
  That stays himself on thee!
Who waits for thy salvation, Lord,
  Shall thy salvation see.

394 *Pilgrimage heavenward.* 7s.

1 CHILDREN of the heavenly King,
  As ye journey, sweetly sing:
Sing your Saviour's worthy praise,
Glorious in his works and ways.

2 Ye are travelling home to God,
In the way the fathers trod;

They are happy now, and ye
Soon their happiness shall see.

3 Shout, ye little flock, and bless'd;
Ye on Jesus' throne shall rest;
There your seat is now prepared,
There your kingdom and reward.

4 Fear not, brethren, for ye stand
On the borders of your land;
Jesus, God's exalted Son,
Bids you undismayed go on.

5 Lord, submissive make us go,
Gladly leaving all below;
Only thou our leader be,
And we still will follow thee.

395 *The Heavenly City.*—Heb. xiii. 14. L. M

1 "WE'VE no abiding city here"—
We seek a city out of sight:
Zion its name—the Lord is there,
It shines with everlasting light.

2 "We've no abiding city here"—
This may distress the worldly mind,
But should not cost the saint a tear,
Who hopes a better rest to find.

3 "We've no abiding city here"—
Then let us live as pilgrims do;
Let not the world our rest appear,
But let us haste from all below.

4 O sweet abode of peace and love,
Where pilgrims, freed from toil, are
Had I the pinions of the dove, [bless'd!
I'd flee to thee, and be at rest.

5 But hush, my soul, nor dare repine;
The time my God appoints is best:
While here, to do his will be *mine*,
And *his* to fix my time of rest.

396 *Pilgrims to Zion* C. P. M.

1 YE pilgrims—partners in distress,
Who, travelling through the wilder-
Are pressing onward still; [ness,
A while forget your griefs and fears,
And look beyond this vale of tears,
To the celestial hill.

2 Beyond the bounds of time and space,
Look forward to that heavenly place,
The saints' secure abode;
On faith's strong eagle-pinions rise,
And trace your passage to the skies,
And view the mount of God.

3 We suffer with our Master here;
But we shall soon with him appear,
And by his side sit down;
To patient faith the prize is sure,
And all that to the end endure
The cross, shall wear the crown.

4 Thrice blessed bliss-inspiring hope,
It lifts the fainting spirits up;
It brings to life the dead!

Our conflicts here will soon be past,
And we together rise at last,
Triumphant with our Head.

5 That great mysterious Deity!—
We soon with open face shall see
The beatific sight; [praise
Shall fill heaven's sounding courts with
And worship 'mid the golden blaze
Of everlasting light.

397 *Heaven anticipated.* C. M.

1 OUR journey is a thorny maze,
But we march upward still;
Forget these troubles of the ways,
And reach at Zion's hill.

2 See the kind angels at the gates,
Inviting us to come!
There Jesus, the forerunner, waits
To welcome trav'llers home!

3 By glimm'ring hopes and gloomy fears
We trace the sacred road;
Through dismal deeps and dangerous
We make our way to God. [snares

4 A thousand savage beasts of prey
Around the forest roam;
But Judah's Lion guards the way,
And guides the strangers home.

5 Eternal glory to the King
Who bears us safely through,
Our tongues shall never cease to sing,
And endless praise renew.

398 *The Way to Zion.*—Isa. xxxv. 8, 10. C. M

1 SING, all ye ransomed of the Lord,
Your great Deliverer sing:
Pilgrims, for Zion's city bound,
Be joyful in your King.

2 See the fair way his hand hath raised;
How peaceful and how plain!
The simplest traveller shall not err,
Nor ask the path in vain.

3 A hand divine shall lead you on,
Through all the blissful road,
Till to the sacred mount you rise,
And see your smiling God.

4 March on in your Redeemer's strength;
Pursue his footsteps still;
On the bright prospect fix your eye,
And press to Zion's hill.

399 *The Saint's Sweet Home.* 11s.

1 'MID scenes of confusion and creature complaints,
How sweet to my soul is communion with saints;
To find at the banquet of mercy there' room,
And feel in the presence of Jesus at home

CHORUS.

Home, home—sweet, sweet home;
Prepare me, dear Saviour, for glory, my home.

2 Sweet bonds that unite all the children (
peace!
And thrice precious Jesus, whose love car
not cease!
Though oft from thy presence in sadness
roam,
I long to behold thee in glory, at home.

3 I sigh from this body of sin to be free,
Which hinders my joy, and communio
with thee;
Though now my temptations like billow
may foam,
All, all will be peace, when I'm with the
at home.

4 While here in the valley of conflict I sta
Oh give me submission, and strength a
my day;
In all my afflictions to thee would I come
Rejoicing in hope of my glorious home.

5 Whate'er thou deniest, oh give me th
grace,
The Spirit's sure witness, and smiles o
thy face;
Indulge me with patience to wait at th
throne,
And find, even now, a sweet foretaste o
home.

6 I long, dearest Lord, in thy beauties t
shine;
No more, as an exile, in sorrow to pine;

And in thy dear image arise from the tomb,
With glorified millions to praise thee at
home.

400 *The Conflict.* L. M.

NATURE may raise up all her strife,
Reluctant to the heavenly life;
Loth in a Saviour's death to share,
Her daily cross compelled to bear.

But grace omnipotent at length
Shall arm the saint with saving strength,
Through the sharp war with aid attend,
And his long conflict sweetly end.

Let faith exert its conquering power;
Say, in thy tempted, trembling hour—
"My God, my Father, save thy son"—
'Tis heard, and all thy fears are done.

But if corruption's strength prevail,
And oft thy pilgrim footsteps fail,
Pray for his grace with louder cries;
So shalt thou cleansed and stronger rise.

401 *Triumph of Faith.* 6. 5.

1 IF life's pleasures charm thee,
Give them not thy heart;
Lest the gift ensnare thee
From thy God to part.

2 If distress befall thee,
Painful though it be,
Let not grief appal thee,
To thy Saviour flee.

3 When earth's prospects fail thee,
Let it not distress:
Better comforts wait thee,
Christ will freely bless.

4 Let not death alarm thee,
Shrink not from his blow;
For the conflict arm thee,
Triumph o'er the foe.

402 *Hope in the Covenant.*—Heb. vi. 17. L. M.

1 HOW oft have sin and Satan strove
To rend my soul from thee, my God;
But everlasting is thy love,
And Jesus seals it with his blood.

2 The oath and promise of the Lord
Join to confirm the wondrous grace;
Eternal power performs the word,
And fills all heaven with endless praise.

3 Amidst temptations, sharp and long,
My soul to this dear refuge flies;
Hope is my anchor, firm and strong,
While tempests blow, and billows rise.

4 The gospel bears my spirit up;
A faithful and unchanging God
Lays the foundation for my hope,
In oaths, and promises, and blood.

403 *The Family of Saints.*—Eph. iii. 15. C. M.

1 COME, let us join our friends above,
Who have obtained the prize,

And, on the eagle-wings of love,
To joy celestial rise.

2 Let saints below in concert sing,
With those to glory gone;
For all the servants of our King,
In heaven and earth, are one.

3 One family, we dwell in him,
One church, above, beneath;
Though now divided by the stream—
The narrow stream of death.

4 One army of the living God,
To his commands we bow;
Part of the host have crossed the flood,
And part are crossing now.

5 Ten thousand to their endless home
This solemn moment fly;
And we are to the margin come,
And soon expect to die.

6 Dear Saviour, be our constant guide;
Then, when the word is given,
Bid the cold waves of death divide,
And land us safe in heaven.

404 *One in Christ.* S. M.

1 LET party names no more
The Christian world o'erspread;
Gentile and Jew, and bond and free,
Are one in Christ their head.

2 Among the saints on earth
Let mutual love be found;

Heirs of the same inheritance,
With mutual blessings crowned.

3 Thus will the church below
Resemble that above,
Where streams of pleasure ever flow,
And every heart is love.

405 *Fellowship.* C. M.

1 OUR souls by love together knit,
Cemented, mixed in one,
One hope, one heart, one mind, one voice,
'Tis heaven on earth begun.

2 Our hearts have often burned within,
And glowed with sacred fire,
While Jesus spoke, and fed, and bless'd,
And filled th' enlarged desire.

3 Lord, when thou mak'st thy jewels up,
And sett'st thy starry crown;
When all thy sparkling gems shall shine,
Proclaimed by thee thine own;

4 May we, a little band of love,
We sinners, saved by grace,
From glory unto glory changed,
Behold thee face to face.

406 *Christian Love.* C. M.

1 HOW sweet, how heavenly is the sight,
When those who love the Lord
In one another's peace delight,
And so fulfill his word;—

2 When each can feel his brother's sigh,
And with him bear a part;
When sorrows flow from eye to eye,
And joy from heart to heart;—

3 When, free from envy, scorn, and pride,
(Our wishes all above,)
Each can his brother's failings hide,
And show a brother's love.

4 Let love, in one delightful stream,
Through every bosom flow;
And union sweet, and dear esteem,
In every action glow.

5 Love is the golden chain that binds
The happy souls above;
And he's an heir of heaven, who finds
His bosom glow with love.

407 *A Welcome to Christian Fellowship.* L. M.

1 COME in, thou blessed of the Lord;
We bid thee come, in Jesus' name;
We welcome thee with one accord,
And trust the Saviour does the same.

2 Those joys which earth cannot afford,
We'll seek in fellowship to prove;
Joined in one spirit to our Lord,
Together bound by mutual love.

3 And while we pass this vale of tears,
We'll make our joys and sorrows known;
We'll share each other's hopes and fears,
And count a brother's cares our own.

4 Once more our welcome we repeat;
Receive assurance of our love:
Oh may we all together meet
Around the throne of God above.

REVIVAL.

408 *Prayer for Revival.* S. M

1 OH for the happy hour
When God will hear our cry,
And send, with a reviving power,
His Spirit from on high.

2 We meet, we sing, we pray,
We listen to the word,
In vain—we see no cheering ray,
No cheering voice is heard.

3 Our prayers are faint and dull,
And languid all our songs,
Where once with joy our hearts were full,
And rapture tuned our tongues.

4 While many crowd thy house,
How few, around thy board,
Meet to recount their solemn vows,
And bless thee as their Lord!

5 Thou, thou alone canst give
Thy gospel sure success;
Canst bid the dying sinner live
Anew in holiness.

6 Come, then, with power divine,
Spirit of life and love;
Then shall our people all be thine,
Our church like that above.

409

The Prosperity of Zion.—Isa. lx. 1. H. M.

1 O ZION, tune thy voice,
And raise thy hands on high;
Tell all the earth thy joys,
And shout salvation nigh:
Cheerful in God,
Arise and shine:
While rays divine
Stream all abroad.

2 He gilds thy morning face
With beams that cannot fade;
His all-resplendent grace
He pours around thy head:
The nations round
Thy form shall view,
With lustre new
Divinely crowned.

3 In honor to his name
Reflect that sacred light,
And loud that grace proclaim
Which makes thy darkness bright:
Pursue his praise,
Till sovereign love,
In worlds above,
The glory raise.

4 There, on his holy hill,
A brighter Sun shall rise,
And with his radiance fill
Those fairer, purer skies:
While round his throne
Ten thousand stars,
In nobler spheres,
His influence own.

410 *Presence of Christ in His Church.* C. P. M.

1 THE Lord into his garden comes,
The spices yield their rich perfumes,
The lilies grow and thrive;
Refreshing showers of grace divine
From Jesus flow to every vine,
And make the dead revive.

2 Oh that this dry and barren ground
In springs of water may abound,
A fruitful soil become;
The desert blossom as the rose,
While Jesus conquers all his foes,
And brings the wanderers home.

3 The glorious day is hastening on,
The gracious work is now begun,
The Saviour now is nigh:
Forgiveness, in his blessed name,
The messengers of peace proclaim;
The sinner need not die.

4 Come, brethren, ye who love the Lord,
Who taste the sweetness of his word,
To his high service come;

Our troubles and our trials here,
Will only make us richer there,
When we arrive at home.

5 There, when we come to reign above,
And all surround the throne of love,
We'll drink a full supply;
Our Shepherd will before us go,
And lead where heavenly fountains flow,
That never will run dry.

411 *Joy over the repenting Sinner.* C. M.

1 OH, how divine, how sweet the joy,
When but one sinner turns,
And with a humble, broken heart,
His sin and error mourns!

2 Pleased with the news, the saints below
In songs their tongues employ;
Beyond the skies the tidings go,
And heaven is filled with joy.

3 Well pleased the Father sees and hears
The conscious sinner's moan;
Jesus receives him in his arms,
And claims him for his own.

4 Nor angels can their joys contain,
But kindle with new fire:
"The sinner lost is found," they sing,
And strike the sounding lyre.

412 *Blind Bartimeus.* 8. 7.

1 "MERCY, O thou Son of David!"
Thus blind Bartimeus prayed:

"Others by thy word are saved,
Now to me afford thine aid."

2 Many for his crying chid him,
But he called the louder still;
Till the gracious Saviour bid him—
"Come, and ask me what you will."

3 Money was not what he wanted,
Though by begging used to live;
But he asked, and Jesus granted
Alms, which none but he could give.

4 "Lord, remove this grievous blindness,
Let my eyes behold the day"—
Straight he saw, and won by kindness,
Followed Jesus in the way.

5 Oh, methinks I hear him praising,
Publishing to all around—
"Friends, is not my case amazing?
What a Saviour I have found!

6 "Oh that all the blind but knew him,
And would be advised by me;
Surely they would hasten to him,
He would cause them all to see."

413 *Converting Grace.*—Ps. xlv. 3, 5. C. M.

1 HAIL, mighty Jesus, how divine
Is thy victorious sword!
The stoutest rebel must resign,
At thy commanding word.

2 Deep are the wounds thine arrows give,
They pierce the hardest heart;

Thy smiles of grace the slain revive,
And joy succeeds to smart.

3 The strongest holds of Satan yield
To thine all-conquering hand;
When once thy glorious arm's revealed,
No rebel can withstand.

414 *Prayer for a Revival.*—Ps. lxxxv. 6. 8. 7. 4.

1 SAVIOUR, visit thy plantation;
Grant us, Lord, a gracious rain;
All will come to desolation,
Unless thou return again.
Lord, revive us;
All our help must come from thee.

2 Keep no longer at a distance;
Shine upon us from on high,
Lest, for want of thine assistance,
Every plant should droop and die.

3 Let our mutual love be fervent,
Make us prevalent in prayers;
Let each one esteemed thy servant
Shun the world's bewitching snares.

4 Break the tempter's fatal power;
Turn the stony heart to flesh;
And begin, from this good hour,
To revive thy work afresh.

415 *The Conversion of Sinners.* C. M

1 HOW much the hearts of those revive
Who love and fear the Lord,

When sinners dead are made alive
By his all-quickening word.

2 The ministers of Christ rejoice,
When souls the word receive;
When sinners hear the Saviour's voice,
And in the Lord believe.

3 The church of God their praises join,
And of salvation sing;
They glorify the grace divine
Of their victorious King.

4 On us, our Saviour, shed thy light;
Thy work, O Lord, revive:
May we enjoy that blessed sight—
Dead sinners made alive.

5 Then will thy saints aloud rejoice,
And join the hosts above,
To praise thy name with cheerful voice,
And magnify thy love.

KINGDOM OF CHRIST.

416 *Love to the Church.* S. M.

1 I LOVE thy kingdom, Lord,
The house of thine abode,
The church our bless'd Redeemer saved
With his own precious blood.

2 I love thy church, O God;
Her walls before thee stand,

Dear as the apple of thine eye,
And graven on thy hand.

3 If e'er to bless thy sons
My voice or hands deny,
These hands let useful skill forsake,
This voice in silence die.

4 If e'er my heart forget
Her welfare or her wo,
Let every joy this heart forsake,
And every grief o'erflow.

5 Beyond my highest joy
I prize her heavenly ways,
Her sweet communion, solemn vows,
Her hymns of love and praise.

6 For her my tears shall fall,
For her my prayers ascend;
To her my cares and toils be given,
Till toils and cares shall end.

417 *Zion.*—Ps. lxxxvii. 3. 8. 7.

1 GLORIOUS things of thee are spoken,
Zion, city of our God!
He whose word can ne'er be broken,
Formed thee for his own abode:
On the rock of ages founded,
What can shake thy sure repose?
With salvation's walls surrounded,
Thou may'st smile at all thy foes.

2 Here the streams of living waters,
Springing from eternal love,

Well supply thy sons and daughters,
  And all fear of want remove:
Who can faint while such a river
  Ever flows, their thirst t' assuage—
Grace which, like the Lord, the giver,
  Never fails from age to age?

3 Saviour, if in Zion's city
  Thou record my worthless name,
Let the world deride or pity,
  I may well endure the shame:
Fading is the worldling's pleasure,
  All his boasted pomp and show;
Solid joys and lasting treasure
  None but Zion's children know.

418 *Safety of the Church.* 7s. Double

1 SEE the gospel church secure,
  See it founded on the rock;
All her promises are sure,
  Her high bulwarks who can shock?
Count her every precious shrine,
  Tell, to after-ages tell—
Fortified by power divine,
  Zion is established well.

2 In the city of our God,
  In his holy mount below,
Publish, spread his name abroad,
  All his truth and goodness show.
Zion's God is all our own,
  On his mercy we rely;

We his pardoning love have known,
His we live, and his we die.

419 *Awake, O Zion!*—Isa. lii. 1. L. M.

1 AWAKE, awake, O Zion, wake;
Thy beautiful attire put on:
Rise from the dust, thy garments shake;
The dark and mourning hours are gone.

2 Loose from thy neck the hostile bands,
O captive daughter, and behold
Thine exiles flock from all the lands,
And hasten to their parent fold.

3 See, Ethiopia, at thy gates,
Is stretching forth her hands to God;
And there, with all her treasures, waits
To enter thy divine abode.

4 Put on thy strength, break forth in joy;
Whence did these ransomed children come?
Bless'd Zion! bless'd in thine employ,
With singing bring these exiles home.

420 *The God of Zion.* 8. 7. 4.

1 ZION stands, by hills surrounded;
Zion, kept by power divine:
All her foes shall be confounded,
Though the world in arms combine.
Happy Zion,
What a favored lot is thine!

2 Every human tie may perish;
Friend to friend unfaithful prove;

Mothers cease their own to cherish;
Heaven and earth at last remove;
But no changes
Can attend Jehovah's love.

3 In the furnace God may prove thee,
Thence to bring thee forth more bright,
But can never cease to love thee;
Thou art precious in his sight.
God is with thee—
God thine everlasting light.

421 *The Church triumphant.* 11s.

1 DAUGHTER of Zion, awake from thy sadness;
Awake, for thy foes shall oppress thee no more;
Bright o'er thy hills dawns the day-star of gladness,
Arise, for the night of thy sorrow is o'er.

2 Strong were thy foes, but the arm that subdued them,
And scattered their legions, was mightier far;
They fled, like the chaff, from the scourge that pursued them;
Vain were their steeds and their chariots of war.

3 Daughter of Zion, the power that hath saved thee,
Extolled with the harp and the timbrel should be;

Shout! for the foe is destroyed that enslaved
thee,
Th' oppressor is vanquished, and Zion is
free.

422 *Promises to the Church.*—Isa. lx. 15, 20. 8. 7.

1 HEAR what God the Lord hath spoken;
"O my people, faint and few,
Comfortless, afflicted, broken,
Fair abodes I build for you:
Thorns of heart-felt tribulation
Shall no more perplex your ways:
You shall name your walls Salvation,
And your gates shall all be praise.

2 "There, like streams that feed the garden,
Pleasures, without end, shall flow;
For the Lord, your faith rewarding,
All his bounty shall bestow:
Still in undisturbed possession,
Peace and righteousness shall reign;
Never shall you feel oppression—
Hear the voice of war again.

3 "Ye no more your suns descending,
Waning moons no more shall see;
But, your griefs for ever ending,
Find eternal noon in me.
God will rise, and shining o'er you,
Change to day the gloom of night;
He, the Lord, will be your glory,
God your everlasting light."

423 *Good Tidings to Zion.*—Isa. lii. 7. 8. 7. 4

1 ON the mountain's top appearing,
Lo, the sacred herald stands;
Welcome news to Zion bearing,
Zion long in hostile lands:
Mourning captive,
God himself will loose thy bands.

2 Has thy night been long and mournful,
All thy friends unfaithful proved?
Have thy foes been proud and scornful,
By thy sighs and tears unmoved?
Cease thy mourning,
Zion still is well beloved.

3 God, thy God, will now restore thee,
He himself appears thy friend;
All thy foes shall flee before thee,
Here their boasts and triumphs end;
Great deliverance
Zion's King will surely send.

4 Enemies no more shall trouble;
All thy warfare now is past;
For thy shame thou shalt have double,
Days of peace are come at last:
All thy conflicts
End in everlasting rest.

424 *The Lord reigneth.* 8. 7.

1 JESUS comes! let Earth and Ocean
Pour their treasures at his feet;

Sea-born isles, with glad devotion,
  Haste your promised Lord to greet.
What though, high their shadows rearing,
  Clouds and darkness vail his throne?
Truth, in all his ways appearing,
  Tells us—he is Christ alone.

2 Heaven his glory is revealing,
  Farthest worlds confess his sway;
Millions, at his altar kneeling,
  Cast their idol-bonds away.
Salem hears—exulting Salem
  Hears, and of his judgments sings,
While, with joy, her daughters hail him
  Lord of lords, and King of kings.

425 *The Dominion of Jesus.*—Phil. ii. 10. L. M.

1 YES—mighty Jesus, thou shalt reign,
  Till all thy haughty foes submit;
Till hell, and all her trembling train,
  Become the footstool of thy feet.

2 Then rescued souls shall bless thy power;
  Thine arm shall full salvation bring:
Thy saints, in that illustrious hour,
  Shall conquer with their conquering
    King.

3 And when, through brilliant gates of gold,
  Thou lead'st thy chosen to the skies,
May we the shining pomp behold,
  And partners of the triumph rise.

4 Then, ranged thy blazing throne around,
The Saviour's honors we'll proclaim;
While heaven's transported realms resound
Thy mighty deeds and glorious name.

426 "*He shall reign.*"—Rev. xi. 15. 7s.

1 HARK! the song of Jubilee—
Loud as mighty thunders roar,
Or the fullness of the sea,
When it breaks upon the shore.

2 Hallelujah! for the Lord,
God Omnipotent, shall reign:
Hallelujah! let the word
Echo round the earth and main.

3 Hallelujah! hark! the sound,
From the centre to the skies,
Wakes, above, beneath, around,
All creation's harmonies.

4 See Jehovah's banners furled,
Sheathed his sword! he speaks—'tis [done,
And the kingdoms of this world
Are the kingdoms of his Son.

5 He shall reign from pole to pole,
With illimitable sway:
He shall reign, when, like a scroll,
Yonder heavens have passed away.

6 Then the end—beneath his rod
Man's last enemy shall fall:
Hallelujah! Christ in God,
God in Christ, is all in all.

427 *Rejoice in the Lord.*—Ps. ii. 6. H. M.

1 REJOICE, the Lord is king,
Your God and King adore;
Mortals, give thanks, and sing,
And triumph evermore:
Lift up the heart, lift up the voice,
Rejoice aloud, ye saints, rejoice.

2 Rejoice, the Saviour reigns,
The God of truth and love;
When he had purged our stains,
He took his seat above. Lift up, &c.

3 His kingdom cannot fail,
He rules o'er earth and heaven;
The keys of death and hell
Are to our Jesus given. Lift up, &c.

4 He all his foes shall quell,
Shall all our sins destroy,
And every bosom swell
With pure, seraphic joy. Lift up, &c.

5 Rejoice in glorious hope;
Jesus, the Judge, shall come,
And take his servants up
To their eternal home.
We soon shall hear th' archangel's voice,
The trump of God shall sound—Rejoice.

428 *Christ a Conqueror.*—Ps. xlv. 4. C. M.

1 JESUS, immortal King, arise;
Assert thy rightful sway,

Till earth, subdued, its tribute brings,
And distant lands obey.

2 Ride forth, victorious Conqueror, ride
Till all thy foes submit,
And all the powers of hell resign
Their trophies at thy feet.

3 Send forth thy word, and let it fly
The spacious earth around;
Till every soul beneath the sun
Shall hear the joyful sound.

4 From sea to sea—from shore to shore,
May Jesus be adored;
And earth, with all her millions, shout
Hosanna to the Lord.

429 *The Messiah.* 7. 6. Iambic

1 HAIL to the Lord's anointed,
Great David's greater Son!
Hail, in the time appointed,
His reign on earth begun:
He comes to break oppression,
To set the captive free;
To take away transgression,
And rule in equity.

2 He comes, with succor speedy,
To those who suffer wrong;
To help the poor and needy,
And bid the weak be strong:
To give them songs for sighing,
Their darkness turn to light,

Whose souls, condemned and dying,
Were precious in his sight.

3 For him shall prayer unceasing
And daily vows ascend;
His kingdom still increasing,
A kingdom without end:
The mountain dews shall nourish
A seed in weakness sown,
Whose fruit shall spread and flourish,
And shake like Lebanon.

4 O'er every foe victorious,
He on his throne shall rest,
From age to age more glorious,
All-blessing and all-bless'd:
The tide of time shall never
His covenant remove:
His name shall stand for ever;
That name to us is—Love.

430 *The Reign of Christ.* 7s. Double.

1 SEE the ransomed millions stand,
Palms of conquest in their hand;
This before the throne their strain—
Hell is vanquished, death is slain.
Blessing, honor, glory, might,
Are the Conqu'ror's native right;
Thrones and powers before him fall,
Lamb of God, and Lord of all.

2 Hasten, Lord, the promised hour;
Come in glory and in power;

Still thy foes are unsubdued;
Nature sighs to be renewed:
Time has nearly reached its sum;
All things, with the bride, say—come.
Jesus, whom all worlds adore,
Come, and reign for evermore.

431 *Exhortation to Effort.* 8. 7

1 WHILE the heralds of salvation
Christ's abounding grace proclaim,
Let his friends, of every station,
Gladly join to spread his fame.

2 May his kingdom be promoted;
May the world the Saviour know;
Be my all to him devoted;
To my Lord my all I owe.

3 Praise the Saviour, all ye nations;
Praise him, all ye hosts above;
Shout, with joyful acclamations,
His divine, victorious love.

432 *The Latter-day Glory.*—Mic. iv. 1—5. C. M

1 BEHOLD, the mountain of the Lord,
In latter days, shall rise
On mountain tops, above the hills,
And draw the wond'ring eyes.

2 To this the joyful nations round,
All tribes and tongues, shall flow;
"Up to the hill of God," they say,
"And to his house we'll go."

3 The beams that shine on Zion's hill
Shall lighten ev'ry land;
The King who reigns in Salem's towers
Shall all the world command.

4 No longer hosts encountering hosts,
Their millions slain deplore;
They hang the trumpet in the hall,
And study war no more.

5 Come, then—oh come from every land,
To worship at his shrine:
And walking in the light of God,
With holy beauties shine.

433 *Christ's Exaltation.* H. M.

1 GOD is gone up on high,
With a triumphant noise;
The clarions of the sky
Proclaim th' angelic joys;
Join, all on earth, rejoice and sing,
Glory ascribe to glory's King.

2 God in the flesh below,
For us he reigns above;
Let all the nations know
The Saviour's conquering love,
Join, all, &c.

3 High on his holy seat,
He bears the righteous sway;
His foes beneath his feet
Shall sink and die away.
Join, all, &c.

4 His foes and our's are one—
Satan, the world, and sin;
But he shall tread them down,
And bring his kingdom in.
Join, all, &c.

434 *Increase of the Church.*—Isa. lx. 5, 6. H. M.

1 RISE, gracious God, and shine
In all thy saving might;
And prosper each design
To spread thy glorious light:
Let healing streams of mercy flow,
That all the earth thy truth may know.

2 Oh bring the nations near,
That they may sing thy praise:
Let all the people hear,
And learn thy holy ways:
Reign, mighty God, assert thy cause,
And govern by thy righteous laws.

3 Put forth thy glorious power;
The nations then will see,
And earth present her store
In converts born of thee:
God, our own God, his church will bless,
And earth shall yield her full increase.

435 *Christ's universal Reign.* L. M

1 JESUS shall reign where'er the sun
Does his successive journeys run;
His kingdom stretch from shore to shore,
'Till moons shall wax and wane no more.

2 For him shall endless prayer be made,
And praises throng to crown his head;
His name, like sweet perfume, shall rise
With every morning sacrifice.

3 People and realms of every tongue
Dwell on his love with sweetest song;
And infant voices shall proclaim
Their early blessings on his name.

4 Blessings abound where'er he reigns,
The prisoner leaps to lose his chains,
The weary find eternal rest,
And all the sons of want are bless'd.

436 *Praise from all Nations.* L. M.

1 FROM all that dwell below the skies,
Let the Creator's praise arise:
Let the Redeemer's name be sung
Through every land—by every tongue.

2 Eternal are thy mercies, Lord;
Eternal truth attends thy word:
Thy praise shall sound from shore to shore,
Till suns shall rise and set no more.

437 *The Reign of Christ.* 8. 7

1 HARK, ten thousand harps and voices
Sound the note of praise above;
Jesus reigns, and heaven rejoices;
Jesus reigns, the God of love.

2 King of glory, reign for ever—
Thine an everlasting crown:

Nothing from thy love shall sever
Those whom thou hast made thine own.

3 Saviour, hasten thine appearing;
Bring, oh bring the glorious day,
When, the gospel summons hearing,
Heathen nations will obey.

438 *Spread of the Gospel.* C. M.

1 GREAT God, the nations of the earth
Are by creation thine;
And in thy works, from nature's birth,
Thy power and glory shine.

2 But, Lord, thy greater love hath sent
Thy gospel to our race;
Unvailing thy divine intent
Of rich redeeming grace.

3 Soon may these gracious tidings roll
The spacious earth around,
Till every tribe and every soul
Shall hear the joyful sound.

4 When, to her sable sons conveyed,
Shall Afric learn thy word,
And vassals, long enslaved, become
The freemen of the Lord?

5 When shall the scattered wanderers meet,
That now in darkness rove,
And, gathered round Immanuel's feet,
Sing of his saving love?

6 O Lord, each faithful effort own,
To spread the gospel-rays;

And rear on sin's demolished throne
The temples of thy praise.

439 *The Jubilee proclaimed.* H. M.

1 BLOW ye the trumpet, blow—
The gladly solemn sound;
Let all the nations know,
To earth's remotest bound—
The year of jubilee is come;
Return, ye ransomed sinners, home.

2 Exalt the Lamb of God,
The sin-atoning Lamb;
Redemption by his blood
Through all the lands proclaim.
The year, &c.

3 Ye who have sold for nought
The heritage above,
Receive it back unbought,
The gift of Jesus' love.
The year, &c.

4 Ye slaves of sin and hell,
Your liberty receive;
And safe in Jesus dwell,
And bless'd in Jesus live.
The year, &c.

5 The gospel-trumpet hear—
The news of pardoning grace;
Ye happy souls, draw near,
Behold your Saviour's face.
The year, &c

440

Thy Kingdom come.—Matt vi. 10. S. M.

1 O GOD of sovereign grace,
We bow before thy throne,
And plead, for all the human race,
The merits of thy Son.

2 Spread through the earth, O Lord,
The knowledge of thy ways;
And let all lands with joy record
The great Redeemer's praise.

441

Success of the Gospel. 7. 6. Iambic.

1 THE morning light is breaking,
The darkness disappears;
The sons of earth are waking
To penitential tears:
Each breeze that sweeps the ocean,
Brings tidings from afar,
Of nations in commotion,
Prepared for Zion's war.

2 See heathen nations bending
Before the God we love,
And thousand hearts ascending
In gratitude above;
While sinners, now confessing,
The gospel call obey,
And seek the Saviour's blessing—
A nation in a day.

3 Bless'd river of salvation,
Pursue thy onward way;

Flow thou to every nation,
  Nor in thy richness stay;
Stay not till all the lowly
  Triumphant reach their home;
Stay not till all the holy
  Proclaim—the Lord is come.

442 *The Gospel Light.*—Isa. lii. 10. C. M.

1 STRETCH, O my soul, thine ardent wing,
  And hail the dawning light;
Behold, what scenes, what visions spring
  Of infinite delight.

2 Soon shall the glorious eastern Star
  Above the mountains rise;
And rays celestial, beaming far,
  Illume e'en polar skies.

3 If angels in their sphere rejoice
  One rescued soul to greet,
How will they raise th' enraptured voice
  Whole continents to meet.

4 Siberia spreads her frozen arms,
  Released from sin and chains;
And Sharon's rose exhales its charms
  On Afric's sultry plains.

5 From Java to the farthest west
  The heavenly light shall reach;
And truth divine its power attest,
  In every clime and speech.

6 Shed, Sun of righteousness, thy rays
  On every land of night;

Till all the heathen sing thy praise,
And hail the cheerful light.

443 *Spread of the Gospel.* 8. 7. 4.

1 YES, we trust the day is breaking;
Joyful times are near at hand;
God, the mighty God, is speaking
By his word, in every land:
When he chooses,
Darkness flies at his command.

2 While the foe becomes more daring,
While he enters like a flood,
God, the Saviour, is preparing
Means to spread his truth abroad;
Every language
Soon shall tell the love of God.

3 God of Jacob, high and glorious,
Let thy people see thy hand;
Let the gospel be victorious
Through the world in every land:
And the idols
Perish, Lord, at thy command.

444 *The Fountain.*—Zech. xiii. 1. 8. 7. 4.

1 SEE from Zion's sacred mountain
Streams of living water flow;
God has opened there a fountain
Which supplies the world below:
They are blessed
Who its sovereign virtues know.

2 Through ten thousand channels flowing,
Streams of mercy find their way;
Life and health and joy bestowing,
Making all around look gay:
O ye nations,
Hail the long expected day.

3 Gladdened by the flowing treasure,
All enriching as it goes,
Lo, the desert smiles with pleasure,
Buds and blossoms as the rose:
Every object
Sings for joy where'er it flows.

4 Trees of life, the banks adorning,
Yield their fruit to all around;
Those who eat are saved from mourning,
Pleasure comes, and hopes abound:
Fair their portion—
Endless life with glory crowned.

445 *The Gospel Tidings.* H. M.

1 HARK! hark!—the notes of joy
Roll o'er the heavenly plains,
And seraphs find employ
For their sublimest strains;
Some new delight in heaven is known,
Loud sound the harps around the throne.

2 Bear, bear the tidings round;
Let every mortal know
What love in God is found,
What pity he can show;

Ye winds that blow, ye waves that roll,
Bear the glad news from pole to pole.

3 Strike, strike the harps again,
To great Immanuel's name;
Arise, ye sons of men,
And all his grace proclaim;
Angels and men, wake every string,
'Tis God the Saviour's praise we sing.

446 *Jesus reigns.* 7s.

1 WAKE the song of jubilee,
Let it echo o'er the sea;
Now is come the promised hour;
Jesus reigns with sovereign power.

2 All ye nations, join and sing,
"Christ of lords and kings is King."
Let it sound from shore to shore—
Jesus reigns for evermore.

3 Now the desert lands rejoice,
And the islands join their voice;
Yea, the whole creation sings—
"Jesus is the King of kings!"

447 *The Millennium.* H. M.

1 RISE, Sun of glory, rise,
And chase those shades of night,
Which now obscure the skies,
And hide thy sacred light:
Oh chase those dismal shades away,
And bring the bright millennial day.

2 Now send thy Spirit down
On all the nations, Lord;
With great success to crown
The preaching of thy word;
That heathen lands may own thy sway,
And cast their idol gods away.

3 Then shall thy kingdom come
Among our fallen race,
And all the earth become
The temple of thy grace,
Whence pure devotion shall ascend,
And songs of praise, till time shall end.

448 "*Watchman, what of the Night?*" 7s. Double.

1 WATCHMAN, tell us of the night,
What its signs of promise are.
Traveller, o'er yon mountain's height,
See that glory-beaming star!
Watchman, does its beauteous ray
Aught of hope or joy foretell?
Traveller, yes; it brings the day—
Promised day of Israel.

2 Watchman, tell us of the night;
Higher yet that star ascends.
Traveller, blessedness and light,
Peace and truth its course portends.
Watchman, will its beams alone
Gild the spot that gave them birth?
Traveller, ages are its own,
See, it bursts o'er all the earth!

3 Watchman, tell us of the night,
For the morning seems to dawn.

Traveller, darkness takes its flight,
  Doubt and terror are withdrawn.
Watchman, let thy wanderings cease;
  Hie thee to thy quiet home.
Traveller, lo! the Prince of Peace—
  Lo! the Son of God is come!

449 *The Heathen.*—Acts xvi. 9. 7. 6. Iambic

1 FROM Greenland's icy mountains,
  From India's coral strand,
Where Afric's sunny fountains
  Roll down their golden sand;
From many an ancient river,
  From many a palmy plain,
They call us to deliver
  Their land from error's chain.

2 What though the spicy breezes
  Blow soft o'er Ceylon's isle—
Though every prospect pleases,
  And only man is vile?
In vain with lavish kindness
  The gifts of God are strown;
The heathen, in his blindness,
  Bows down to wood and stone.

3 Shall we, whose souls are lighted
  With wisdom from on high—
Shall we to men benighted
  The lamp of life deny?
Salvation! oh, salvation!
  The joyful sound proclaim,
Till earth's remotest nation
  Has learned Messiah's name.

4 Waft—waft, ye winds, his story,
And you, ye waters, roll,
Till, like a sea of glory,
It spreads from pole to pole;
Till o'er our ransomed nature,
The Lamb for sinners slain,
Redeemer, King, Creator,
In bliss returns to reign.

450 *Fulfillment of Prophecy implored.* L. M.

1 GREAT King of Zion, now arise,
Thy glorious promises fulfill;
Behold thy church in mourning lies,
Yet waiting for thy mercy still.

2 O God, how long?—thy people cry;
When shall our prayers acceptance gain?
Look from thy lofty throne on high,
And break the prisoners' heavy chain.

3 Let Asia's millions hear thy voice;
Send them thy heralds to proclaim
Salvation—bid them soon rejoice
In Jesus, our Immanuel's name.

4 Let Africa, with all her tribes,
Be rescued from the spoiler's hand;
Nor lust of power, nor golden bribes,
Draw murderers there to waste her land.

5 Let every nation under heaven,
In all their various tongues, receive
The glorious gospel thou hast given,
Renounce their idols, and believe.

451 *Christians Debtors to the Heathen.* L. M.

1 CHRISTIANS, the glorious hope ye know,
Which soothes the heart in every wo;
While heathens helpless, hopeless, lie;
No ray of glory meets their eye.

2 Christians, ye taste the heavenly grace
Which cheers believers in their race;
Uncheered by grace, through heathen gloom,
See millions hastening to the tomb.

3 Christians, ye prize the Saviour's blood,
In which the soul is cleansed for God;
Millions of souls in darkness dwell,
Uncleansed from sin—exposed to hell.

4 To distant lands that grace convey,
Which trains the soul for endless day;
Oh strive that heathens soon may view
That precious blood which cleanseth you.

452 *Prayer for the Spirit.* H. M.

1 SOVEREIGN of worlds above,
And Lord of all below,
Thy faithfulness and love,
Thy power and mercy show:
Fulfill thy word;
Thy Spirit give;
Let heathens live
And praise the Lord.

2 On lands that lie beneath
Foul superstition's sway,
Whose horrid shades of death
Admit no heavenly ray,
Bless'd Spirit shine,
Their hearts illume;
Dispel the gloom
With light divine.

3 Few be the years that roll,
Ere all shall worship thee;
The travail of his soul
Soon let the Saviour see;
O God of grace,
Thy power employ,
Fill earth with joy,
And heaven with praise.

453 *Divine Power invoked.*—Isa. li. 9. L. M.

1 ARM of the Lord, awake, awake,
Put on thy strength, the nations shake,
And let the world, adoring, see
Triumphs of mercy wrought by thee.

2 Say to the heathen, from thy throne,
"I am Jehovah—God alone:"
Thy voice their idols shall confound,
And cast their altars to the ground.

3 No more let human blood be spilt—
Vain sacrifice for human guilt!
But to each conscience be applied
The blood that flowed from Jesus' side.

4 Almighty God, thy grace proclaim,
In every land of every name;
Let adverse powers before thee fall,
And crown the Saviour—Lord of all.

454 *Prayer for the Heathen.* 8. 7. 4

1 O'ER the realms of pagan darkness
Let the eye of pity gaze:
See the kindreds of the people
Lost in sin's bewildering maze;
Darkness brooding
On the face of all the earth.

2 Light of them who sit in error—
Rise and shine, thy blessings bring;
Light, to lighten all the Gentiles—
Rise with healing in thy wing;
To thy brightness
Let all kings and nations come.

3 Let the heathen, now adoring
Idol gods of wood and stone,
Come, and worshiping before him,
Serve the living God alone.
Let thy glory
Fill the earth as floods the sea.

4 Thou to whom all power is given,
Speak the word—at thy command
Let the company of preachers
Spread thy name from land to land:
Lord, be with them
Till the world and time shall end.

455 *"Have mercy upon Zion."*—Ps. cii. 13. L. M.

1 SOVEREIGN of worlds, display thy power;
Be this thy Zion's favored hour:
Bid the bright morning star arise,
And point the nations to the skies.

2 Speak, and the world shall hear thy voice;
Speak, and the desert shall rejoice;
Scatter the gloom of heathen night,
And bid all nations hail the light.

456 *Peace and Light.* 7s. 6 lines.

1 PRINCE of Peace, the world is thine,
Come, oh come, with power divine;
While the hosts of hell oppose,
Come to triumph o'er thy foes.
Then, beneath thy gentle reign,
Earth shall bud and bloom again.

2 Sun of righteousness, illume
Nations long involved in gloom.
Wait we till the morn's faint ray
Brightens into perfect day;
Pray we till the shades of night
Fly before thy glorious light.

457 *Restoration of Israel.* C. M.

1 JERUSALEM, Jerusalem,
My heart is pained for thee;
Jerusalem, Jerusalem,
I long to see thee free.

2 Thy halcyon days of wealth and praise
Have faded from our view;
And thou art left, of all bereft,
To show what God can do.

3 Bright scenes await thy future state;
For Israel's land shall bless
Earth's ruined race with truths of grace,
And Jesus Christ confess.

4 Descend again, on earth to reign,
Almighty Prince of Peace;
Thy promised seed for mercy plead,
And look for their release.

458 *The out-cast Nation.*—Ps. liii. 6. 7. 6. Iambic.

1 OH that the Lord's salvation
Were out of Zion come,
To heal his ancient nation,
To lead his outcasts home.
How long the holy city
Shall heathen feet profane?
Return, O Lord, in pity;
Rebuild her walls again.

2 Let fall thy rod of terror;
Thy saving grace impart;
Roll back the vail of error;
Release the fettered heart.
Let Israel, home returning,
Their lost Messiah see;
Give oil of joy for mourning,
And bind thy church to thee.

459 *"I will gather thee."*—Isa. xliii. 5. C. M.

1 DAUGHTER of Zion, from the dust
Exalt thy fallen head:
Again in thy Redeemer trust,
He calls thee from the dead.

2 Awake, awake, put on thy strength,
Thy beautiful array;
The day of freedom dawns at length,
The Lord's appointed day.

3 Rebuild thy walls, thy bounds enlarge,
And send thy heralds forth:
Say to the south, "Give up thy charge,
And keep not back, O north."

4 They come, they come;—thine exiled
Where'er they rest or roam, [bands,
Have heard thy voice in distant lands,
And hasten to their home.

5 Thus, though the universe shall burn,
And God his works destroy,
With songs thy ransomed shall return,
And everlasting joy.

460 *Prayer for the Jews.* L. M.

1 OH, why should Israel's sons, once bless'd,
Still roam the scorning world around,
Disowned of heaven, by man oppressed,
Outcasts from Zion's hallowed ground?

2 O God of Israel, view their race;
Back to thy fold the wanderers bring;

Teach them to seek thy slighted grace,
To hail in Christ their promised King.

3 The vail of darkness rend in twain,
Which hides their Shiloh's glorious light;
The severed olive-branch again
Back to its parent stock unite.

4 While Judah views his birth-right gone,
With contrite shame his bosom move
The Saviour he denied, to own,
The Lord he crucified, to love.

5 Haste, glorious day, expected long,
When Jew and Greek one prayer shall raise,
With eager feet one temple throng,
One God with grateful rapture praise.

461 *The Harvest ready.*—John iv. 35. 7s.

1 SEE the ripened, waving grain
Beckon for the reaper's hand,
Ripe and ready—yet in vain
Comes the sign from foreign land.

2 See yon fair and fruitful field,
Shaken by the whirlwind's breath;
See its wasting harvest yield
To th' unsparing reaper—death.

3 Wherefore named we Jesus' name,
If we shun his work to share?
Who will take the cross, the shame?
Who will for the field prepare?

4 Christian, doubt not, shrink not thou;
God will be thy trust, thy stay;
He the cloud to shade thy brow,
He the light to guide thy way.

462 *Go forth and reap.* C. M.

1 LOOK up, the harvest fields are white,
And bends the ripening grain;
Go forth and reap, lest fall the night,
And day be given in vain.

2 See, India, from her jeweled throne,
Bows down the listening ear,
And her unnumbered thousands own
The dawn of mercy near.

3 A slanting ray of freedom's sun
Has glanced on Afric's shore;
Swiftly and wide the tidings run
That darkness reigns no more.

4 Go forth—the lamp of truth is bright—
And bid its heavenly ray
Dispel the lingering shades of night,
And chase their gloom away.

5 We plant the cross; but, Lord, thy breath
Alone has power to raise,
From the dark silent vale of death,
An army to thy praise.

463 "*The Morning cometh.*"—Isa. xxi. 12. 11s.

1 WAKE, Isles of the South, your redemption is near;
No longer repose in the borders of gloom;

The strength of his chosen in love will appear,
And light shall arise on the verge of the tomb.

2 The billows that girt you, the wild waves that roar,
The zephyrs that play where the ocean-storms cease,
Shall bear the rich freight to your desolate shore,
Shall waft the glad tidings of pardon and peace.

3 On the islands that sit in the regions of night,
The lands of despair, to oblivion a prey,
The morning will open with healing and light;
The bright Star of Bethlehem will usher the day.

4 The heathen will hasten to welcome the time,
The day-spring the prophet in vision once saw—
When the beams of Messiah shall gladden each clime,
And the isles of the ocean shall wait for his law.

464 *"Come over and help us."* 8. 7.

1 HARK! what mean those lamentations,
Rolling sadly through the sky?

'Tis the cry of heathen nations—
"Come and help us, or we die!"

2 Hear the heathens' sad complaining;
Christians, hear their dying cry;
And, the love of Christ constraining,
Haste to help them, ere they die.

465 *The Missionary.* 6. 4

1 SOUND, sound the truth abroad,
Bear ye the word of God
Through the wide world!
Tell what our Lord has done,
Tell how the day is won,
And from his lofty throne
Satan is hurled.

2 Speed on the wings of love;
Jesus, who reigns above,
Bids us to fly;
They who his message bear,
Should neither doubt nor fear;
He will their friend appear,
He will be nigh.

3 When on the mighty deep,
He will their spirits keep,
Stayed on his word;
When in a foreign land,
No other friend at hand,
Jesus will by them stand,
Jesus their Lord.

4 Ye who, forsaking all,
At your loved Master's call,
Comforts resign—

Soon will your work be done,
Soon will the prize be won,
Brighter than yonder sun
Then shall ye shine.

466 *The Ambassador of the Cross.* 7s

1 GO, ye messengers of God,
Like the beams of morning fly;
Take the wonder-working rod,
Wave the banner-cross on high.

2 Where the lofty minaret
Gleams along the morning skies,
Wave it till the crescent set,
And the "Star of Jacob" rise.

3 Go to many a tropic isle,
In the bosom of the deep,
Where the skies for ever smile,
And th' oppressed for ever weep.

4 O'er the negro's night of care
Pour the living light of heaven;
Chase away the fiend despair,
Bid him hope to be forgiven.

5 Where the golden gates of day
Open on the palmy East,
Wide the bleeding cross display,
Spread the gospel's richest feast.

6 Bear the tidings round the ball,
Visit every soil and sea;
Preach the cross of Christ to all—
Christ, whose love is full and free.

467 *The Messenger of Mercy.* C. M.

GO, messenger of peace and love,
To nations plunged in shades of night;
Like angels sent from fields above,
Be thine to shed celestial light.

Go, to the hungry food impart;
To paths of peace the wanderer guide,
And lead the thirsty, panting heart,
Where streams of living water glide.

3 Go, bid the bright and morning star
From Bethlehem's plains resplendent shine,
And, piercing through the gloom afar,
Shed heavenly light and love divine.

4 To India's various castes proclaim
The gospel's soft but powerful voice;
And at the bless'd Redeemer's name
Let ocean's lonely isles rejoice.

5 From north to south, from east to west,
Messiah yet shall reign supreme;
His name by every tongue confessed,
His praise the universal theme.

6 Then faint not in the day of toil,
When harvest waits the reaper's hand;
Go, gather in the glorious spoil,
And joyous in his presence stand.

468 *Missionaries sent forth.* 8. 7. 4.

1 MEN of God, go, take your stations;
Darkness reigns throughout the earth;

Go—proclaim among the nations
Joyful news of heavenly birth;
Bear the tidings
Of the Saviour's matchless worth.

2 When exposed to fearful dangers,
Jesus will his own defend;
Borne afar 'midst foes and strangers,
Jesus will appear your friend;
He hath promised
To be with you to the end.

469 *Missionaries sent forth.* L. M.

1 YE Christian heroes, go, proclaim
Salvation through Immanuel's name;
To distant climes the tidings bear,
And plant the Rose of Sharon there.

2 He'll shield you with a wall of fire,
With flaming zeal your breasts inspire,
Bid raging winds their fury cease,
And hush the tempests into peace.

3 And when our labors all are o'er,
Then we shall meet to part no more;
Meet, with the blood-bought throng to
And crown our Jesus Lord of all. [fall—

470 *The Missionary Ship.*

1 BLOW fresh, ye favoring breezes—blow,
And round the canvass, like swells of
Ye rolling waters, lie smooth below; [snow:
And over the skies
May no storms arise,
For the sowers go forth to sow.

2 They go, in lands by the heathen trod
To sow the seed of the word of God;
From the root of Jesse to show the rod,
'Mid the desert's gloom,
Till the "Branch" shall bloom
O'er its idols beneath the sod.

3 Shine clear, O sun, on the sparkling sea:
Of Him who nameth himself by thee
The light—life-giving, and pure, and [free—
To the blind to show,
Far away they go;
And with leaves of the healing tree.

4 Speed on, bright ship, in thy grandeur fair;
We give thy helm to an angel's care,
Salvation's heralds unharmed to bear
To their distant goal;
For the priceless soul
Is the jewel which draws them there.

5 From friends and home in their far remove,
Around them hover, thou heavenly Dove:
Descend, sweet Comforter, from above,
To strengthen their bands,
And hold up their hands,
For their labor of faith and love.

6 O thou the beams of whose chambers lie
Below the flood and above the sky,
'Mid shadows of death thy friends be nigh,
Till glory divine
From the cross shall shine,
And death, in its radiance, die.

THE SABBATH.

471 *Saturday Evening.* 11. 8.

1 LET the cares of the week all be banished far hence,
To devotion now let us be given;
May the work of the Sabbath this evening commence,
And our souls be preparing for heaven.

2 Let us search well the bosom, if aught can be found
To hinder the growth of the seed;
And earnestly pray God would clear from the ground
Each rank and injurious weed.

3 And oh that a dew from the Lord may descend,
To rest in abundance on all;
For without it no blessing the word will attend,
Though preached by Apollos or Paul.

4 And may the Redeemer his presence bestow,
Delighting each heart with his love;
And give us to taste, in his dwelling below,
The joys of his temple above.

472 *Saturday Evening.* L. M. 6 lines.

1 SWEET is the last, the parting ray,
That ushers placid evening in;

When, with the still, expiring day,
The Sabbath's peaceful hours begin;
How grateful to the anxious breast
The sacred hours of holy rest!

2 Hushed is the tumult of the day,
And worldly cares and business cease;
While soft the vesper breezes play,
To hymn the glad return of peace:
Delightful season! kindly given
To turn the wandering thoughts to heaven.

3 Oft as this peaceful hour shall come,
Lord, raise my thoughts from earthly things,
And bear them to my heavenly home,
On faith and hope's celestial wings,
Till the last gleam of life decay,
In one eternal Sabbath-day.

473 *The Sabbath welcomed.* S. M.

1 WELCOME, sweet day of rest,
That saw the Lord arise;
Welcome to this reviving breast,
And these rejoicing eyes.

2 The King himself comes near,
And feasts his saints to-day;
Here we may sit, and see him here,
And love and praise and pray.

3 One day amidst the place
Where my dear Lord has been,
Is sweeter than ten thousand days
Of pleasurable sin.

4 My willing soul would stay
  In such a frame as this,
And sit and sing herself away
  To everlasting bliss.

474 *The Sabbath welcomed.* 7s. Double

1 WELCOME, sacred day of rest;
  Sweet repose from worldly care;
Day above all days the best,
  When our souls for heaven prepare;
Day when our Redeemer rose,
  Victor o'er the hosts of hell:
Thus he vanquished all our foes;
  Let our lips his glory tell.

2 Gracious Lord, we love this day,
  When we hear thy holy word,
When we sing thy praise, and pray;
  Earth can no such joys afford.
But a better rest remains—
  Heavenly Sabbaths, happier days,
Rest from sin, and rest from pains,
  Endless joys, and endless praise.

475 *Divine Blessing implored.* H. M

1 WELCOME, delightful morn,
  Thou day of sacred rest;
I hail thy kind return;
  Lord, make these moments bless'd.
From the low train of mortal toys,
I soar to reach immortal joys.

2 Now may the King descend,
And fill his throne of grace;
Thy sceptre, Lord, extend,
While saints address thy face:
Let sinners feel thy quickening word,
And learn to know and fear the Lord.

3 Descend, celestial Dove,
With all thy quickening powers;
Disclose a Saviour's love,
And bless these sacred hours:
Then shall my soul new life obtain,
Nor Sabbaths be indulged in vain.

476 *The Day of Rest.* L. M.

1 ANOTHER six days' work is done;
Another Sabbath is begun:
Return, my soul, enjoy thy rest,
Improve the day thy God has blessed.

2 Come, bless the Lord, whose love assigns
So sweet a rest to wearied minds;
Provides an antepast of heaven,
And gives, this day, the food of seven.

3 Oh that our thoughts and thanks may rise,
As grateful incense, to the skies;
And draw from heaven that sweet repose,
Which none, but he that feels it, knows.

4 This heavenly calm within the breast
Is the dear pledge of glorious rest
Which for the church of God remains—
The end of cares, the end of pains.

5 In holy duties let the day—
In holy pleasures pass away;
How sweet a Sabbath thus to spend,
In hope of one that ne'er shall end!

477 *The Day of Rest.* C. M

1 WHEN the worn spirit wants repose,
And sighs her God to seek,
How sweet to hail the evening's close
That ends the weary week!

2 How sweet to hail the early dawn
That opens on the sight,
When first the soul-reviving morn
Beams its new rays of light!

3 Sweet day; thine hours too soon will cease
Yet, while they gently roll,
Breathe, Holy Spirit, source of peace,
A Sabbath o'er my soul.

4 When will my pilgrimage be done,
The world's long week be o'er,
That Sabbath dawn which needs no sun,
That day which fades no more?

478 *Unfruitfulness lamented.* C. M.

1 LONG have I sat beneath the sound
Of thy salvation, Lord;
But still how weak my faith is found,
And knowledge of thy word!

2 Oft I frequent thy holy place,
And hear almost in vain;

How small a portion of thy grace
  My memory can retain!

3 How cold and feeble is my love,
  How negligent my fear,
How low my hope of joys above,
  How few affections there!

4 Great God, thy sovereign power impart
  To give thy word success;
Write thy salvation in my heart,
  And make me learn thy grace.

5 Show my forgetful feet the way
  That leads to joys on high;
There knowledge grows without decay,
  And love shall never die.

479 *Public Worship.* L. M.

1 LORD, how delightful 'tis to see
  A whole assembly worship thee!
At once they sing—at once they pray—
They hear of heaven, and learn the way.

2 I have been there, and still would go;
'Tis like a heaven enjoyed below:
Not all that careless sinners say,
Shall tempt me to forget this day.

3 Oh write upon my memory, Lord,
The texts and doctrines of thy word;
That I may break thy laws no more,
But love thee better than before.

4 With thoughts of Christ and things divine,
Fill up this foolish heart of mine;

That, finding pardon through his blood,
I may lie down and wake with God.

480 *Detention from the Sanctuary.* C. M.

1 THOUSANDS, O Lord of hosts, to-day
Within thy temple meet;
And tens of thousands throng to pay
Their homage at thy feet.

2 They sing thy deeds, as I have sung,
In sweet and solemn lays;
Were I among them, my glad tongue
Might learn new themes of praise.

3 The dew lies thick on all the ground,
Shall my poor fleece be dry?
The manna rains from heaven around,
Shall I of hunger die?

4 Behold thy prisoner, loose my bands,
If 'tis thy gracious will;
If not, contented in thy hands
Behold thy prisoner still.

5 I may not to thy courts repair,
Yet here thou surely art;
Oh give me here a house of prayer,
Here Sabbath joys impart.

481 *Sabbath Evening.* 6s.

1 THE light of Sabbath eve
Is fading fast away;
What record will it leave,
To crown the closing day?

Is it a Sabbath spent,
  Of fruitless time destroyed;
Or have these moments lent
  Been sacredly employed?

2 How dreadful and how drear,
  In yon dark world of pain,
Will Sabbaths lost appear,
  That cannot come again!
Then, in that hopeless place,
  The wretched soul will say,
"I had those hours of grace,
  But cast them all away."

3 To waste these Sabbath hours
  Oh may we never dare;
Nor taint with thoughts of ours
  These sacred days of prayer:
But may our Sabbaths here
  Inspire our hearts with love;
And prove a foretaste clear
  Of that sweet rest above.

482 *Sabbath Evening.* C. M.

1 FREQUENT the day of God returns,
  To shed its quickening beams,
And yet how slow devotion burns;
  How languid are its flames!

2 Accept our faint attempts to love,
  Our frailties, Lord, forgive;
We would be like thy saints above,
  And praise thee while we live.

3 Increase, O Lord, our faith and hope,
And fit us to ascend
Where the assembly ne'er breaks up,
The Sabbath ne'er shall end;

4 Where we shall breathe in heavenly air,
With heavenly lustre shine;
Before the throne of God appear,
And feast on love divine;

5 Where we in high seraphic strains
Shall all our powers employ;
Delighted range th' ethereal plains,
And take our fill of joy.

483 *The eternal Sabbath.* L. M.

1 THINE earthly Sabbaths, Lord, we love,
But there's a nobler rest above;
To that our longing souls aspire,
With cheerful hope and strong desire.

2 No more fatigue—no more distress,
Nor sin, nor death shall reach the place;
No groans shall mingle with the songs
Which warble from immortal tongues.

3 No rude alarms of raging foes,
No cares to break the long repose;
No midnight shade, no clouded sun,
But sacred, high, eternal noon.

4 O long expected day, begin;
Dawn on these realms of wo and sin:
Fain would we leave this weary road,
And sleep in death, to rest in God.

SPECIAL OCCASIONS.

484

Close of the Year. C. M.

1 AWAKE, ye saints, and raise your eyes,
And raise your voices high;
Awake, and praise that sovereign love
That shows salvation nigh.

2 On all the wings of time it flies;
Each moment brings it near;
Then welcome each declining day,
Welcome each closing year.

3 Not many years their rounds shall run,
Nor many mornings rise,
Ere all its glories stand revealed
To our admiring eyes.

4 Ye wheels of nature, speed your course;
Ye mortal powers, decay;
Fast as ye bring the night of death,
Ye bring eternal day.

485

The New Year. 5. 11.

1 COME, let us anew
Our journey pursue,
Roll round with the year,
And never stand still till the Master ap-
His adorable will [pear:
Let us gladly fulfill,
And our talents improve, [love.
By the patience of hope, and the labor of

2 Our life is a dream;
Our time, as a stream,
Glides swiftly away,
And the fugitive moment refuses to stay:
The arrow is flown—
The moment is gone—
The millennial Year
Rushes on to our view, and Eternity's here!

3 Oh that each, in the day
Of his coming, may say,
"I have fought my way through;
I have finished the work which thou gav'st me to do."
Oh that each from his Lord
May receive the glad word,
"Well and faithfully done!
Enter into my joy, and sit down on my throne."

486 *New Year:—Blessing implored.* C. M.

1 NOW, gracious Lord, thine arm reveal,
And make thy glory known;
Now let us all thy presence feel,
And soften hearts of stone.

2 Help us to venture near thy throne,
And plead a Saviour's name:
For all that we can call our own
Is vanity and shame.

3 From all the guilt of former sin
May mercy set us free;

And let the year we now begin,
Begin and end with thee.

4 Send down thy Spirit from above,
That saints may love thee more,
And sinners now may learn to love,
Who never loved before.

5 And when before thee we appear,
In our eternal home,
May growing numbers worship here,
And praise thee in our room.

487 *New Year:—Goodness of God.* L. M.

1 GREAT God, we sing that mighty hand
By which supported still we stand:
The opening year thy mercy shows,
Let mercy crown it till it close.

2 By day, by night, at home, abroad,
Still we are guarded by our God;
By his incessant bounty fed,
By his unerring counsel led.

3 With grateful hearts the past we own;
The future—all to us unknown—
We to thy guardian care commit,
And, peaceful, leave before thy feet.

4 In scenes exalted or depressed,
Be thou our joy, and thou our rest;
Thy goodness all our hopes shall raise,
Adored through all our changing days.

5 When death shall interrupt our songs,
And seal in silence mortal tongues,

We'll rise to sing thy praise above,
And glory in thy boundless love.

488

Close of the Year. 7s. Double.

1 WHILE, with ceaseless course, the sun
Hasted through the former year,
Many souls their race have run,
Never more to meet us here:
Fixed in an eternal state,
They have done with all below;
We a little longer wait,
But how little—none can know.

2 As the winged arrow flies
Speedily the mark to find;
As the lightning from the skies
Darts, and leaves no trace behind—
Swiftly thus our fleeting days
Bear us down life's rapid stream;
Upward, Lord, our spirits raise,
All below is but a dream.

3 Thanks for mercies past receive;
Pardon of our sins renew;
Teach us henceforth how to live
With eternity in view:
Bless thy word to young and old;
Fill us with a Saviour's love;
And when life's short tale is told,
May we dwell with thee above.

489

Spared another Year. H. M.

1 THE Lord of earth and sky,
The God of ages praise,

Who reigns enthroned on high—
Ancient of endless days;
Who lengthens out our trial here,
And spares us yet another year.

2 Barren and withered trees,
We cumbered long the ground;
No fruit of holiness
On our dead souls was found;
Yet doth he us in mercy spare
Another and another year.

3 When justice bared the sword,
To cut the fig-tree down,
The pity of the Lord
Cried, "Let it still alone."
The Father mild inclined his ear,
And spared us yet another year.

4 Jesus, thy speaking blood
From God obtained the grace;
Who therefore hath bestowed
On us a longer space;
Thou didst in our behalf appear,
And lo, we see another year.

5 Then dig about our root,
Break up our fallow ground,
And let our gracious fruit
To thy great praise abound;
Oh let us all thy praise declare,
And fruit unto perfection bear.

490 *Dedication of a Place of Worship.* H. M.

1 GREAT King of Glory, come,
And with thy favor crown
This temple as thy dome,
This people as thine own:
Beneath this roof oh deign to show
How God can dwell with men below.

2 Here may thine ears attend
Our interceding cries,
And grateful praise ascend,
All-fragrant, to the skies:
Here may thy word melodious sound,
And spread celestial joys around.

3 Here may th' attentive throng
Imbibe thy truth and love,
And converts join the song
Of seraphim above;
And willing crowds surround thy board,
With sacred joy and sweet accord.

4 Here may our unborn sons
And daughters sound thy praise,
And shine like polished stones,
Through long succeeding days:
Here, Lord, display thy saving power,
While temples stand, and men adore.

491 *Dedication of a Place of Worship.* L. M.

1 AND will the great, eternal God
On earth establish his abode?

And will he, from his radiant throne,
Avow our temple for his own?

2 These walls we to thine honor raise,
Long may they echo to thy praise;
And thou, descending, fill the place
With choicest tokens of thy grace.

3 Here let the great Redeemer reign,
With all the glories of his train;
While power divine his word attends,
To conquer foes, and cheer his friends.

4 And in the great decisive day,
When God the nations shall survey,
May it before the world appear
That crowds were born to glory here.

492 *Zion.*—Ps. lxxxvii. 2. L. M. 6 lines.

1 ENTHRONED in light, eternal God,
The highest heaven is thine abode;
Yet thou with us wilt deign to dwell;
Thou lov'st the gates of Zion well.
On Salem's peaceful hill we raise
A sacred temple to thy praise.

2 Here let the pilgrim find the road
That leads the wandering soul to God;
Here sorrow lift her tearful eye,
Allured to brighter scenes on high;
The weary spirit find repose,
And at the cross forget her woes.

3 Our God, our fathers' God, we raise
This sacred temple to thy praise;

Here, safe beneath thy sheltering wing,
Shall contrite souls their offerings bring,
Till called to soar, and join the song
Which swells amid the heavenly throng.

493 *Bethesda.* 6. 5

1 COME to Bethesda's pool,
All ye who need it;
Let not its waters cool
Mantle unheeded:
Here bring each grief and pain;
Here bring each sinful stain;
Here wash the vilest clean—
Come, all who need it.

2 Is there one impotent
On its brink lying?
Is there one penitent,
Bitterly sighing?—
Courage, thou helpless one;
Cheer up thou sorrowing;
Here God's eternal Son
Raiseth the dying.

3 Now, holy Messenger,
Over us bending,
Come, every bosom stir,
Kindly descending;
While in this temple we
Offer our praise to thee,
Here let thy presence be
Aiding, defending.

494

The Pastor welcomed. L. M.

1 WE bid thee welcome, in the name
Of Jesus, our exalted Head;
Come as a servant; so he came,
And we receive thee in his stead.

2 Come as a shepherd; guard and keep
This fold from hell, and earth, and sin;
Nourish the lambs, and feed the sheep,
The wounded heal, the lost bring in.

3 Come as an angel, hence to guide
A band of pilgrims on their way;
That, safely walking at thy side,
We fail not, faint not, turn nor stray.

4 Come as a teacher sent from God,
Charged his whole counsel to declare;
Lift o'er our ranks the prophet's rod,
While we uphold thy hands with prayer.

5 Come as a messenger of peace,
Filled with the Spirit, fired with love:
Live to behold our large increase,
And die to meet us all above.

495

Prayer for the Pastor. L. M.

1 WITH heavenly power, O Lord, defend
Him whom we now to thee commend;
His person bless, his soul secure,
And make him to the end endure.

2 Gird him with all-sufficient grace;
Direct his feet in paths of peace;

Thy truth and faithfulness fulfill,
And help him to obey thy will.

3 Before him thy protection send;
Oh love him, save him to the end;
Nor let him, as thy pilgrim, rove
Without the convoy of thy love.

4 Enlarge, inflame, and fill his heart;
In him thy mighty power exert;
That thousands yet unborn may praise
The wonders of redeeming grace

496 *Watchfulness.*—Luke xii. 37. S. M

1 YE servants of the Lord,
Each in his office wait,
Observant of his heavenly word,
And watchful at his gate.

2 Let all your lamps be bright,
And trim the golden flame:
Gird up your loins as in his sight,
For awful is his name.

3 Watch—'tis your Lord's command;
And while we speak, he's near;
Mark the first signal of his hand,
And ready all appear.

4 Oh happy servant he
In such a posture found!
He shall his Lord with rapture see,
And be with honor crowned.

497 *Zion's Watchmen.*—Heb. xiii. 17. C. M.

1 LET Zion's watchmen all awake,
And take th' alarm they give:
Now let them from the mouth of God
Their solemn charge receive.

2 'Tis not a cause of small import
The pastor's care demands;
But what might fill an angel's heart,
And filled a Saviour's hands.

3 They watch for souls, for which the Lord
Did heavenly bliss forego;
For souls which must for ever live
In raptures or in wo.

4 May they that Jesus whom they preach,
Their own Redeemer see;
Lord, watch thou daily o'er their souls,
That they may watch for thee.

498 *Preachers sent forth.* S. M.

1 YE messengers of Christ,
His sovereign voice obey:
Arise, and follow where he leads,
And peace attend your way.

2 The Master whom you serve
Will needful strength bestow;
Depending on his promised aid,
With sacred courage go.

3 Go, spread a Saviour's fame,
And tell his matchless grace;

Redemption by his blood proclaim
To Adam's guilty race.

4 Mountains shall sink to plains,
And hell in vain oppose:
The cause is God's, and must prevail,
In spite of all his foes.

499 *Bearers of glad Tidings.*—Isa. lii. 7. S. M.

1 HOW beauteous are their feet
Who stand on Zion's hill;
Who bring salvation on their tongues,
And words of peace reveal!

2 How charming is their voice!
How sweet the tidings are!
"Zion, behold thy Saviour—King,
He reigns and triumphs here."

3 How happy are our ears,
That hear this joyful sound
Which kings and prophets waited for,
And sought, but never found!

4 How blessed are our eyes,
That see this heavenly light!
Prophets and kings desired it long,
But died without the sight.

5 The watchmen join their voice,
And tuneful notes employ;
Jerusalem breaks forth in songs,
And deserts learn the joy.

6 The Lord makes bare his arm,
Through all the earth abroad;

Let every nation now behold
  Their Saviour and their God.

500 *"This do in remembrance of me."* C. M.

1 ACCORDING to thy gracious word,
  In meek humility,
This will I do, my dying Lord,
  I will remember thee.

2 Thy body, broken for my sake,
  My bread from heaven shall be;
Thy testamental cup I take,
  And thus remember thee.

3 Gethsemane can I forget?
  Or there thy conflict see,
Thine agony and bloody sweat,
  And not remember thee?

4 When to the cross I turn my eyes,
  And rest on Calvary,
O Lamb of God, my sacrifice,
  I must remember thee—

5 Remember thee and all thy pains,
  And all thy love to me;
Yea, while a breath, a pulse remains,
  Will I remember thee.

6 And when these failing lips grow dumb,
  And mind and memory flee,
When thou shalt in thy kingdom come,
  Jesus, remember me.

501 *The Table of the Lord.*—Luke xiv. 23. C. M.

1 HOW sweet and awful is the place
With Christ within the doors,
While everlasting love displays
The choicest of her stores.

2 While all our hearts, in praise and song,
Join to admire the feast,
Each of us cries, with thankful tongue,
"Lord, why was I a guest?"

3 "Why was I made to hear thy voice,
And enter while there's room—
When thousands make a wretched choice,
And rather starve than come?"

4 'Twas the same love that spread the feast,
That sweetly forced us in;
Else we had still refused to taste,
And perished in our sin.

5 Pity the nations, O our God,
Constrain the earth to come;
Send thy victorious word abroad,
And bring the strangers home.

6 We long to see thy churches full,
That all the chosen race
May, with one voice and heart and soul,
Sing thy redeeming grace.

502 *Christ crucified.* L. M.

1 WHEN on the cross my Lord I see,
Bleeding to death for wretched me,

Satan and sin no more can move,
For I am all transformed to love.

2 Come, sinners, view the Lamb of God,
Wounded, and dead, and bathed in blood!
Behold his side, and venture near;
The well of endless life is here.

3 Here I forget my cares and pains;
I drink; yet still my thirst remains;
Only the fountain-head above
Can satisfy the thirst of love.

4 Oh that I thus could always feel!
Lord, more and more thy love reveal;
Then my glad tongue shall loud proclaim
The grace and glory of thy name.

503 *The Memorials of our absent Lord.* L. M.

1 JESUS is gone above the skies,
Where our weak senses reach him not;
And carnal objects court our eyes
To thrust our Saviour from our thought.

2 He knows what wandering hearts we have,
Apt to forget his lovely face;
And to refresh our minds he gave
These kind memorials of his grace.

3 Let sinful sweets be all forgot,
And earth grow less in our esteem;
Christ and his love fill every thought,
And faith and hope be fixed on him.

4 While he is absent from our sight,
'Tis to prepare our souls a place,

That we may dwell in heavenly light,
And live for ever near his face.

504 *Redeeming Grace.* C. M.

1 LORD, at thy table we behold
The wonders of thy grace;
But most of all admire that we
Should find a welcome place—

2 We who are all defiled with sin,
And rebels to our God;
We who have crucified thy Son,
And trampled on his blood!

3 What strange, surprising grace is this,
That we, so lost, have room!
Jesus our weary souls invites,
And freely bids us come.

4 Ye saints below, and hosts of heaven,
Join all your sacred powers:
No theme is like redeeming love;
No Saviour is like ours.

505 *The amazing Love of Christ.* L. M

1 COME, let me love, or is my mind
Hardened to stone, or froze to ice?
I see the blessed Fair One bend,
And stoop t' embrace me from the skies!

2 Oh, 'tis a thought would melt a rock,
And make a heart of iron move,
That those sweet lips, that heavenly look,
Should seek and wish a mortal love!

3 I was a traitor doomed to fire,
Bound to sustain eternal pains;
He flew on wings of strong desire,
Assumed my guilt, and took my chains.

4 Infinite grace! almighty charms!
Stand in amaze, ye rolling skies!
Jesus, the God, extends his arms,
Hangs on the cross of love, and dies.

5 Did pity ever stoop so low,
Dressed in divinity and blood?
Was ever rebel courted so,
In groans of an expiring God?

6 Sure I must love; or are my ears
Still deaf, nor will my passions move?
Lord, melt this stubborn heart to tears;
This heart shall yield to death or love.

506 "*Suffer little children,*" &c.—Mark x. 14. C. M.

1 SEE Israel's gentle Shepherd stand,
With all-engaging charms;
Hark, how he calls the tender lambs,
And folds them in his arms.

2 "Permit them to approach," he cries,
"Nor scorn their humble name;
For 'twas to bless such souls as these
The Lord of angels came."

3 We bring them, Lord, in thankful hands,
And yield them up to thee;
Joyful that we ourselves are thine,
Thine let our offspring be.

4 If orphans they are left behind,
Thy guardian care we trust;
That care shall heal our bleeding hearts,
If weeping o'er their dust.

507 *The Promise to Abraham.* C. M.

1 HOW large the promise, how divine,
To Abra'm and his seed—
"I'll be a God to thee and thine,
Supplying all their need."

2 The words of his extensive love
From age to age endure;
The angel of the covenant proves,
And seals the blessings sure.

3 Jesus the ancient faith confirms,
To our great fathers given;
He takes young children to his arms,
And calls them heirs of heaven.

4 Our God, how faithful are his ways!
His love endures the same;
Nor from the promise of his grace
Blots out the children's name.

508 *Kindness of the Saviour.* L. M.

1 WITH thankful hearts our songs we raise,
To celebrate the Saviour's praise;
Yet who but saints in heaven above,
Can tell the riches of his love?

2 His love, with gentle accents, sheds
A blessing on our infants' heads;
Bids us for infants seek his face,
And ask for them renewing grace.

3 He, the good Shepherd, kindly leads
The wand'rer, and the hungry feeds;
Deigns in his arms the lambs to bear,
And makes them his peculiar care.

4 Jesus, to thy protecting wing
Our helpless little ones we bring;
Oh grant them grace and strength that they
May find and keep the heavenward way.

509 *Blessings implored.* C. M.

1 OUR children, Lord, in faith and prayer,
We now devote to thee;
Let them thy covenant mercies share,
And thy salvation see.

2 In early days their hearts secure
From worldly snares, we pray;
And let them to the end endure
In every righteous way.

3 Grant us before them, Lord, to live
In holy faith and fear;
And then to heaven our souls remove,
And bring our children there.

510 *Public Fast.* C. M.

1 SEE, gracious God, before thy throne
Thy mourning people bend;

'Tis on thy sovereign grace alone
Our humble hopes depend.

2 Tremendous judgments from thy hand
Thy dreadful power display:
Yet mercy spares this guilty land,
And still we live to pray.

3 What numerous crimes increasing rise,
Through this apostate land!
What land so favored of the skies,
Yet thoughtless of thy hand?

4 How changed, alas, are truths divine,
For error, guilt, and shame!
What impious numbers, bold in sin,
Disgrace the Christian name!

5 Oh, turn us, turn us, mighty Lord,
By thy resistless grace:
Then shall our hearts obey thy word,
And humbly seek thy face.

511 *Prayer for Rain.* C. M

1 NOW may the Lord of earth and skies
Regard us when we call;
'Tis he who bids the vapors rise,
And showers abundant fall.

2 On thee, our God, we all depend
For life, and health, and food;
Oh make refreshing showers descend,
And crown the year with good.

3 Let grace come down, like copious rain,
On Zion's drooping field;

So shall our souls revive again,
And fruit abundant yield.

4 Then smiling nature shall express
Her mighty Maker's praise;
And we, the children of thy grace,
Join her harmonious lays.

512 *Tract Distribution.* 8. 7. 4.

1 LORD of glory, who didst honor
David's humble sling and stone,
Ancient Israel to deliver—
Now as weak an effort own;
Bless the labor
Which our feeble hands have done.

2 'Tis the gospel seed we're sowing
On the good and fallow ground;
Bearing, weeping, without knowing
Which shall fail and which abound:
Holy Spirit,
Let it verdant spring around.

3 When the harvest-time is ended,
When the Master counts our sheaves,
Oh let those by us attended,
Be as numerous as the leaves
Which we scatter,
And a dying world receives.

513 *Providential Deliverance.* C. M.

1 JUST snatched from danger and from
My thankful voice I raise; [death,

And fain emit my feeble breath
  In grateful hymns of praise.

2 As on destruction's brink aghast
  I stood with panting breath,
And thought that moment was my last,
  And looked for instant death;

3 Just in the moment of despair
  I raised my fainting cry;
My Saviour heard the broken prayer,
  His hand unseen was nigh.

4 Oh, blessings on his name, and praise,
  Who saved me from above;
Be my spared life and rescued days
  Devoted to his love.

514 *Temperance Hymn.* S. M.

1 MOURN for the thousands slain,
  The youthful and the strong;
Mourn for the wine-cup's fatal reign,
  And the deluded throng.

2 Mourn for the tarnished gem—
  For Reason's light divine,
Quenched from the soul's bright diadem,
  Where God had bid it shine.

3 Mourn for the ruined soul—
  Eternal life and light
Lost by the fiery, maddening bowl,
  And turned to hopeless night.

4 Mourn for the lost—but call,
  Call to the strong, the free;

Rouse them to shun that dreadful fall,
And to the refuge flee.

5 Mourn for the lost—but pray,
Pray to our God above,
To break the fell destroyer's sway,
And show his saving love.

515 *The Maternal Prayer-meeting.* C. M.

1 WE gather at the mercy-seat,
Oppressed with anxious care,
And at our great Redeemer's feet,
We pour the mother's prayer.

2 A feeble band, to him we fly,
And in our weakness dare
Address him in the mother's sigh,
And in the mother's prayer.

3 In the rich blessings of his love
He calls the child to share;
And he will listen from above,
And hear the mother's prayer.

4 Now on our burdened hearts, O Lord,
Our children we would bear;
Fulfill the promise of thy word,
And grant the mother's prayer.

5 "Save, Lord," we will not cease to cry,
Nor of thy grace despair;
For thou wilt not the gift deny,
Nor spurn the mother's prayer.

516 *Marriage.* C. M.

1 SINCE Jesus freely did appear
To grace a marriage feast,
O Lord, we ask thy presence here,
To make a wedding guest.

2 Upon the bridal pair look down,
Who now have plighted hands;
Their union with thy favor crown,
And bless the nuptial bands.

3 With gifts of grace their hearts endow,
Of all rich dowries best;
Their substance bless, and peace bestow,
To sweeten all the rest.

4 In purest love their souls unite,
That they, with Christian care,
May make domestic burdens light,
By taking mutual share.

5 On every soul assembled here,
Oh make thy face to shine;
Thy goodness more our hearts can cheer,
Than richest food or wine.

517 *The Sailor's Friend.* C. M.

1 OF old did Jesus condescend
To calm the raging sea?
Yes, he was then the Sailor's Friend,
And such he still would be.

2 Not to sustain our mortal breath
We raise the earnest cry;

Lord, save our precious souls from death,
And make us fit to die.

3 Then blow, ye winds, ye surges roar;
'Twill not our souls appal,
Though waves and billows pass us o'er,
And deep to deep should call.

4 But oh, without that blessed hope,
Without a Saviour near,
What desperate courage bears us up;
What madness not to fear!

5 Jesus, on thee our hopes we cast,
No more thy wrath defy;
Thou art the anchor sure and fast;
On thee our souls rely.

6 Soon shall the sea give up its dead;
And should our graves be there,
With joy we'll quit our watery bed,
To meet thee in the air.

518 *A Propitious Gale desired.* L. M.

1 AT anchor laid, remote from home,
Toiling, I cry, "Sweet Spirit come;
Celestial breeze, no longer stay,
But swell my sails, and speed my way.

2 "Fain would I mount, fain would I glow,
And loose my cable from below;
But I can only spread my sail— [gale."
Thou, thou must breathe th' auspicious

519 *The aged Christian's Prayer.*—Ps. lxxi. 9. C. M.

1 GOD of my childhood and my youth,
The guide of all my days,
I have declared thy heavenly truth,
And told thy wondrous ways.

2 Wilt thou forsake my hoary hairs,
And leave my fainting heart?
Who shall sustain my sinking years,
If God, my strength, depart?

3 Let me thy power and truth proclaim
To the surviving age,
And leave the savor of thy name
When I shall quit the stage.

4 The land of silence and of death
Attends my next remove;
Oh may these poor remains of breath
Teach the wide world thy love.

520 *Spring.* C. M.

1 THE icy chains that bound the earth
Are now dissolved and gone;
Waked by the sun, the blooming spring
Puts her new livery on.

2 My soul, in every scene admire
The wisdom and the power;
Behold thy God in every plant,
In every opening flower.

3 Yet in his word the God of grace
More clearly writes his name;

The wonders of redeeming love
My noblest song shall claim.

4 With warmest beams, thou God of grace,
Shine on this heart of mine,
Turn thou my winter into spring,
And be the glory thine.

521 *The Harvest.* L. M.

1 GREAT God, as seasons disappear,
And changes mark the rolling year,
Thy favor still has crowned our days,
And we would celebrate thy praise.

2 The harvest-song would we repeat;
Thou givest us the finest wheat:
The joys of harvest we have known;
The praise, O Lord, is all thine own.

3 Another harvest comes apace;
Prepare our spirits by thy grace,
That we may calmly meet the blow
The sickle gives to lay us low.

4 That when the angel-reapers come,
To gather sheaves to thy bless'd home,
Our spirits may be borne on high,
To thy safe garner in the sky.

522 *Autumn.*—Isa. lxiv. 6. 8. 7.

1 SEE the leaves around us falling,
Dry and withered to the ground;
Thus to thoughtless mortals calling,
In a sad and solemn sound:

2 "Ye on length of days presuming,
Think how soon our course has fled;
We were lately fresh and blooming,
Now are withered, dry, and dead.

3 "Cease presumptuous hopes to cherish,
Prize the seasons as they fly;
Like the leaves you rise and flourish,
Like the leaves must droop and die.

4 "But to those in Jesus planted
By a true and living faith,
Shall unfading spring be granted,
And a triumph over death."

523 *National Thanksgiving.* L. M

1 PRAISE to the Lord, who bows his ear
Propitious to his people's prayer;
And though deliverance long delay,
Answers in his well-chosen day.

2 Lord, may thy goodness cause our land,
Preserved by thine almighty hand,
The tribute of its love to bring
To thee, our Saviour and our King.

3 So shall each public temple raise
A song of triumph to thy praise;
And every peaceful private home
To thee a temple shall become.

4 Still be it our supreme delight
To walk as in thine awful sight;
And in thy precepts and thy fear,
Till life's last hour, to persevere.

524 *Drought.* C. M.

1 THE sun, that minister of love,
Who from the naked ground
Calls forth the hidden scenes to birth,
And spreads their beauties round;

2 At the dread order of his God,
Now darts destructive fires;
Hills, plains, and vales are parched with
And blooming life expires. [drought,

3 Like burnished brass, the heaven around
In angry terror burns,
While the earth lies a joyless waste,
And into iron turns.

4 Oh pity, Lord, our deep distress,
Nor with our land contend;
Bid the avenging skies relent,
And showers of mercy send.

CHILDHOOD AND YOUTH.

525 *Invitation to the Young.*—Prov. viii. 17. C. M.

1 YE hearts with youthful vigor warm,
In smiling crowds draw near,
And turn from every mortal charm,
A Saviour's voice to hear.

2 He, Lord of all the worlds on high,
Stoops to converse with you;

And lays his radiant glories by,
Your friendship to pursue.

3 "The soul that longs to see my face,
Is sure my love to gain;
And those that early seek my grace,
Shall never seek in vain."

4 What object, Lord, my soul should move,
If once compared with thee?
What beauty should command my love,
Like what in Christ I see?

5 Away—ye false, delusive toys,
Vain tempters of the mind!
'Tis here I fix my lasting choice,
And here true bliss I find.

526 *Blessedness of early Piety.* C. M.

1 HAPPY the child whose early years
Receive instruction well;
Who hates the sinner's path, and fears
The road that leads to hell.

2 When we devote our youth to God,
'Tis pleasing in his eyes;
A flower, when offered in the bud,
Is no vain sacrifice.

3 'Twill save us from a thousand snares
To mind religion young:
Grace will preserve our following years,
And make our virtues strong.

4 To thee, Almighty God, to thee
Our childhood we resign;

'Twill please us to look back and see
That our whole lives were thine.

5 Let the sweet work of prayer and praise
Employ our youngest breath:
Thus we're prepared for longer days,
Or fit for early death.

527 *Jesus the Child's Pattern.* 8. 7

1 JESUS Christ, my Lord and Saviour,
Once became a child like me;
Oh that in my whole behavior
He my pattern still might be.

2 All my nature is unholy,
Pride and passion dwell within;
But the Lord was meek and lowly,
And was never known to sin.

3 Lord, assist a feeble creature,
Guide me by thy word of truth;
Condescend to be my teacher,
Through my childhood and my youth.

4 Often shall I be forgetful
Of the lessons thou hast taught,
Idle, passionate, and fretful,
Or indulging foolish thought.

5 Then permit me not to harden
In my sin, and be content;
But bestow a gracious pardon,
And assist me to repent.

528 *The sanctified Child.* C. M.

1 BY cool Siloam's shady rill
How sweet the lily grows;
How sweet the breath, beneath the hill,
Of Sharon's dewy rose.

2 And such the child, whose early feet
The paths of peace have trod;
Whose secret heart, with influence sweet,
Is upward drawn to God.

3 O thou whose infancy was found
With heavenly rays to shine,
Whose years, with changeless virtue [crowned,
Were all alike divine;

4 Dependent on thy bounteous breath,
We seek thy grace alone,
In childhood, manhood, and in death,
To keep us still thine own.

529 *The Power and Greatness of God.* C. M.

1 HOW glorious is our heavenly King,
Who reigns above the sky!
How shall a child presume to sing
His dreadful majesty?

2 How great his power is, none can tell,
Nor think how large his grace;
Not men below, nor saints that dwell
On high, before his face.

3 Not angels that stand round the Lord
Can search his secret will;

But they perform his holy word,
And sing his praises still.

4 Then let me join this heavenly train,
And my first offerings bring;
Th' eternal God will not disdain
To hear an infant sing.

5 My heart resolves, my tongue obeys,
And angels shall rejoice,
To hear their mighty Maker's praise
Sound from a feeble voice.

530 *The Hosannas of Children.* 7.6. Iambic

1 WHEN, his salvation bringing,
To Zion Jesus came,
The children all stood singing
Hosanna to his name.
Nor did their zeal offend him;
But as he rode along,
He let them still attend him,
And smiled to hear their song.

2 And since the Lord retaineth
His love for children still,
Though now as King he reigneth
On Zion's heavenly hill,
We'll flock around his banner,
Who sits upon the throne;
And cry aloud, "Hosanna
To David's royal Son."

3 For, should we fail proclaiming
Our great Redeemer's praise,

The stones, our silence shaming,
Might well hosannas raise.
But shall we only render
The tribute of our words?
No, while our hearts are tender,
They too shall be the Lord's.

531 *"Thou God seest me."* C. M.

1 ALMIGHTY God, thy piercing eye
Strikes through the shades of night,
And our most secret actions lie
All open to thy sight.

2 There's not a sin that we commit,
Nor wicked word we say,
But in thy dreadful book 'tis writ,
Against the judgment day.

3 Lord, at thy feet ashamed I lie,
Upward I dare not look;
Pardon my sins, or else I die—
Oh blot them from thy book.

4 Remember all the dying pains
That my Redeemer felt,
And let his blood wash out my stains,
And answer for my guilt.

5 Oh may I now for ever fear
T' indulge a sinful thought;
Since the great God can see, and hear,
And writes down every fault.

532 *Prayer of a Child.*

1 O JESUS, delight of my soul,
My Saviour, my Shepherd divine;

I yield to thy blessed control;
My body and spirit are thine.

2 The love I can never deserve,
That bids me be happy in thee;
My God and my King I will serve,
Whose favor is heaven to me.

3 How can I thy goodness repay,
By nature so weak and defiled?
Myself I have given away;
Oh call me thy own little child.

4 And art thou my Father above?
Will Jesus abide in my heart?
Oh bind me so fast with thy love,
That I never from thee shall depart.

533 *The Praises of Children.* 7s

1 GLORY to the Father give,
God in whom we move and live:
Children's prayers he deigns to hear;
Children's songs delight his ear.

2 Glory to the Son we bring,
Christ our Prophet, Priest and King;
Children, raise your sweetest strain
To the Lamb, for he was slain.

3 Glory to the Holy Ghost;
Be this day a Pentecost;
Children's minds may he inspire,
Touch their lips with holy fire.

4 Glory in the highest be
To the blessed Trinity,

For the gospel from above,
For the word, that "God is love."

534 *The Sabbath-School.* C. M

1 THERE is a glorious world of light,
Above the starry sky,
Where saints departed, clothed in white,
Adore the Lord most high.

2 And hark, amid the sacred songs
Those heavenly voices raise,
Ten thousand thousand infant tongues
Unite in perfect praise.

3 Those are the hymns that we shall know,
If Jesus we obey;
That is the place where we shall go,
If found in wisdom's way.

4 This is the joy we ought to seek,
And make our chief concern;
For this we come from week to week,
To read, and hear, and learn.

5 Soon will our earthly race be run,
Our mortal frame decay;
Children and teachers, one by one,
Must die, and pass away.

6 Great God, impress the serious thought,
This day, on every breast;
That both the teachers and the taught
May enter to thy rest.

535 *The Sabbath-School.* L. M.

1 HOSANNAS by an infant train
  Were once within the temple sung,
While Jesus listened to the strain,
  And poured his blessing on the throng.

2 Lord, may thy Spirit seal the truth
  On every heart, with power divine;
Renew and sanctify these youth,
  And make these children wholly thine.

3 May we our humble voices raise
  Responsive to the heavenly host,
In strains of everlasting praise
  To Father, Son, and Holy Ghost.

536 *The Sabbath-School Teacher.* C. M.

1 BLESS'D work, the youthful mind to
  And turn the rising race [win,
From the deceitful paths of sin,
  To seek redeeming grace.

2 Children our kind protection claim;
  And God will well approve,
When infants learn to lisp his name,
  And their Redeemer love.

3 Be ours the bliss in wisdom's way
  To guide untutored youth,
And show the mind which went astray,
  The way, the life, the truth.

4 Thy Spirit, Father, on us shed,
And bless this good design;
The honors of thy name be spread,
And all the glory thine.

DEATH.

537 *Uncertainty of Life* C. M

1 BENEATH our feet and o'er our head
Is equal warning given:
Beneath us lie the countless dead,
Above us is the heaven.

2 Death rides on every passing breeze,
And lurks in every flower;
Each season has its own disease,
Its peril every hour.

3 Our eyes have seen the rosy light
Of youth's soft cheek decay,
And fate descend in sudden night
On manhood's middle day.

4 Our eyes have seen the steps of age
Halt feebly to the tomb;
And yet shall earth our hearts engage,
And dreams of days to come?

5 Turn, mortal, turn; thy danger know:
Where'er thy foot can tread,
The earth rings hollow from below,
And warns thee of her dead.

6 Turn, Christian, turn; thy soul apply
To truths divinely given:
The forms which underneath thee lie,
Shall live, for hell or heaven.

538 *Time fleeting.* 7. 6

1 TIME is winging us away
To our eternal home;
Life is but a winter's day,
A journey to the tomb:
Youth and vigor soon will flee,
Blooming beauty lose its charms;
All that's mortal soon will be
Enclosed in death's cold arms.

2 Time is winging us away
To our eternal home;
Life is but a winter's day,
A journey to the tomb:
But the Christian shall enjoy
Health and beauty soon above;
Far beyond the world's alloy,
Secure in Jesus' love.

539 *Thoughts of Death.* C. M.

1 MY soul, come, meditate the day,
And think how near it stands,
When thou must quit this house of clay,
And fly to unknown lands.

2 And you, my eyes, look down and view
The hollow gaping tomb;

This gloomy prison waits for you,
  Whene'er the summons come.

3 Oh, could we die with those that die,
  And place us in their stead,
Then would our spirits learn to fly,
  And converse with the dead.

4 Then should we see the saints above,
  In their own glorious forms,
And wonder why our souls should love
  To dwell with mortal worms.

5 We should almost forsake our clay
  Before the summons come,
And pray, and wish our souls away
  To their eternal home.

540 *Death and the Judgment.* S. M.

1 AND am I born to die—
  To lay this body down?
And must my trembling spirit fly
  Into a world unknown?

2 Soon as from earth I go,
  What scenes will burst on me!
Eternal happiness or wo
  Must then my portion be!

3 Waked by the trumpet's sound,
  I from my grave shall rise,
And see the Judge with glory crowned,
  And see the flaming skies!

4 Shall I then leave my tomb
  With triumph, or regret?

A fearful, or a joyful doom,
A curse, or blessing meet?

5 Will angel bands convey
Their brother to the bar?
Or devils drag my soul away,
To meet its sentence there?

6 O thou who did'st atone,
Dispel my anxious fear;
And when thou comest on thy throne,
May I with joy appear.

541 "*I would not live alway.*"—Job vii. 16. 11s.

1 I WOULD not live alway; I ask not to stay
Where storm after storm rises dark o'er the way:
The few fleeting mornings that dawn on us here
Are enough for life's sorrows—enough for its cheer.

2 I would not live alway; no, welcome the tomb;
Since Jesus hath lain there, I dread not its gloom;
There sweet be my rest, till he bid me arise,
To hail him in triumph descending the skies.

3 Who, who would live alway, away from
his God,
Away from yon heaven, that blissful abode,
Where rivers of pleasure flow o'er the
bright plains,
And the noontide of glory eternally reigns?

4 Where the saints of all ages in harmony
meet,
Their Saviour and brethren transported to
greet;
While anthems of rapture unceasingly roll,
And the smile of the Lord is the feast of
the soul.

542 *Reflections after Sickness.* S M

1 JUST o'er the grave I hung—
No pardon met my eyes,
As blessings never greet the slain,
And hope shall never rise.

2 I saw, beyond the tomb,
The awful Judge appear,
Prepared to scan, with strict account,
My blessings wasted here.

3 How mourned my sinking soul
The Sabbath's hours divine,
The day of grace, that precious day,
Consumed in sense and sin.

4 The work—the mighty work
Of life—so long delayed!

Repentance yet to be begun,
 Upon a dying bed!

5 Ye sinners, fear the Lord,
 While yet 'tis called to-day;
Soon will the awful voice of death
 Command your souls away.

6 Soon will the harvest close,
 The summer soon be o'er;
And soon your injured, angry God
 Will hear your prayers no more.

543 *The Grave.* 8. 4.

1 THERE is a calm for those who weep,
 A rest for weary pilgrims found:
They softly lie, and sweetly sleep,
 Low in the ground.

2 The storm that wrecks the winter sky
No more disturbs their deep repose,
Than summer evening's latest sigh,
 That shuts the rose.

3 Thou traveller in the vale of tears,
To realms of everlasting light,
Through time's dark wilderness of years,
 Pursue thy flight.

4 Whate'er thy lot—where'er thou be—
Confess thy folly, kiss the rod;
And in thy chastening sorrows see
 The hand of God.

5 Though long of winds and waves the sport,
Condemned in wretchedness to roam,
Thou soon shalt reach a sheltering port,
A quiet home.

544 *The tolling Bell.* L. M.

1 OFT as the bell, with solemn toll,
Speaks the departure of a soul,
Let each one ask himself, "Am I
Prepared, should I be called to die?"

2 Only this frail and fleeting breath
Preserves me from the jaws of death;
Soon as it fails, at once I'm gone,
And plunged into a world unknown.

3 Lord Jesus, help me now to flee,
And seek my hope alone in thee;
Apply thy blood, thy Spirit give,
Subdue my sins, and let me live.

4 Then when the solemn bell I hear,
If saved from guilt, I need not fear;
Nor would the thought distressing be—
Perhaps it next may toll for me.

545 *Consolations in Sickness.* C. M.

1 WHEN languor and disease invade
This trembling house of clay,
'Tis sweet to look beyond my pains,
And long to fly away.

2 Sweet to look inward, and attend
The whispers of his love;

Sweet to look upward to the place
 Where Jesus pleads above.

3 Sweet to reflect how grace divine
 My sins on Jesus laid;
Sweet to remember that his blood
 My debt of suffering paid.

4 Sweet on his faithfulness to rest,
 Whose love can never end;
Sweet on his covenant of grace
 For all things to depend.

5 Sweet, in the confidence of faith,
 To trust his firm decrees;
Sweet to lie passive in his hands,
 And know no will but his.

6 Sweet to rejoice in lively hope
 That, when my change shall come,
Angels will hover round my bed,
 And waft my spirit home.

546 *Hope in Affliction.* C. M.

1 WHEN musing sorrow weeps the past,
 And mourns the present pain,
How sweet to think of peace at last,
 And feel that death is gain.

2 'Tis not that murmuring thoughts arise,
 And dread a Father's will;
'Tis not that meek submission flies,
 And would not suffer still;

3 It is that heaven-taught faith surveys
 The path that leads to light;

And longs her eagle-plumes to raise,
And lose herself in sight.

4 It is that hope with ardor glows
To see Him face to face,
Whose dying love no language knows
Sufficient art to trace.

5 It is that harrassed conscience feels
The pangs of struggling sin;
And sees, though far, the hand that heals,
And ends the strife within.

6 Oh let me wing my hallowed flight
From earth-born wo and care;
And soar above these clouds of night,
My Saviour's bliss to share.

547 *The Saviour's Presence in Death.* L. M

1 WHY should we start and fear to die?
What timorous worms we mortals are!
Death is the gate of endless joy,
And yet we dread to enter there.

2 The pains, the groans, the dying strife,
Fright our approaching souls away;
Still we shrink back again to life,
Fond of our prison and our clay.

3 Oh, if my Lord would come and meet,
My soul would stretch her wings in haste,
Fly fearless through death's iron gate,
Nor feel the terrors as she passed.

4 Jesus can make a dying bed
Feel soft as downy pillows are;

While on his breast I lean my head,
And breathe my life out sweetly there.

548 *The Fear of Death subdued.* C. M.

1 WHEN downward to the darksome tomb
I thoughtful turn my eyes,
Frail nature trembles at the gloom,
And anxious fears arise.

2 Why shrinks my soul?—in death's embrace
Once Jesus captive slept;
And angels, hovering o'er the place,
His lowly pillow kept.

3 Thus shall they guard my sleeping dust,
And, as the Saviour rose,
The grave again shall yield her trust,
And end my deep repose.

4 My Lord, before to glory gone,
Shall bid me come away;
And calm and bright shall break the dawn
Of heaven's eternal day.

5 Then let my faith each fear dispel,
And gild with light the grave;
To him my loftiest praises swell,
Who died from death to save.

549 *Support in Death.* 7. 4.

1 WHEN the vale of death appears,
Faint and cold this mortal clay,
Kind Forerunner, soothe my fears,

Light me through the darksome way;
Break the shadows,
Usher in eternal day.

2 Starting from this dying state,
Upward bid my soul aspire,
Open thou the crystal gate,
To thy praise attune my lyre:
Dwell for ever—
Dwell on each immortal wire.

3 When the mighty trumpet blown,
Shall the judgment dawn proclaim,
From the central, burning throne,
Mid creation's final flame,
With the ransomed,
Judge and Saviour, own my name.

550 *Triumph over Death.* C. M.

1 OH for an overcoming faith,
To cheer my dying hours;
To triumph o'er the monster death,
And all his frightful powers.

2 Joyful, with all the strength I have,
My quivering lips should sing—
"Where is thy boasted victory, grave?
And where the monster's sting?"

3 If sin be pardoned, I'm secure;
Death has no sting beside:
The law gives sin its damning power,
But Christ, my ransom, died.

4 Now to the God of victory
Immortal thanks be paid,
Who makes us conquerors, while we die,
Through Christ our living head.

551 *Support in Death.* C. M.

1 WHEN bending o'er the brink of life
My trembling soul shall stand,
Waiting to pass death's awful flood,
Great God, at thy command;

2 When every long-loved scene of life
Stands ready to depart;
When the last sigh that shakes the frame
Shall rend this bursting heart;

3 O thou great source of joy supreme,
Whose arm alone can save,
Dispel the darkness that surrounds
The entrance to the grave.

4 Lay thy supporting, gentle hand,
Beneath my sinking head;
And with a ray of love divine
Illume my dying bed.

5 Leaning on thy dear faithful breast,
May I resign my breath;
And in thy fond embraces lose
The bitterness of death.

552 *Rejoicing in view of Death.* C. M.

1 AND let this feeble body fail,
And let it droop and die;

My soul shall quit this mournful vale,
  And soar to worlds on high;

2 Shall join the disembodied saints,
  And find its long-sought rest—
That only bliss for which it pants—
  In my Redeemer's breast.

3 In hope of that immortal crown,
  I now the cross sustain;
And gladly wander up and down,
  And smile at toil and pain.

4 Oh, what are all my sufferings here,
  If, Lord, thou count me meet
With that enraptured host t' appear,
  And worship at thy feet?

5 Give joy or grief—give ease or pain,
  Take life or friends away,
But let me find them all again
  In that eternal day.

553 *Hope of the Resurrection.* S. M.

1 AND must this body die;
  This mortal frame decay?
And must these active limbs of mine
  Lie mouldering in the clay?

2 God, my Redeemer, lives,
  And often from the skies
Looks down, and watches all my dust,
  Till he shall bid it rise.

3 Arrayed in glorious grace
  Shall these vile bodies shine;

And every shape and every face
Look heavenly and divine.

4 These lively hopes we owe
To Jesus' dying love;
We would adore his grace below,
And sing his power above.

5 Dear Lord, accept the praise
Of these our humble songs,
Till tunes of nobler sound we raise
With our immortal tongues.

554 *Death of pious Friends.* C. M.

1 WHY do we mourn departing friends,
Or shake at death's alarms?
'Tis but the voice that Jesus sends,
To call them to his arms.

2 Are we not tending upward too,
As fast as time can move?
Nor should we wish the hours more slow,
To keep us from our love.

3 Why should we tremble to convey
Their bodies to the tomb?
There the dear flesh of Jesus lay,
And left a long perfume.

4 The graves of all the saints he bless'd,
And softened every bed;
Where should the dying members rest,
But with the dying Head?

5 Thence he arose, ascended high,
And showed our feet the way:

Up to the Lord our flesh shall fly,
At the great rising day.

555 *Rest and Resurrection.* C. M.

1 THROUGH sorrow's night, and danger's [path,
Amid the deepening gloom,
We, soldiers of an injured King,
Are marching to the tomb.

2 There, when the turmoil is no more,
And all our powers decay,
Our cold remains in solitude
Shall sleep the years away.

3 Our labors done, securely laid
In this our last retreat,
Unheeded, o'er our silent dust,
The storms of life shall beat.

4 Yet not thus lifeless, thus inane,
The vital spark shall lie;
For o'er life's wreck that spark shall rise
To seek its kindred sky.

5 These ashes too, this little dust,
Our Father's care shall keep,
Till the last angel rise and break
The long and dreary sleep.

6 Then love's soft dew o'er every eye
Shall shed its mildest rays;
And the long silent dust shall burst
With shouts of endless praise.

556 *Funeral of a Young Person.* C. M.

1 WHEN blooming youth is snatched away
By death's resistless hand,
Our hearts the mournful tribute pay
Which pity must demand.

2 While pity prompts the rising sigh,
Oh may this truth, impress'd
With awful power—"I too must die"—
Sink deep in every breast.

3 Let this vain world engage no more;
Behold the gaping tomb!
It bids us seize the present hour;
To-morrow death may come.

4 The voice of this alarming scene
May every heart obey;
Nor be the heavenly warning vain,
Which calls to watch and pray.

5 Oh let us fly—to Jesus fly—
Whose powerful arm can save;
Then shall our hopes ascend on high,
And triumph o'er the grave.

557 *Death of a Child.* C. M.

1 THE once loved form, now cold and dead,
Each mournful thought employs;
And nature weeps her comforts fled,
And withered all her joys.

2 Hope looks beyond the bounds of time,
When what we now deplore

Shall rise in full, immortal prime,
And bloom to fade no more.

3 Then cease, fond nature, cease thy tears;
Religion points on high;
There everlasting spring appears,
And joys which cannot die.

558 *Death of a Minister.* C. M.

1 NOW let our mourning hearts revive,
And all our tears be dry;
Why should those eyes be drowned in grief,
Which view a Saviour nigh?

2 What though the arm of conquering death
Does God's own house invade?
What though the prophet and the priest
Be numbered with the dead?

3 Though earthly shepherds dwell in dust
The aged and the young—
The watchful eye in darkness closed,
And mute th' instructive tongue;—

4 Th' eternal Shepherd still survives,
New comfort to impart;
His eye still guides us, and his voice
Still animates our heart.

5 "Lo, I am with you," saith the Lord,
"My church shall safe abide;
For I will ne'er forsake my own,
Whose souls in me confide."

559 *Death of an aged Minister.* S. M.

1 "SERVANT of God, well done,
Rest from thy loved employ:
The battle fought, the victory won,
Enter thy Master's joy."

2 The voice at midnight came,
He started up to hear;
A mortal arrow pierced his frame,
He fell—but felt no fear.

3 Tranquil amidst alarms,
It found him on the field,
A veteran slumbering on his arms,
Beneath his red-cross shield.

4 The pains of death are past,
Labor and sorrow cease;
And life's long warfare closed at last,
His soul is found in peace.

5 Soldier of Christ, well done;
Praise be thy new employ;
And while eternal ages run,
Rest in thy Saviour's joy.

560 *Death of the Righteous.* L. M.

1 HOW bless'd the righteous when they die,
When holy souls retire to rest!
How mildly beams the closing eye!
How gently heaves th' expiring breast!

2 So fades a summer cloud away;
So sinks the gale when storms are o'er;

So gently shuts the eye of day;
So dies a wave along the shore.

3 Farewell, conflicting hopes and fears,
Where lights and shades alternate dwell;
How bright th' unchanging morn appears!
Farewell, inconstant world, farewell.

4 Life's duty done, as sinks the clay,
Light from its load the spirit flies;
While heaven and earth combine to say,
"How bless'd the righteous when he dies!"

561 *The departing Saint.* 8.7

1 HAPPY soul, thy days are ended,
All thy mourning days below:
Go, by angel guards attended,
To the sight of Jesus go.
Waiting to receive thy spirit,
Lo, the Saviour stands above;
Shows the purchase of his merit,
Reaches out the crown of love.

2 Struggle through thy latest passion
To thy dear Redeemer's breast,
To his uttermost salvation,
To his everlasting rest.
For the joy he sets before thee,
Bear a momentary pain;
Die, to live the life of glory—
Suffer, with thy Lord to reign.

562 *The departing Saint.* 7s. Double.

1 DYING saint, to glory rise,
Seek thy mansion in the skies;
Go to shine before his throne
Who hath bought thee for his own;
Lo, he beckons from on high;
Fearless, to his presence fly:
Thine the merit of his blood,
Thine the righteousness of God.

2 Shudder not to pass the stream,
Venture all thy care on him;
Him whose dying love and power
Stilled its tossing, hushed its roar.
Safe is the expanded wave,
Gentle as a summer's eve;
Not one object of his care
Ever suffered shipwreck there.

563 *The dying Christian to his Soul.*

1 VITAL spark of heavenly flame,
Quit, oh quit this mortal frame:
Trembling, hoping, lingering, flying—
Oh, the pain, the bliss of dying!
Cease, fond nature, cease thy strife,
And let me languish into life.

2 Hark! they whisper—angels say,
"Sister spirit, come away:"
What is this absorbs me quite,
Steals my senses, shuts my sight,

Drowns my spirits, draws my breath—
Tell me, my soul—can this be death?

3 The world recedes—it disappears—
Heaven opens on my eyes!—my ears
With sounds seraphic ring!
Lend, lend your wings; I mount! I fly!
O grave, where is thy victory?
O death, where is thy sting?

564 *Death of a Saint.* 7s. Double

1 LO, the prisoner is released,
Lightened of his fleshly load;
Where the weary are at rest,
He is gathered unto God.
Lo, the pain of life is past,
All his warfare now is o'er;
Death and hell behind are cast,
Grief and suffering are no more.

2 Yes, the Christian's course is run,
Ended is the glorious strife:
Fought the fight, the work is done,
Death is swallowed up of life!
Borne aloft on angel-wings,
Far from earth the spirit flies;
Finds his God, and sits and sings,
Triumphing in Paradise.

3 Join we then with one accord,
In the new, the joyful song:
Absent from our glorious Lord
We shall not continue long:

We shall quit the house of clay,
We a better lot shall share;
We shall see the realms of day,
Meet our happy brother there.

565 *Funeral Hymn.* 12. 11.

1 THOU art gone to the grave, but we will not deplore thee,
Though sorrows and darkness encompass the tomb;
The Saviour has passed through its portals before thee,
And the lamp of his love is thy guide through the gloom.

2 Thou art gone to the grave; we no longer behold thee,
Nor tread the rough paths of the world by thy side;
But the wide arms of mercy are spread to enfold thee;
And sinners may hope, since the Sinless has died.

3 Thou art gone to the grave, and its mansion forsaking,
Perchance thy weak spirit in doubt lingered long;
But the sunshine of heaven beamed bright on thy waking,
And full on thine ear burst the seraphim's song.

4 Thou art gone to the grave, but we will
not deplore thee,
Since God was thy ransom, thy guardian, thy guide;
He gave thee, he took thee, and he will
restore thee;
And death has no sting, since the Saviour has died.

566 *Funeral Hymn.* C. M.

1 WHILE to the grave our friends are
Around their cold remains [borne,
How all the tender passions mourn,
And each fond heart complains.

2 But down to earth, alas, in vain
We bend our weeping eyes;
Ah, let us leave these seats of pain,
And upward learn to rise.

3 Jesus, who left his bless'd abode,
(Amazing grace!) to die,
Marked, when he rose, the shining road
To his bright courts on high.

4 To those bright courts when hope ascends,
The tears forget to flow;
Hope views our absent happy friends,
And calms the swelling wo.

5 Then let our hearts repine no more
That earthly comfort dies;
But lasting happiness explore,
And ask it from the skies.

567 *The Tomb and the Resurrection.* L. M.

1 UNVAIL thy bosom, faithful tomb,
Take this new treasure to thy trust,
And give these sacred relics room
To seek a slumber in the dust.

2 Nor pain, nor grief, nor anxious fear
Invade thy bounds; no mortal woes
Can reach the peaceful sleeper here,
While angels watch the soft repose.

3 So Jesus slept—God's dying Son
Passed through the grave, and blessed the bed:
Rest here, bless'd saint, till from his throne
The morning break and pierce the shade.

4 Break from his throne, illustrious morn;
Attend, O earth, his sovereign word;
Restore thy trust—a glorious form
Called to ascend and meet the Lord.

568 *"To die is gain."* 8s.

1 REJOICE for a brother deceased;
Our loss is his infinite gain;
A soul out of prison released,
And freed from its bodily chain;
With songs let us follow his flight,
And mount with his spirit above;
Escaped to the mansions of light,
And lodged in the Eden of love.

2 Our brother the haven has gained,
Outflying the tempest and wind;
His rest he has sooner obtained,
And left his companions behind,
Still tossed on a sea of distress,
Hard toiling to make the bless'd shore,
Where all is assurance and peace,
And sorrow and sin are no more.

3 There all the ship's company meet,
Who sailed with the Saviour beneath;
With shouting each other they greet,
And triumph o'er trouble and death:
The voyage of life's at an end,
The mortal affliction is past:
The age that in heaven they spend,
For ever and ever shall last.

THE JUDGMENT.

569 *The Judgment.*—Mal. iii. 2. S. M

1 AND will the Judge descend?
And must the dead arise,
And not a single soul escape
His all-discerning eyes?

2 How will my heart endure
The terrors of that day,
When earth and heaven, before his face
Astonished, shrink away?

3 But, ere that trumpet shakes
The mansions of the dead,
Hark! from the gospel's cheering sound
What joyful tidings spread!

4 Ye sinners, seek his grace,
Whose wrath ye cannot bear;
Fly to the shelter of his cross,
And find salvation there.

5 So shall that curse remove,
By which the Saviour bled;
And the last awful day shall pour
His blessings on your head.

570 *The Sinner warned.* 8. 7. 4.

1 WHEN th' eternal Judge, descending,
Shall enthroned in glory come,
Sinner, at his bar attending,
Thou wilt hear thy awful doom:
Speechless, hopeless,
Thou wilt hear thy awful doom.

2 O'er thy folly then lamenting,
Filled with dread of future pain,
Cries of bitter anguish venting,
Thou wilt mourn and weep in vain;
Called to judgment,
Thou wilt mourn and weep in vain.

3 There will sit thy slighted Saviour,
With the marks of dying love;
Oh that thou would'st seek his favor,
While invited from above:
Golden moments—
While invited from above.

4 Swift thy days of grace are fleeting,
Canst thou linger and delay?
Lo! the hours, their calls repeating,
Hasten on the judgment-day;
Hours of mercy
Hasten on the judgment-day.

571 *The Judgment anticipated.* C. M.

1 WHEN, rising from the bed of death,
O'erwhelmed with guilt and fear,
I see my Maker face to face,
Oh, how shall I appear?

2 If now, while pardon may be found,
And mercy may be sought,
My heart with inward horror shrinks,
And trembles at the thought,—

3 When thou, O Lord, shalt stand disclosed
In majesty severe,
And sit in judgment on my soul,
Oh how shall I appear?

572 *"Watch and Pray."* S. M

1 THOU Judge of quick and dead,
Before whose bar severe,
With holy joy or guilty dread,
We all shall soon appear;

2 Our cautioned souls prepare
For that tremendous day,
And fill us now with watchful care,
And stir us up to pray.

3 Oh may we all be found
Obedient to thy word,
Attentive to the trumpet's sound,
And looking for our Lord.

4 Oh may we all ensure
A lot among the bless'd;
And watch a moment to secure
An everlasting rest.

573 *The Day of Judgment.* 8. 7. 4.

1 DAY of judgment—day of wonders!
Hark, the trumpet's awful sound,
Louder than a thousand thunders,
Shakes the vast creation round!
How the summons
Will the sinner's heart confound!

2 See the Judge, our nature wearing,
Clothed in majesty divine!
You who long for his appearing,
Then shall say, "This God is mine;"
Gracious Saviour,
Own me in that day for thine.

3 At his call, the dead awaken,
Rise to life from earth and sea;
All the powers of nature, shaken
By his looks, prepare to flee:
Careless sinner,
What will then become of thee?

4 But to those who have confessed,
Loved, and served the Lord below,

He will say, "Come near, ye blessed,
See the kingdom I bestow:
You for ever
Shall my love and glory know."

574 *The Day of Judgment.* C. M.

1 THAT awful day will surely come;
Th' appointed hour makes haste,
When I must stand before my Judge,
And pass the solemn test.

2 Thou lovely chief of all my joys,
Thou sovereign of my heart,
How could I bear to hear thy voice
Pronounce the sound—depart!

3 Oh, wretched state of deep despair—
To see my God remove,
And fix my doleful station where
I must not taste his love!

4 Oh tell me that my worthless name
Is graven on thy hands;
Show me some promise in thy book,
Where my salvation stands.

575 *The Sleep of the Grave.* 9. 8.

1 ON man's last sleep, in rending thunder,
The last loud judgment-trump will break;
The sinner, in despair and wonder,
From out his silent death-dreams wake;
His deep grave gaping near the stone
That signal-sound hath overthrown.

2 With fear and wild amazement smitten,
His eyes to heaven for mercy roll;
But read, in flaming letters written,
The sentence of his ruined soul:
In vain he seeks a frightful death,
Within the lightning's blasting breath.

3 O Saviour, when that fearful morning
Reveals thee on the quick-winged cloud,
The last loud trump, with signal warning,
Breaking the slumber of my shroud,
And earth and sea have passed away—
Be thou my trembling spirit's stay.

THE ETERNAL STATE.

576 *Rest in Heaven.* C. M. Peculiar

1 THERE is an hour of peaceful rest
To mourning wanderers given;
There is a joy for souls distressed,
A balm for every wounded breast—
'Tis found above, in heaven.

2 There is a home for weary souls,
By sin and sorrow driven;
When tossed on life's tempestuous shoals
Where storms arise, and ocean rolls,
And all is drear—'tis heaven.

3 There faith lifts up her cheerful eye,
The heart no longer riven,

And views the tempest passing by,
Sees evening shadows quickly fly,
And all serene in heaven.

4 There fragrant flowers immortal bloom,
And joys supreme are given;
There rays divine disperse the gloom—
Beyond the confines of the tomb
Appears the dawn of heaven.

577 *Heaven anticipated.* C. M.

1 OUR sins and sorrows, how they rise!
How loud the tempests roar!
But death shall land our weary souls
Safe on the heavenly shore.

2 There to fulfill his high commands
Our speedy feet shall move;
No sin shall clog our active zeal,
Or cool our burning love.

3 There shall we sit, and sing, and tell
The wonders of his grace,
Till heavenly raptures fire our hearts,
And smile in every face.

4 For ever his dear sacred name
Shall dwell upon our tongue;
And Jesus and salvation be
The close of every song.

578 *Heavenly Rest.* S. M.

AND is there, Lord, a rest
For weary souls designed,

Where not a care shall stir the breast,
Or sorrow entrance find?

2 Is there a blissful home,
Where kindred minds shall meet,
And live and love, nor ever roam
From that serene retreat?

3 Are there bright happy fields,
Where nought that blooms shall die;
Where each new scene fresh pleasure
And healthful breezes sigh? [yields,

4 Are there celestial streams
Where living waters glide,
With murmurs sweet as angel dreams,
And flowery banks beside?

5 For ever blessed they,
Whose joyful feet shall stand,
While endless ages waste away,
Amid that glorious land.

6 My soul would thither tend,
While toilsome years are given;
Then let me, gracious God, ascend
To sweet repose in heaven.

579 *"They that sow in Tears," &c.* C. M. Double.

1 THERE is an hour of hallowed peace
For those with cares distressed,
When sighs and sorrowing tears shall
And all be hushed to rest. [cease,
'Tis then the soul is freed from fears
And doubts which here annoy;

And they who oft have sown in tears,
Shall reap again with joy.

2 There is a home of sweet repose,
Where storms assail no more;
The stream of endless pleasure flows
On that celestial shore.
There smiling peace with love appears,
And bliss without alloy;
There they who once have sown in tears,
Now reap eternal joy.

3 When the revealing hour is near
Which shall unvail the tomb,
When, filled with doubt and trembling fear,
We pass the valley's gloom,
Wilt thou, bless'd Jesus, calm these fears;
Let praise our lips employ;
That we who here have sown in tears,
May reap in heaven with joy.

580 *Life and Death eternal.* S. M.

1 OH, where shall rest be found,
Rest for the weary soul?
'Twere vain the ocean-depths to sound,
Or pierce to either pole.

2 The world can never give
The bliss for which we sigh;
'Tis not the whole of life to live,
Nor all of death to die.

3 Beyond this vale of tears,
There is a life above,

Unmeasured by the flight of years—
  And all that life is love.

4 There is a death whose pang
  Outlasts the fleeting breath;
Oh, what eternal horrors hang
  Around the second death.

5 Lord God of truth and grace,
  Teach us that death to shun;
Lest we be banished from thy face,
  And evermore undone.

581 *The Mourner comforted.* C. M. Double.

1 OH weep not for the joys that fade
  Like evening lights away,
For hopes, that, like the stars decayed,
  Have left thy mortal day;
The clouds of sorrow will depart,
  And brilliant skies be given;
For bliss awaits the holy heart,
  Amid the bowers of heaven.

2 Oh weep not for the friends that pass
  Into the lonely grave,
As breezes sweep the withered grass
  Along the restless wave;
For though thy pleasures may depart,
  And mournful days be given,
Yet bliss awaits the holy heart,
  When friends rejoin in heaven.

582

The Saints in Glory. 7s. Double.

1 HIGH in yonder realms of light,
Dwell the raptured saints above;
Far beyond our feeble sight,
Happy in Immanuel's love:
Once they knew, like us below,
Pilgrims in this vale of tears,
Torturing pain, and heavy wo,
Gloomy doubts, distressing fears.

2 Oft the big unbidden tear,
Stealing down the furrowed cheek,
Told, in eloquence sincere,
Tales of wo they could not speak.
But these days of weeping o'er,
Pass'd this scene of toil and pain,
They shall feel distress no more—
Never, never weep again.

3 'Mid the chorus of the skies,
'Mid th' angelic lyres above,
Hark! their songs melodious rise,
Songs of praise to Jesus' love!
Happy spirits, ye are fled
Where no grief can entrance find;
Lulled to rest the aching head,
Soothed the anguish of the mind.

4 All is tranquil and serene,
Calm and undisturbed repose;
There no cloud can intervene,
There no angry tempest blows;

Every tear is wiped away,
  Sighs no more shall heave the breast,
Night is lost in endless day,
  Sorrow—in eternal rest.

583 *The Vision of Christ.* C. M.

1 FROM thee, my God, my joys shall rise,
  And run eternal rounds,
Beyond the limits of the skies,
  And all created bounds.

2 The holy triumphs of my soul
  Shall death itself outbrave,
Leave dull mortality behind,
  And fly beyond the grave.

3 There, where my blessed Jesus reigns,
  In heaven's unmeasured space,
I'll spend a long eternity
  In pleasure and in praise.

4 Millions of years my wondering eyes
  Shall o'er thy beauties rove;
And endless ages I'll adore
  The glories of thy love.

584 *Happiness of Heaven.* 8s.

1 OH when shall we sweetly remove,
  And enter our heavenly rest;
Return to the Zion above,
  And join in the songs of the bless'd?
Oh when shall we dwell with our King,
  Where sorrow and pain are no more,

Where saints our Immanuel sing,
And cherub and seraph adore.

2 Our Saviour, thou knowest our prayer;
We long thy appearing to see;
Resigned to the burden we bear,
But hoping to triumph with thee:
To mourn for thy coming is sweet,
To weep at thy longer delay;
But thou whom we hasten to meet,
Wilt chase all our sorrows away.

585 *Heavenly Love.* S. M.

1 LOVE fills all heaven with light;
Love tunes the lyres above;
Angels and saints their songs unite,
And every voice is love.

2 That holy, happy throng
In sweet accordance move;
Jesus their everlasting song,
And every accent love.

3 Soon will the church below
Unite with that above;
The Saviour's blissful presence know,
And sing redeeming love.

586 *Happiness of Heaven.* 8s.

1 WE speak of the realms of the bless'd,
That country so bright and so fair;
And oft are its glories confess'd,
But what must it be to be there!

2 We speak of its freedom from sin,
From sorrow, temptation, and care,
From trials without and within—
But what must it be to be there!

3 We speak of its service of love,
The robes which the glorified wear,
The church of the first-born above—
But what must it be to be there!

4 Do thou, Lord, 'midst pleasure or wo,
For heaven my spirit prepare;
And shortly I also shall know
And feel what it is to be there.

587 *The everlasting Song.* C. M.

1 EARTH has engrossed my love too long;
'Tis time I lift my eyes
Upward, dear Father, to thy throne,
And to my native skies.

2 There the bless'd Man, my Saviour, sits;
The God! how bright he shines!
And scatters infinite delights
On all the happy minds.

3 Seraphs, with elevated strains,
Circle the throne around;
And move and charm the starry plains
With an immortal sound.

4 Jesus, the Lord, their harps employs;
Jesus, thy love they sing;
Jesus, the life of all our joys,
Sounds sweet from every string.

5 Now let me mount and join their song,
And be an angel too;
My heart, my hand, my ear, my tongue—
Here's joyful work for you.

6 I would begin the music here,
And so my soul should rise:
Oh for some heavenly notes to bear
My passions to the skies!

7 There ye that love my Saviour sit,
There I would fain have place,
Among your thrones, or at your feet,
So I might see his face.

588 *The Saints in Heaven.* 7. 6

1 TO their Lord believers go,
When from the flesh they fly;
Glorious joys ordained to know,
They mount above the sky;
In that bright, celestial place,
They without a vail shall see
Their Redeemer's heavenly face,
And with him ever be.

2 When they once have entered there,
Their mourning days are o'er;
Sin and pain and want and care
And sighing are no more:
Subject then to no decay,
Heavenly bodies they put on,
Swifter than the lightning's ray,
And brighter than the sun.

3 While eternal ages roll,
Their anthems they shall raise;
God the portion of the soul,
And its employment praise:
Upward, Lord, our souls would rise,
We would join that happy throng;
Swell the chorus of the skies,
And praise in endless song.

589 *Friendship in Heaven.* 6. 8.

1 FRIEND after friend departs:
Who hath not lost a friend?
There is no union here of hearts,
That finds not here an end:
Were this frail world our final rest,
Living or dying, none were bless'd.

2 Beyond the flight of time,
Beyond the reign of death,
There surely is some blessed clime
Where life is not a breath,
Nor life's affections transient fire,
Whose sparks fly upwards and expire.

3 There is a world above,
Where parting is unknown;
A long eternity of love,
Formed for the good alone;
And faith beholds the dying here,
Translated to that glorious sphere.

4 Thus star by star declines,
Till all are passed away:

As morning high and higher shines,
To pure and perfect day:
Nor sink those stars in empty night,
But hide themselves in heaven's own light.

590 *The Christian's Hope.* L. M.

1 WHAT sinners value, I resign;
Lord, 'tis enough that thou art mine;
I shall behold thy blissful face,
And stand complete in righteousness.

2 This life's a dream, an empty show;
But the bright world to which I go
Hath joys substantial and sincere;
When shall I wake and find me there?

3 Oh, glorious hour! Oh bless'd abode!
I shall be near and like my God;
And flesh and sin no more control
The sacred pleasures of the soul.

4 My flesh shall slumber in the ground
Till the last trumpet's joyful sound;
Then burst the chains with sweet surprise,
And in my Saviour's image rise.

591 *The Heavenly Jerusalem.* C. M.

1 JERUSALEM, my happy home—
Name ever dear to me,
When shall my labors have an end,
In joy and peace, in thee?

2 Oh when, thou city of my God,
Shall I thy courts ascend,

Where congregations ne'er break up,
And Sabbaths have no end?

3 There happier bowers than Eden's bloom,
Nor sin nor sorrow know:
Bless'd seats, through rude and stormy scenes,
I onward press to you.

4 Why should I shrink at pain and wo,
Or feel, at death, dismay?
I've Canaan's goodly land in view,
And realms of endless day.

5 Apostles, martyrs, prophets there
Around my Saviour stand;
And soon my friends in Christ below
Will join the glorious band.

6 Jerusalem, my happy home—
My soul still pants for thee;
Then shall my labors have an end,
When I thy joys shall see.

592 *Heavenly Glory.* 7. 6. Iambic.

1 THERE is a holy city,
A happy world above,
Beyond the starry regions,
Built by the God of love:
An everlasting temple;
And saints, arrayed in white,
There serve their great Redeemer,
And dwell with him in light.

2 The meanest child of glory
Outshines the radiant sun;

But who can speak the splendor
Of Jesus on the throne?
There now he sits exalted,
Who hung upon the tree;
The elders fall before him,
The angels bend the knee.

3 Is this the man of sorrows,
Who stood at Pilate's bar,
Condemned by haughty Herod,
And by his men of war?
Lo! now the mighty conqueror
Who spoiled the powers below,
And ransomed many captives
From everlasting wo.

4 The hosts of saints around him
Redeeming grace adore;
Recount their toils and conflicts,
And tell their sufferings o'er;
Then turn and bow to Jesus,
Who brought them on their way,
From earthly tribulation
To everlasting day.

593 *The Heavenly Canaan.* C. M.

1 THERE is a land of pure delight,
Where saints immortal reign;
Where endless day excludes the night,
And pleasures banish pain.

2 There everlasting spring abides,
And never-withering flowers:

Death, like a narrow sea, divides
  This heavenly land from ours.

3 Sweet fields beyond the swelling flood
  Stand dressed in living green;
So to the Jews old Canaan stood,
  While Jordan rolled between.

4 But timorous mortals start and shrink
  To cross this narrow sea;
And linger shivering on the brink,
  And fear to launch away.

5 Oh, could we make our doubts remove,
  Those gloomy doubts that rise,
And see the Canaan that we love,
  With unbeclouded eyes;

6 Could we but climb where Moses stood,
  And view the landscape o'er;
Not Jordan's stream, nor death's cold flood,
  Should fright us from the shore.

594 *"We shall see him as he is."* C. M.

1 FATHER, I long, I faint to see
  The place of thine abode;
I'd leave the earthly courts, and flee
  Up to thy seat, my God.

2 Here I behold thy distant face,
  And 'tis a pleasant sight;
But to abide in thine embrace
  Is infinite delight.

3 I'd part with all the joys of sense,
  To gaze upon thy throne;

Pleasure springs fresh for ever thence,
Unspeakable, unknown.

4 There all the heavenly hosts are seen;
In shining ranks they move;
And drink immortal vigor in,
With wonder and with love.

5 Then at thy feet, with awful fear,
Th' adoring armies fall;
With joy they shrink to nothing there,
Before th' eternal All.

6 The more thy glories strike my eyes,
The humbler I shall lie;
Thus, while I sink, my joys shall rise
Immeasurably high.

595 THE LORD'S PRAYER. S. M.

1 OUR heavenly Father, hear
The prayer we offer now:
Thy name be hallowed, far and near,
To thee all nations bow.

2 Thy kingdom come; thy will
On earth be done in love,
As saints and seraphim fulfill
Thy perfect law above.

3 Our daily bread supply,
While by thy word we live;
The guilt of our iniquity
Forgive, as we forgive.

4 From dark temptation's power,
From Satan's wiles defend;
Deliver in the evil hour,
And guide us to the end.

5 Thine, then, for ever be
Glory and power divine;
The sceptre, throne, and majesty
Of heaven and earth are thine.

6 Thus humbly taught to pray,
By thy beloved Son,
Through him we come to thee, and say—
All for his sake be done.

DOXOLOGIES.

596 *Invocation of the Trinity.* 6. 4.

1 COME, thou Almighty King,
Help us thy name to sing,
Help us to praise:
Father all glorious,
O'er all victorious,
Come, and reign over us,
Ancient of days.

2 Jesus, our Lord, arise,
Scatter our enemies,
And make them fall;
Let thine almighty aid

Our sure defence be made;
Our souls on thee be stayed—
Lord, hear our call.

3 Come, thou incarnate Word,
Gird on thy mighty sword;
Our prayer attend:
Come, and thy people bless,
And give thy word success;
Spirit of holiness,
On us descend.

4 Come, holy Comforter,
Thy sacred witness bear,
In this glad hour;
Thou who almighty art,
Now rule in every heart,
And ne'er from us depart,
Spirit of power.

5 To the great One in Three,
The highest praises be,
Hence evermore:
His sovereign majesty
May we in glory see,
And to eternity
Love and adore.

597 *Praise to the Trinity.* H. M.

1 WE give immortal praise
To God the Father's love,
For all our comforts here,
And better hopes above;

He sent his own eternal Son
To die for sins that man had done.

2 To God the Son belongs
Immortal glory too,
Who saved us by his blood
From everlasting wo;
And now he lives, and now he reigns,
And sees the fruit of all his pains.

3 To God the Holy Ghost
Immortal praise we give;
Whose new-creating power
Makes the dead sinner live;
His work completes the great design,
And fills the soul with joy divine.

4 Almighty God, to thee
Be endless honors done;
The undivided Three,
And the mysterious One:
Where reason fails, with all her powers,
There faith prevails, and love adores.

598 *Praise to the Trinity.* 7s. Double.

1 HOLY, holy, holy Lord,
God, the Father and the Word,
God the Comforter, receive
Blessing more than we can give;
Joining those beyond the sky,
Who adore the Lord most high,
We our hearts and voices raise,
Echoing thine eternal praise.

2 Happy they who never rest,
With thy heavenly presence bless'd;
They the heights of glory see,
Sound the depths of Deity.
Fain with them our souls would vie;
Sink as low, and mount as high;
Fall, o'erwhelmed with love, or soar;
Shout, or silently adore.

599 *"Our God for ever and ever."* 8s.

1 THIS God is the God we adore,
Our faithful, unchangeable Friend,
Whose love is as large as his power,
And neither knows measure nor end.

2 'Tis Jesus, the First and the Last,
Whose Spirit shall guide us safe home;
We'll praise him for all that is past,
And trust him for all that's to come.

600 *Praise to the Trinity.* S. M.

1 LET God the Father live
For ever on our tongues:
Sinners from his first love derive
The ground of all their songs.

2 Ye saints, employ your breath
In honor of the Son,
Who bought your souls from hell and death,
By offering up his own.

3 Give to the Spirit praise
Of an immortal strain;

Whose light and power and grace conveys
Salvation down to men.

4 To the great One in Three,
That seals the grace in heaven,
The Father, Son, and Spirit, be
Eternal glory given.

601 L. M.

TO God the Father, God the Son,
And God the Spirit, Three in One,
Be honor, praise, and glory given,
By all on earth, and all in heaven.

602 L. M.

PRAISE God, from whom all blessings flow;
Praise him, all creatures here below;
Praise him above, ye heavenly host,
Praise Father, Son, and Holy Ghost.

603 C. M.

LET God, the Father and the Son
And Spirit be adored,
Where there are works to make him known,
Or saints to love the Lord.

604 C. M. Double.

1 THE God of mercy be adored,
Who calls our souls from death;
Who saves by his redeeming word,
And new-creating breath.

2 To praise the Father and the Son
And Spirit, all divine,
The One in Three, and Three in One,
Let saints and angels join.

605 S. M.

YE angels round the throne,
And saints who dwell below,
Worship the Father, praise the Son,
And bless the Spirit too.

606 H. M.

TO God the Father's throne
Perpetual honors raise;
Glory to God the Son,
To God the Spirit praise:
With all our powers, eternal King,
Thy name we sing, while faith adores.

607 C. P. M.

TO Father, Son, and Holy Ghost,
Be praise amid the heavenly host,
And in the church below;
From whom all creatures draw their breath,
By whom redemption blessed the earth,
From whom all comforts flow.

608 7s.

SING we to our God above,
Praise eternal as his love:
Praise him all ye heavenly host,
Father, Son, and Holy Ghost.

609

7s. 6 lines.

FATHER, Son, and Holy Ghost,
One in Three, and Three in One,
As by the celestial host,
Let thy will on earth be done:
Praise by all to thee be given,
Glorious Lord of earth and heaven.

610

7s. Double.

FATHER, Son, and Holy Ghost,
One in Three, and Three in One,
As by the celestial host,
Let thy will on earth be done;
Sing we to our God above
Praise eternal as his love;
Praise by all to thee be given,
Glorious Lord of earth and heaven.

611

7. 6.

FATHER, God, thy love we praise,
Which gave thy Son to die;
Jesus, full of truth and grace,
Alike we glorify:
Spirit, Comforter divine,
Praise by all to thee be given,
Till we in full chorus join,
And earth is changed to heaven.

612

8. 7.

1 MAY the grace of Christ our Saviour,
And the Father's boundless love,

With the Holy Spirit's favor,
Rest upon us from above.

2 Thus may we abide in union
With each other and the Lord,
And possess, in sweet communion,
Joys which earth cannot afford.

613

8. 7. 4.

GLORY be to God the Father,
Glory to th' eternal Son;
Sound aloud the Spirit's praises;
Join the elders round the throne;
Hallelujah,
Hail the glorious Three in One.

614

6. 4.

TO the great One in Three
The highest praises be,
Hence evermore;
His sovereign majesty
May we in glory see,
And to eternity
Love and adore.

615

5. 6.

BY angels in heaven
Of every degree,
And saints upon earth,
All praise be addressed
To God in Three persons,
One God ever blessed:
As it has been, and now is,
And always shall be.

616

11s.

O FATHER Almighty, to thee be addressed,
With Christ and the Spirit, one God ever bless'd,
All glory and worship from earth and from heaven,
As was, and is now, and shall ever be given.

617

12s.

ALL glory and praise to the Father be given,
The Son and the Spirit, from earth and from heaven;
As was, and is now, be supreme adoration,
And ever shall be to the God of salvation.

618

7. 6. Iambic.

FROM all in earth and heaven,
To God, the Three in One,
Be boundless glory given,
And ceaseless service done;
Co-equal praise to Father,
To Son, to Spirit be;
One God they reign together,
One Holy Trinity.

TABLE OF METRES.

C. M.	Common Metre.
L. M.	Long Metre.
S. M.	Short Metre.
H. M.	Hallelujah Metre.
C. P. M.	Common Particular Metre.
5. 6. . . . . *like*	"Though troubles assail."
6. 4. . . . . "	"Come, thou almighty King."
6. 5. . . . . "	"When shall we meet again?"
7s. . . . . "	"Children of the heavenly King."
7. 6. . . . . "	"Rise, my soul, and stretch thy wings."
7. 6. (Iambic,). . "	"From Greenland's icy mountains."
8s. . . . . "	"My gracious Redeemer I love."
8. 7. . . . . "	"Come, thou fount of every blessing."
8. 7. 4. . . . . "	"Lord, dismiss us with thy blessing."
11s. (Anapestic,) "	"How firm a foundation, ye saints of the Lord."
11s. (Dactylic,) . "	"Daughter of Zion, awake from thy sadness."
11. 8. . . . . "	"O Thou in whose presence my soul," &c.
12s. . . . . "	"The voice of free grace, cries escape," &c.

Note.—Metres of which there are but single specimens in the book, are not inserted in the above table.

CLASSIFICATION OF SUBJECTS.

INDEX OF SUBJECTS.

PASSAGES OF SCRIPTURE

ALLUDED TO IN THE HYMNS.

INDEX OF FIRST LINES.

* Ascribed by some to Whitefield.

www.ingramcontent.com/pod-product-compliance
Lightning Source LLC
LaVergne TN
LVHW020927110826
845150LV00004B/786